Resurrection

GUIDES FOR THE PERPLEXED

Bloomsbury's *Guides for the Perplexed* are clear, concise and accessible introductions to thinkers, writers and subjects that students and readers can find especially challenging. Concentrating specifically on what it is that makes the subject difficult to grasp, these books explain and explore key themes and ideas, guiding the reader towards a thorough understanding of demanding material.

Guides for the Perplexed available from Bloomsbury include:

Atonement: A Guide for the Perplexed, Adam Johnson
Balthasar: A Guide for the Perplexed, Rodney Howsare
Benedict XVI: A Guide for the Perplexed, Tracey Rowland
Bonhoeffer: A Guide for the Perplexed, Joel Lawrence
Calvin: A Guide for the Perplexed, Paul Helm
De Lubac: A Guide for the Perplexed, David Grumett
Luther: A Guide for the Perplexed, David M. Whitford
Pannenberg: A Guide for the Perplexed, Timothy Bradshaw
Pneumatology: A Guide for the Perplexed, Daniel Castelo
Political Theology: A Guide for the Perplexed, Elizabeth Phillips
Postliberal Theology: A Guide for the Perplexed, Ronald T. Michener
Schleiermacher: A Guide for the Perplexed, Theodore Vial
Scripture: A Guide for the Perplexed, William Lamb
Tillich: A Guide for the Perplexed, Andrew O'Neill
Wesley: A Guide for the Perplexed, Jason A. Vickers
Žižek: A Guide for the Perplexed, Sean Sheehan

Forthcoming *Guides for the Perplexed* available from Bloomsbury include:

Barth: A Guide for the Perplexed, Paul T. Nimmo
Catholic Social Teaching: A Guide for the Perplexed, Anna Rowlands
Ecumenism: A Guide for the Perplexed, R. David Nelson
God-Talk: A Guide for the Perplexed, Aaron B. James and Ryan S. Peterson
Prayer: A Guide for the Perplexed, Ashley Cocksworth
Salvation: A Guide for the Perplexed, Ivor J. Davidson
Schillebeeckx: A Guide for the Perplexed, Stephan van Erp

A GUIDE FOR THE PERPLEXED

Resurrection

Lidija Novakovic

Bloomsbury T&T Clark
An imprint of Bloomsbury Publishing Plc

BLOOMSBURY
LONDON · OXFORD · NEW YORK · NEW DELHI · SYDNEY

Bloomsbury T&T Clark

An imprint of Bloomsbury Publishing Plc

Imprint previously known as T&T Clark

50 Bedford Square	1385 Broadway
London	New York
WC1B 3DP	NY 10018
UK	USA

www.bloomsbury.com

BLOOMSBURY, T&T CLARK and the Diana logo are trademarks of Bloomsbury Publishing Plc

First published 2016

© Lidija Novakovic, 2016

Lidija Novakovic has asserted her right under the Copyright, Designs and Patents Act, 1988, to be identified as Author of this work.

All rights reserved. No part of this publication may be reproduced or transmitted in any form or by any means, electronic or mechanical, including photocopying, recording, or any information storage or retrieval system, without prior permission in writing from the publishers.

No responsibility for loss caused to any individual or organization acting on or refraining from action as a result of the material in this publication can be accepted by Bloomsbury or the author.

British Library Cataloguing-in-Publication Data
A catalogue record for this book is available from the British Library.

ISBN HB: 978-0-56762-981-4
　　　PB: 978-0-56702-815-0
　　ePDF: 978-0-56765-569-1
　　ePub: 978-0-56765-570-7

Library of Congress Cataloging-in-Publication Data
Novakovic, Lidija.
Resurrection : a guide for the perplexed / by Lidija Novakovic.
pages cm
Includes bibliographical references and index.
ISBN 978-0-567-62981-4 (hardback)-- ISBN 978-0-567-02815-0 (pbk.)
1. Jesus Christ--Resurrection. I. Title.
BT482.N68 2016
232'.5--dc23
2015024320

Typeset by Fakenham Prepress Solutions, Fakenham, Norfolk NR21 8NN

*To my husband Ivo
and our children, Andreja and Matthew*

CONTENTS

Preface ix

Introduction 1
1 Resurrection Hope in Second Temple Judaism 5
2 Non-Narrative Traditions about Jesus' Resurrection 49
3 Narratives about the Discovery of the Empty Tomb 77
4 Narratives about the Appearances of the Risen Jesus 103
5 Jesus' Resurrection and History 127
6 Jesus' Resurrection and Theology 161

Bibliography 189
Index 197

PREFACE

My interest in the resurrection of Jesus was sparked while I was a student at the Baptist Theological Seminary Rüschlikon, Switzerland, when Günter Wagner, my New Testament Professor, began his seminar in New Testament theology with this topic. Thorwald Lorenzen, my Systematic Theology Professor at Rüschlikon, made me aware of the importance of the resurrection for Christian discipleship. During my PhD studies at Princeton Theological Seminary, Donald Juel, my Doktorvater, and James H. Charlesworth, my mentor in the PTS Dead Sea Scrolls Project, introduced me to Jewish literature of the Second Temple period, which is instrumental for the understanding of the emergence of the belief in resurrection. As a biblical scholar, I have continued to investigate various questions pertaining to Jesus' resurrection, but my major publication in this field explores the use of Israel's Scripture in the early Christian interpretations of the resurrection. I wish to thank Anna Turton, Commissioning Editor for T&T Clark, for inviting me to write this volume in the *Guides for the Perplexed* series. I am especially grateful for her patience and graceful extension of the deadlines for the submission of the manuscript. I also wish to thank my departmental chair, Bill Bellinger, and my colleagues in the Department of Religion at Baylor University for their friendship and continuous support of this project. Special thanks are due to my graduate assistant, Amanda Brobst-Renaud, for her editorial work and helpful feedback about the contents of the manuscript. I would like to extend my deepest gratitude to my husband, Ivo, with whom I had many stimulating conversations about the issues addressed in this book, and to our children Andreja and Matthew, whose interest in this project contributed to its completion.

Introduction

The belief in the resurrection of Jesus is one of the basic tenets of Christianity. The Apostle Paul passionately contends that 'if Christ has not been raised, then our proclamation has been in vain and your faith has been in vain' (1 Cor. 15.14). Yet there is hardly any topic that has been less understood than the resurrection. For many Christians today, Paul's statement means that Christianity stands or falls with the empty tomb. They insist that Jesus has been physically raised from the dead and that no other interpretation of this event represents a genuinely Christian view. Others allege that the belief in a literal resurrection of the physical body contradicts the known laws of nature and prefer to talk about spiritual or metaphorical resurrection. People of different faiths, agnostics and atheists frequently regard the belief in Jesus' resurrection as a Christian legend. Still others pay more attention to the Easter eggs and the Easter bunny than to the real reason for Easter celebration. In addition, for numerous Christian believers, what happened to the dead Jesus is not directly related to the question of what will happen to them when they die. They may confess that Jesus has been bodily raised from the grave, but they believe that upon death their immortal souls will go straight to heaven.

In the autumn of 2013, I taught an undergraduate course on the resurrection of Jesus. On the first day of class, I asked the students to define resurrection. What follows are some of the most representative answers that I got.

Resurrection means actually coming back to life again after death. The functions of eating, drinking, and sleeping are no longer necessary, but are still possible.

Resurrection consists in bringing something back to life that has fully died. In death, the spirit leaves the body, and resurrection rejoins body and spirit.

Resurrection involves reanimation of a corpse.

There are a few types of resurrection, which result in varying results after resurrection, i.e. the possibility of death after resurrection and no possibility of death after resurrection.

Resurrection is a supernatural event in which one has physically died and been buried but is then brought back to life by an external, non-material force.

Resurrection is the act of a body or soul surpassing the physical state of death. The body does not advance in age during death.

A common element in these definitions is the emphasis on the bodily aspect of resurrection. Other issues, especially those related to the characteristics of the resurrected body, are less clear or outright baffling. Some students confused resurrection with resuscitation. There was also an apparent tendency to combine the idea of the immortality of the soul with the concept of the resurrection of the body. The class discussion revealed that many students were oblivious to the differences in the gospel resurrection narratives. Hardly anyone knew anything about the religious milieu in which the Christian proclamation of Jesus' resurrection began.

This book seeks to clarify these and other issues pertaining to the resurrection of Jesus. Similar to other *Guides for the Perplexed*, its target audience is upper-level students or interested readers who may have some general knowledge on this subject but find specific ideas related to the resurrection challenging or downright bewildering. My basic assumption is that we cannot talk about the nature and meaning of this event unless we understand what the followers of Jesus meant when they declared that he was raised from the dead. Although many first-century Jews expected the resurrection of the dead on the last day, the Christian claim that this had already happened to one individual within the realm of history was unprecedented. Yet the language and the concepts that the early Christians used to describe Jesus' resurrection were not novel. They were derived from their prior beliefs about the world, God and afterlife, i.e. from their existing worldview. This worldview was shaped, for the most part, by religious ideas that were developed in Second Temple Judaism. One such belief was the belief in the resurrection of the dead. This belief, however, was by no means uniform. As we will see in the first chapter of this book, some Jews presumed that God would use the earthly bodies to fashion the resurrected bodies, while others believed that mortal bodies were not really needed because God could create them *ex nihilo*. The issue on which all of them agreed, however, was that the resurrection would be a corporate event at the end of time.

The next three chapters of this book are devoted to the New Testament evidence for the resurrection of Jesus. Given the nature of this project, only the most significant passages in the epistolary literature and the gospels are considered. Early Christian interpreters differ with regard to who saw Jesus alive, what the nature of his risen body was and whether the empty tomb was widespread knowledge or an assumption based on prior beliefs. Unlike Paul, who emphasizes the discontinuity between the earthly body and the risen body, the evangelists seek to establish the continuity between the crucified Jesus and the risen Jesus. One of the tasks of this book is to explain these differences by explicating the religio-historical context in which they were formulated.

Chapter 5 addresses one of the most controversial questions in the study of the resurrection of Jesus – its historicity. Rather than presenting various scholarly views on this subject, I have reviewed major arguments for and against the historicity of the empty tomb, as well as major arguments for and against the objectivity of Jesus' appearances. My goal here is not only to explain the contentious issues but also to assess the strengths and weaknesses of individual arguments. This review is prefaced by a succinct discussion of the nature of historical enquiry, which seeks to clarify methodological confusion that characterizes many debates about the historicity of Jesus' resurrection. At the end of this chapter, I address the guiding question of this book: Why did Jesus' followers claim that he was raised from the dead? This is a historical question that could be answered despite the fragmentary character of the available evidence. With regard to the question of whether Jesus' resurrection itself could be proved with historical arguments, however, I join those scholars who claim that this question is not the object of historical enquiry.

The last chapter of the book discusses the implications of Jesus' resurrection for Christian theology. This theme includes four topics: eschatology (the relevance of Jesus' resurrection for Christian hope), Christology (the relevance of Jesus' resurrection for Jesus' messianic identity), theology (the relevance of Jesus' resurrection for our understanding of God) and ethics (the relevance of Jesus' resurrection for Christian living). In each case, I seek to explain the newness of the Christian proclamation vis-à-vis its religious background. My hope is that after reading this book the audience will be able to understand better the exegetical, historical and theological issues pertaining to the resurrection of Jesus, whether they are discussed in the church, in classroom or in scholarly literature.

1

Resurrection Hope in Second Temple Judaism

Belief in resurrection emerged as a specifically Jewish concept of afterlife. Its defining characteristic is the idea that some sort of embodied life will be restored after an interim period of 'death-as-a-state'. Both aspects of this definition – restoration of the body and an interval between one's death and one's resurrection – are nicely articulated in the ingenious formulation coined by N. T. Wright, who describes resurrection as bodily 'life *after* "life after death"'.[1] Scholars customarily emphasize the difference between the Jewish idea of the resurrection of the body and the Platonic idea of immortality of the soul and other Hellenistic beliefs about afterlife, such as the shadowy existence of the dead in Hades. This distinction remains valid even if one considers various stories about reanimated corpses or people being taken bodily into a divine realm after death that were popular among lower classes – such ideas about post-mortem embodied life did not find wider acceptance. Plutarch's comments on this subject are quite illustrative of the general attitude toward afterlife in the Greco-Roman world:

> At any rate, to reject entirely the divinity of human virtue, were impious and base; but to mix heaven with earth is foolish. Let us therefore take the safe course and grant, with Pindar, that 'Our bodies all must follow death's supreme behest, but something living still survives, an image of life, for this alone comes from the gods.' Yes, it comes from them, and to them it returns, not

with its body, but only when it is most completely separated and set free from the body, and becomes altogether pure, fleshless, and undefiled. For 'a dry soul is best', according to Heracleitus, and it flies from the body as lightning flashes from a cloud. But the soul which is contaminated with body, and surfeited with body, like a damp and heavy exhalation, is slow to release itself and slow to rise towards its source. We must not, therefore, violate nature by sending the bodies of good men with their souls to heaven, but implicitly believe that their virtues and their souls, in accordance with nature and divine justice, ascend from men to heroes, from heroes to demi-gods, and from demi-gods, after they have been made pure and holy, as in the final rites of initiation, and have freed themselves from mortality and sense, to gods, not by civic law, but in very truth and according to right reason, thus achieving the fairest and most blessed consummation. (Plutarch, *Rom.* 28.6–8; Perrin, LCL)

In contrast to such adamant denial of any participation of the body in life after death, resurrection hope upholds the restoration of embodied life. The main difficulty in studying the concept of resurrection in Jewish literature, however, comes from the fact that the idea of embodiment does not provide a clear criterion for the selections of texts that should be considered. To begin with, the expectation of a restored embodied life is not identical to the expectation of the restoration of the same kind of physicality that characterizes pre-mortem existence. Reviving the dead, that is, bringing someone back to the same life he or she formerly had, is resuscitation, not resurrection. Such a person will, like everyone else, eventually die again. Resurrection refers to an embodied afterlife that is not characterized by mortality. There is thus a certain discontinuity between pre-mortem and post-mortem bodies. Moreover, while for many contemporary readers the idea of embodiment is related to the distinction between material and immaterial entities, for people in antiquity spiritual beings, even souls, were composed of some kind of material, or 'stuff', however 'fiery' or 'airy' it might be.[2] How dense, then, should the post-mortem restored life be in order to be regarded as an embodied life? Finally, there is a problem of continuity between pre-mortem and post-mortem bodies. Second Temple Jewish texts are not unanimous with regard to the manner and the degree of the expected transformation of the decaying corpses into the new immortal bodies.

There are nevertheless certain elements that any working definition of resurrection should include, which can be used for identifying the passages that speak about resurrection hope: (1) reference to literal death; (2) revival of the dead after an interim period of lifelessness; and (3) a new embodied post-mortem life that stands in continuity but is not identical with pre-mortem existence. Whether a text contains the verbs 'rise', 'arise', 'raise' and the like is not decisive, though it is important. This procedure is, admittedly, to some degree circular. We are using the above criteria to distinguish the resurrection texts in order to learn from these texts what Jews in the Second Temple period believed about the resurrection of the dead. Without these preliminary definitions, however, we will not be able to distinguish between various conceptions of afterlife that can be found in the extant Jewish literature. These criteria are broad enough to allow the inclusion of a range of texts that refer to bodily resurrection, yet differ with regard to when this event will take place, what the characteristics of resurrected bodies are, how they are related to pre-mortem bodies and how individual identity is preserved. The first part of this chapter offers a survey of relevant passages in the Jewish Scriptures, while the second part contains a discussion of relevant passages in early Jewish writings that were not accepted into the Hebrew canon.[3]

1. The Idea of Resurrection in the Jewish Scriptures

Unlike Israel's neighbours, who have shown considerable interest in the fate of the dead (e.g. the Egyptian cult of the dead and the Mesopotamian cult of ancestral veneration), the authors of the Jewish Scriptures do not reveal much interest in the questions of afterlife. This does not mean that the Hebrew Bible is completely silent on this subject, but only that the texts about afterlife are relatively sparse. Yet even this handful of texts betrays a surprising diversity. Some passages (Deut. 26.14; Isa. 14.9; 26.14; Ps. 88.11; 106.28; Prov. 2.18; 9.18; 21.16; Job 26.5–6) reveal a belief in Sheol as the abode of the shades of the departed, whereas other texts indicate that in some circles the notion of afterlife was completely rejected (Job 14.12–14; Sir. 17.28; 41.4; Eccl. 9.5–10). A more contested piece of evidence is found in certain psalms, such as Psalms 16.9–10 and 73.23–26, which is interpreted by some scholars as a longing for beatific vision after death and by others as merely a desire to remain continuously in God's presence. The Greek translation of these psalms further complicates the matter, because several expressions, such as the assertion in Psalm 15.10 LXX (Ps. 16.10 in the Hebrew Bible), 'you will not abandon my soul to Hades or give your devout to see corruption', could be understood, in the opinion of some interpreters, as references to resurrection. Without denying the possibility that later readers, such as Luke's portrayal of Peter in Acts 2.31, could have understood these formulations as evidence for resurrection hope, this interpretation remains doubtful in its original historical and literary setting.

There is a general agreement that Daniel 12.1–3 contains the clearest evidence for belief in resurrection in the Hebrew Bible. Before discussing this text, however, it would be helpful to review three scriptural passages that use the resurrection imagery in the context of the restoration of Israel: Ezekiel 37.1–14; Hosea 6.1–3 and possibly Isaiah 26.19. Even though they do not fulfil the criteria specified above, they use the language that became instrumental for the development of resurrection hope.

1.1. Ezekiel 37.1–14

The vision of the valley of dry bones that are revived by God's spirit provides the most graphic description of the revival of the dead in the Hebrew Scriptures. The process of revivification consists of two major stages: (1) assembling of dry bones, followed by the gradual appearance of sinews, flesh and skin, and (2) reanimation of the restored corpses through the spirit of God.

> The hand of the LORD came upon me, and he brought me out by the spirit of the LORD and set me down in the middle of a valley; it was full of bones. He led me all around them; there were very many lying in the valley, and they were very dry. He said to me, 'Mortal, can these bones live?' I answered, 'O LORD GOD, you know.' Then he said to me, 'Prophesy to these bones,

> and say to them: O dry bones, hear the word of the LORD. Thus says the LORD GOD to these bones: I will cause breath to enter you, and you shall live. I will lay sinews on you, and will cause flesh to come upon you, and cover you with skin, and put breath in you, and you shall live; and you shall know that I am the LORD.' So I prophesied as I had been commanded; and as I prophesied, suddenly there was a noise, a rattling, and the bones came together, bone to its bone. I looked, and there were sinews on them, and flesh had come upon them, and skin had covered them; but there was no breath in them. Then he said to me, 'Prophesy to the breath, prophesy, mortal, and say to the breath: Thus says the LORD GOD: Come from the four winds, O breath, and breathe upon these slain, that they may live.' I prophesied as he commanded me, and the breath came into them, and they lived, and stood on their feet, a vast multitude. (Ezek. 37.1–10)

The commentary that follows, however, clarifies that this vivid description of the revival of the dead merely functions as an allegory for the political restoration of Israel. The dryness of the bones stands for the loss of hope, the graves represent the exile and the restoration of life signifies the return of the exiles to their homeland.

> Then he said to me, 'Mortal, these bones are the whole house of Israel. They say, "Our bones are dried up, and our hope is lost; we are cut off completely." Therefore prophesy, and say to them, Thus says the LORD GOD: I am going to open your graves, and bring you up from your graves, O my people; and I will bring you back to the land of Israel. And you shall know that I am the LORD, when I open your graves, and bring you up from your graves, O my people. I will put my spirit within you, and you shall live, and I will place you on your own soil; then you shall know that I, the LORD, have spoken and will act, says the LORD.' (Ezek. 37.11–14)

Although these verses leave no doubt that – in its current literary context – the revival of dry bones refers to national restoration, this commentary was largely ignored by some later readers, both Jewish (*Pseudo-Ezekiel*; *Gen. Rab.* 14.5; *Lev. Rab.* 14.9; the Targum to Ezekiel) and Christian (Justin, *1 Apol. 52*; Irenaeus,

Haer. 5.15.1; Tertullian, *Res.* 29–30), who 'decontextualized' the first ten verses and read them as a prophecy of literal resurrection of the dead. This interpretative trajectory is not surprising, though. Fragmentation of a text was a common exegetical practice in early Jewish and Christian literature. It seems that Ezekiel's vision of dry bones supplied the new imagery and vocabulary that contributed to the emergence of resurrection hope and enabled the readers who adopted this belief in life after death to express it in tangible and vivid terms.

1.2. Hosea 6.1–3

In this passage, the prophet implores the audience to repent after a period of crisis in the northern kingdom and promises national restoration that will follow the time of deep despair. Like Ezekiel, Hosea uses resurrection language to communicate his message of hope, but, unlike Ezekiel, he does not attach a clarifying commentary regarding the meaning of this text in its current historical and literary setting.

> Come, let us return to the LORD; for it is he who has torn, and he will heal us; he has struck down, and he will bind us up. After two days he will revive us; on the third day he will raise us up, that we may live before him. Let us know, let us press on to know the LORD; his appearing is as sure as the dawn; he will come to us like the showers, like the spring rains that water the earth. (Hos. 6.1–3)

Two temporal expressions, 'after two days' and 'on the third day', communicate the sense of urgency of God's intervention on Israel's behalf. The second phrase frequently appears in the rabbinic writings, which routinely interpret Hosea 6.2 as a prophecy of the resurrection of the dead at the turn of the ages (*y. Ber.* 5.2; *y. Sanh.* 11.6; *b. Sanh.* 97a; *b. Roš Haš.* 31a; *Gen. Rab.* 56.1; 91.7; *Deut. Rab.* 7.6; *Esth. Rab.* 9.2; *Pirqe R. El.* 51 [73b–74a]; *Midr. Pss.* 22.5; the Targum to Hosea). In these texts, the phrase 'on the third day' functions either as a general reference to the day of salvation or as a specific reference to the resurrection of the dead. It is also likely that either one or both of these meanings lie behind the 'third day' motif that appears in the early Christian confession that Christ 'was raised on the third day in accordance with the scriptures' (1 Cor. 15.4). This interpretative tradition, which was prevalent in the third century CE (although it may have been current already in the first century CE), is similar to the interpretative tradition of Ezekiel 37.1–10; a text that employed resurrection imagery to convey hope for national restoration was later interpreted as a text that spoke of the literal resurrection of the dead.

1.3. Isaiah 26.19

This verse is frequently interpreted as evidence of an early belief in the resurrection of the dead: 'Your dead shall live, their corpses shall rise. O dwellers in the dust, awake and sing for joy! For your dew is a radiant dew, and the earth will give birth to those long dead.' This understanding of the text, however, remains controversial. As we have seen in Ezekiel 37 and Hosea 6, the use of resurrection language and imagery is in and of itself inconclusive. The decisive question is whether the statements about revivification of corpses should be understood literally or metaphorically. In favour of literal interpretation is a possible post-exilic dating of the Isaianic Apocalypse (Isa. 24–27) to which this text belongs, which is consistent with the emergence of resurrection hope. If, however, one ascribes this composition to the eighth-century prophet Isaiah, the literal meaning of Isa. 26.19 appears quite subdued, if not implausible, given the general lack of interest in the question of afterlife in this period.

The current literary context of this passage seems to offer additional support for non-literal interpretation. The preceding verses (Isa. 26.16–18) compare people in distress to the pangs of a pregnant woman who is about to give birth: 'we were with child, we writhed, but we gave birth only to wind' (v. 18a). The verses that follow urge the audience to have patience until God punishes 'the inhabitants of the earth for their iniquity' and the earth discloses 'the blood shed on it' (v. 21). The use of figurative language throughout the chapter may suggest that v. 19 should also be understood figuratively, perhaps as a metaphor for national restoration. This interpretation is also easier to reconcile with the assertion in v. 14, which seems to deny any hope of resurrection:

'The dead do not live; shades do not rise – because you have punished them, and wiped out all memory of them.'

The apparent contradiction between Isaiah 26.19 and Isaiah 26.14, however, could be resolved even if Isaiah 26.19 refers to literal resurrection because its scope seems to be limited to slain Israelites, while the denial of resurrection in Isaiah 26.14 seems to apply only to Israel's enemies. On this reading, resurrection itself functions as a vindication of the righteous and its denial as the punishment of the wicked.[4]

1.4. Daniel 12.1–3

This passage is generally regarded as the clearest, if not the earliest, expression of hope for bodily resurrection in the Jewish Scriptures.

> At that time Michael, the great prince, the protector of your people, shall arise. There shall be a time of anguish, such as has never occurred since nations first came into existence. But at that time your people shall be delivered, everyone who is found written in the book. Many of those who sleep in the dust of the earth shall awake, some to everlasting life, and some to shame and everlasting contempt. Those who are wise shall shine like the brightness of the sky, and those who lead many to righteousness, like the stars forever and ever. (Dan. 12.1–3)

To say that this is the clearest scriptural expression of belief in bodily resurrection could be slightly misleading. What is clear is that the phrase 'those who sleep in the dust of the earth' refers to those who have literally died. Death is metaphorically portrayed as a sleep from which one will awaken, which suggests an interim period of lifelessness. The metaphor of awakening implies the restoration of embodied life that characterized one's existence before 'falling asleep'. We can thus identify all three essential elements of our working definition of resurrection. It is also clear that the expected resurrection will take place in the future after a time of unprecedented anguish, i.e. in the eschatological context. What is less clear, however, is the scope of resurrection (i.e. who is included and who is not) and the degree of continuity between pre-mortem and post-mortem life (i.e. the character of the resurrected state and the manner of preserving one's identity).

The assertion in Daniel 12.2 that some will awake to everlasting life while others to everlasting contempt indicates that the author envisions the resurrection of both the good and the bad. Yet, the introductory phrase 'many of those who sleep in the dust of the earth' suggests that this is not a universal resurrection. Since it has a two-fold purpose – to reward the good and to punish the bad – while also presuming that some people will not be raised from the dead, scholars generally agree that three groups are in view. Those who will experience resurrection belong to either side of the ethical spectrum, i.e. they were either exceptionally virtuous or exceptionally wicked. The third group consists of ordinary people who will simply remain dead. This ethical scenario, which is unique in the Hebrew Scriptures, is most likely the result of the extraordinary historical circumstances in which the Book of Daniel was written. It is usually dated to the Maccabean period (167–164 BCE), when Antiochus IV Epiphanes' persecution of pious Jews who persisted in keeping the Torah created an unprecedented theological dilemma: how is one to understand God's justice if the righteous suffer not because they neglect the Torah but precisely because they obey it? The answer given in the Book of Daniel is that God's justice will ultimately prevail, albeit not in this life, but in the life to come. Those who have endured suffering because of their faithfulness to God's law will be raised to everlasting life while the perpetrators who have committed grave injustices against the righteous will be raised to everlasting contempt. It could thus be said that belief in resurrection, which emerged in the Maccabean period, was both an answer to the question of theodicy in the context of martyrdom and an encouragement to the pious to endure in their fidelity to the Torah.

Daniel 12.3 offers additional information about those who will be raised to everlasting life. They are first described as 'those who are wise' and then as 'those who lead many to righteousness'. The parallel structures of two clauses that constitute this verse (*parallelismus membrorum*) seem to suggest that both expressions refer to the same group. What is less clear, however, is whether this description (i.e. the wise who lead many to righteousness) applies to the entire group that will be rewarded with resurrection or merely to one of its subgroups, such as its religious elite. A possible help in identifying this group could be found in Daniel 11.32–35, which first distinguishes between 'those who violate the covenant' and 'the people who are loyal to their God', and then singles out 'the wise among the people' who 'shall give understanding to many'. Within the historical context of the Book of Daniel, the last group most likely refers to religious leaders who encouraged the faithful to resist the Hellenizing policies of Antiochus IV Epiphanes. If the characterization of the wise who give instruction to others functions as an equivalent of the wise who lead many to righteousness in Daniel 12.1–3, its message seems to be that resurrection to everlasting life represents God's reward of the faithful not only for their willingness to suffer martyrdom on behalf of the Torah but also for their leadership and instruction of others.[5] We should also note that the text does not provide any specific information about the fate of the wrongdoers except that, for this group, resurrection will represent an act of judgement that will lead to shame and everlasting contempt. In this text, then, resurrection functions as a means by which the two groups on the opposite ends of ethical spectrum – those extraordinarily virtuous and those extraordinarily wicked – will receive their respective vindication or condemnation.

With regard to the degree of continuity between pre-mortem and post-mortem life, Daniel 12.1–3 raises more questions than it gives answers. To start with, it is not clear whether the expression 'the dust of the earth' in Daniel 12.2 refers to the graves of the dead from which they will arise or to the shadowy existence of the dead in Sheol, as in Job 17.16. Moreover, the post-mortem life of those who are raised to everlasting life is described as a state of shining 'like the brightness of the sky' and 'like the stars forever and ever' (Dan. 12.3). To some scholars, these descriptions are closer to the popular Hellenistic notions of astral immortality (Aristophanes, *Pax* 832–34; Cicero, *Resp.* 6.13–17) than to some sort of bodily afterlife. The author of Daniel 12.1–3, however, does not claim that the wise will become stars, but only that they will shine like stars. In light of a widespread Jewish tradition of identifying stars with angelic beings (Judg. 5.20; Job 38.7; Dan. 8.10; *1 En.* 90.21; 104.2–6), it is probably more likely that these comparisons mean that the resurrected righteous will become like angels. Even if this text does not presume astral transformation but some sort of angelomorphism, as it is usually assumed, the bodily aspect of the resurrected state remains obscure. While it is clear that the post-resurrection life differs from the pre-mortem existence, it is not clear whether and how the earthly bodies will be transformed. The question of whether the identity of resurrected individuals is preserved through a presumed transformation of their corpses or through some other means also remains vague. To expect more clarity, however, is probably inappropriate given the nascent character of resurrection hope and the highly contextual nature of Daniel's vision. After all, the purpose of this text is not to offer an elaborate treatment of the fate of the dead, but to encourage the faithful to persevere in their obedience to the Torah, even unto martyrdom.

2. The Idea of Resurrection in Early Jewish Literature

In this section, we will examine various passages in the Jewish writings from the Second Temple period that were not eventually accepted into the Jewish canon. Some of these texts predate or are contemporaneous with the scriptural passages surveyed above, which suggests a complex conceptual and literary relationship among them. My goal here is not to explain the development of the idea of resurrection but to reconstruct the religious landscape of Second Temple Judaism pertaining to resurrection hope in order to better understand what Jesus' followers meant when they proclaimed that God raised him from the dead.

2.1. The Book of the Watchers (1 Enoch 1–36)

The ideas about afterlife found in the Book of the Watchers, which is usually dated to the third or early second century BCE, are older than those in Daniel 12.1–3. One of the most interesting texts is found in chapter 22, which describes Enoch's vision of the intermediate state of the spirits of the dead, which are kept in different compartments until the day of judgement.

> From there I travelled to another place. And he showed me to the west a great and high mountain of hard rock. And there were

four hollow places in it, deep and very smooth. Three of them were dark and one, illuminated; and a fountain of water was in the middle of it. And I said, 'How smooth are these hollows and altogether deep and dark to view.' Then Raphael answered me, one of the holy angels who was with me, and said to me, 'These hollow places (are intended) that the spirits of the souls of the dead might be gathered into them. For this very (purpose) they were created, (that) here the souls of all human beings should be gathered. And look, these are the pits for the place of their confinement. Thus they were made until the day (on) which they will be judged, and until the time of the day of the end of the great judgement that will be exacted from them.' There I saw the spirit of a dead man making suit, and his lamentation went up to heaven and cried and made suit. Then I asked Raphael, the watcher and holy one who was with me, and said to him, 'This spirit that makes suit – whose is it – that thus his lamentation goes up and makes suit unto heaven?' And he answered me and said, 'This is the spirit that went forth from Abel, whom Cain his brother murdered. And Abel makes accusation against him until his posterity perishes from the face of the earth, and his posterity is obliterated from the posterity of men.' Then I asked about all the hollow places, why they were separated one from the other. And he answered and said, 'These three were made that the spirits of the dead might be separated. And this has been separated for the spirits of the righteous, where the bright fountain of water is. And this has been created for <the spirits of the> sinners, when they die and are buried in the earth, and judgement has not been executed on them in their life. Here their spirits are separated for this great torment, until the great day of judgement, of scourges and tortures of the cursed forever, that there might be a recompense for their spirits. There he will bind them forever. And this has been separated for the spirits of them that make suit, who make disclosure about the destruction, when they were murdered in the days of the sinners. And this was created for the spirits of the people who will not be pious, but sinners, who were godless, and they were companions with the lawless. And their spirits will not be punished on the day of judgement, nor will they be raised from there.' (*1 En.* 22.1–13)[6]

Some scholars regard this passage as the earliest detailed treatment of the fate of the dead in Judaism, which probably underlies the description of the resurrection of the dead in Daniel 12.1–3.[7] Yet this is not a text about resurrection, but about the interim period between death and the final judgement. Whether the author expects that some kind of resurrection will precede the judgement is unclear. The only mention of 'raising' in this chapter – that the spirits of some people 'will not be punished on the day of judgement, nor will they be raised from there' (*1 En.* 22.13) – is inconclusive, as well as somewhat odd. While the spirits of the dead (called 'the spirits of the souls of the dead' in *1 En.* 22.3) retain certain bodily functions, such as memory and sensitivity to light, thirst and pain, it is not clear whether their 'resurrection', if such an event is envisioned, is imagined in bodily form.

Despite these drawbacks, however, the description of the temporary repositories of the dead in *1 En.* 22.1–13 is compatible with Daniel 12.1–3 and could shed some light on its unusual ethical scenario. The spirits of the righteous are separated from the spirits of the wicked, who are further subdivided into those who have escaped punishment during their lifetime and those who have already received judgement during their pre-mortem existence. While the spirits of the former will eventually be transferred to a place of final retribution, the spirits of the latter will remain where they are. It is this second group of evildoers that is explicitly denied eventual resurrection.

1 Enoch 22.1–13 says nothing about the final destiny of the righteous, but this question is addressed in *1 En.* 24.2–25.7. In the vision described in this text, Enoch sees seven glorious mountains. The seventh mountain, which is in the middle, is encircled with fragrant trees. Among them, there is one special tree, whose fragrance and beauty exceeds all other trees. The explanation that follows clarifies that this tree will be given to the righteous. The interpreting angel, however, does not describe their actual restoration to life, but rather focuses on their final state, which is presented as amazingly long, but not necessarily everlasting, life on earth.

> This high mountain that you saw, whose peak is like the throne of God, is the seat where the Great Holy One, the Lord of glory, the King of eternity, will sit, when he descends to visit the earth in goodness. And (as for) this fragrant tree, no flesh has the right to touch it until the great judgement, in which there will

be vengeance on all and a consummation forever. Then it will be given to the righteous and the pious, and its fruit will be food for the chosen. And it will be transplanted to the holy place, by the house of God, the King of eternity. Then they will rejoice greatly and be glad, and they will enter into the sanctuary. Its fragrances <will be> in their bones, and they will live a long life on the earth, such as your fathers lived also in their days, and torments and plagues and suffering will not touch them. (*1 En.* 25.3–7)

Although this text uses the so-called *Urzeit-Endzeit* (primeval time-end time) typology to describe the restored life on earth, it is not clear whether it presumes bodily resurrection, because the author does not use a typical resurrection vocabulary. While some scholars interpret the assertion that the fragrance of the tree of life will be in the bones of the righteous as an allusion to bodily resurrection, this conclusion remains tentative.

2.2. The Animal Apocalypse (1 Enoch 85–90)

This portion of *1 Enoch*, whose final form is usually dated to c.163 BCE, is an allegorical presentation of Israel's history from the creation of Adam to the Hellenistic period. In this allegory, animals represent human beings or nations: sheep stand for Israel, predatory animals for the nations, and white bulls for Adam and the antediluvian patriarchs. The final section of this work describes the replacement of historical Jerusalem (the 'old house') with the eschatological Jerusalem ('a new house') and then offers the following vision:

And all that had been destroyed and dispersed <by> all the wild beasts and all the birds of heaven were gathered in that house. And the Lord of the sheep rejoiced greatly because they were all good and had returned to that house … And I saw how a white bull was born, and its horns were large. And all the wild beasts and all the birds of heaven were afraid of it and made petition to it continually. And I saw until all their species were changed, and they all became white cattle. (*1 En.* 90.33, 37–38a)

The gathering of the sheep that had been previously destroyed is probably a symbolic reference to the resurrection of righteous

Israelites, while the transformation of the sheep into 'white cattle' may refer to the transformation of their earthly bodies into more glorious bodies. This interpretation, though tentative, is certainly conceivable given the similar dating of the Animal Apocalypse and the Book of Daniel.

2.3. The Epistle of Enoch (1 Enoch 91–105)

The Epistle of Enoch, which is preserved in the concluding chapters of *1 Enoch*, is usually dated to the reign of Alexander Jannaeus (104–78 BCE). It describes the suffering of the righteous who are oppressed by the rich and powerful and promises their vindication in the afterlife.

> Fear not, souls of the righteous; take courage, you pious who have died. And do not grieve because your souls have descended into Sheol with grief, and your body of flesh did not fare in your life according to your piety, because the days that you lived were days of sinners and curses on the earth. (*1 En.* 102.4–5)

> For I have read the tablets of heaven, and I have seen the writing of what must be, and I know the things that are written in them and inscribed concerning you – that good things and joy and honour have been prepared and written down for the souls of the pious who have died; and much good will be given to you in the place of your labours, and your lot will exceed the lot of the living. The souls of the pious who have died will come to life, and they will rejoice and be glad; and their spirits will not perish, nor their memory from the presence of the Great One for all the generations of eternity. (*1 En.* 103.2–4)

> Take courage, then; for formerly you were worn out by evils and tribulations, but now you will shine like the luminaries of heaven; you will shine and appear, and the portals of heaven will be opened for you ... Take courage and do not abandon your hope, for you will have great joy like the angels of heaven. (*1 En.* 104.2, 4)

The author of these passages claims that the souls of the righteous who have died will, after a period of waiting, come to life and ascend to heaven, where they will continue to exist like angels. This sequence – death, an interim period and coming back to life – corresponds to the typical sequence of events in the passages that express resurrection hope. It is thus not surprising that some scholars believe that these passages also presume bodily resurrection. This conclusion, however, remains controversial. The final destiny of the righteous is not portrayed as an embodied life but is akin to angelomorphism, like in Daniel 12.3, with which the author seems to have been familiar. Unlike the Danielic text, however, this passage does not describe the revival of the corpses of the dead but the revival of their spirits and their subsequent exaltation to heaven. This idea seems to be closer to *1 En.* 22.1–13 than to Daniel 12.3. While it would be erroneous to regard this concept of afterlife as a Jewish adaptation of the Greek idea of immortality of the soul, it is also problematic to regard it as bodily resurrection.

2.4. The Similitudes of Enoch (1 Enoch 37–71)

This work, which is usually dated to the end of the first century BCE or the first half of the first century CE, is the only section of *1 Enoch* that provides unambiguous, though not wholly harmonious, evidence of the expectation of bodily resurrection. 'In those days, the earth will restore what has been entrusted to it, and Sheol will restore what it has received, and destruction will restore what it owes' (*1 En.* 51.1). If these three clauses form synonymous parallelism, as it is usually assumed, their corresponding terms are mutually interpretative. If so, the mention of the earth in the first clause could be taken as a reference to the dead and the mention of their restoration as a reference to their bodily resurrection. The statement that appears at the end of this passage, that 'the earth will rejoice and the righteous will dwell on it' (*1 En.* 51.5b), probably indicates that those who will be raised from the dead will continue to live on earth.

A somewhat different picture emerges from *1 En.* 39.3–5a, which envisions the dwelling places of the righteous among the angels in heaven: 'And in those days a whirlwind snatched me up from the face of the earth and set me down within the confines of the heavens. And there I saw another vision – the dwellings of the holy ones, and the resting places of the righteous. There my eyes saw their dwellings with his righteous angels and their resting places with the holy ones.' Some passages offer vivid descriptions of the transformed life of the righteous, such as *1 En.* 58.3 ('The righteous will be in the light of the sun, and the chosen, in the light of everlasting life. The days of their life will have no end, and the days of the holy will be innumerable') or *1 En.* 62.15 ('And the righteous and the chosen will have arisen from the earth, and have ceased to cast down their faces, and have put on the garment of glory'). These diverse descriptions of the post-mortem existence cannot be easily harmonized. Their common denominator is the conviction that the restored life will be different from the earthly life, but when it comes to specific aspects of it, such as the dwelling places of the righteous or the character of their future bodies, the relevant texts are either incoherent or elusive.

2.5. Jubilees

The book of *Jubilees* belongs to the group of exegetical works called 'rewritten Scripture'. This composition, which is usually dated to the second century BCE, offers a retelling of a portion of the Pentateuch, beginning with Genesis 1 and ending with Exodus 14. Between the accounts of the death and burial of Abraham and Jacob's procurement of the right of the firstborn from Esau is a lengthy discussion of the end-time (*Jub.* 23.16–31). The final period of human history is envisioned as a return to the Garden of Eden, characterized by increased health, absence of aging and prolonged human life span. At the end of this depiction of the future, the author offers the following description of the post-mortem destiny of the righteous:

> And then the LORD will heal his servants, and they will rise up and see great peace. And they will drive out their enemies, and the righteous ones will see and give praise, and rejoice forever and ever with joy; and they will see all of their judgements and all of their curses among their enemies. And their bones will rest in the earth, and their spirits will increase joy, and they will know that the LORD is an executor of judgement; but he will show mercy to hundreds and thousands, to all who love him. (*Jub.* 23.30–31)

It is not easy to discern the type of afterlife envisaged in this passage. If the clause 'they will rise up' refers to bodily resurrection, as it is sometimes assumed, the statement that 'their bones will rest in the earth' must be explained. If these two clauses describe two simultaneous actions, the author seems to promote an odd concept of non-bodily resurrection, perhaps as a result of blending of resurrection hope with the idea of immortality of soul. If these two clauses describe two actions that will take place at different times, the concept of bodily resurrection is conceivable only if we presume that the author presents the end-time events in a reversed chronological sequence. On this reading, the clause 'their bones will rest in the earth' describes the time between death and resurrection, while the clause 'they will rise up' describes the actual resurrection that will take place afterwards.[8] This interpretation, however, fails to convince because the statement 'their bones will rest on earth' is immediately followed by the assertion 'and their spirits will increase joy', which suggests a separation between the earthly bodies of the righteous and their spirits. If this text envisions some kind of resurrection, the idea is closer to the exaltation of the spirits of the righteous from Sheol to heaven described in *1 En.* 103.3–4 than to the concept of bodily resurrection.

2.6. Second Maccabees

This writing, which is usually dated to the time between 100 and 63 BCE, describes the persecution of Jews under Antiochus IV Epiphanes. The most vivid expressions of the hope of bodily resurrection are found in chapter 7, which describes the martyrdom of seven brothers and their mother who refused to comply with Antiochus' Hellenizing policies. This account is preceded by a story of the martyrdom of the old Eleazar (2 Macc. 6.18–31), who accepts suffering with a simple declaration that no one will escape God's punishment: 'Even if for the present I would avoid the punishment of mortals, yet whether I live or die I will not escape the hands of the Almighty. Therefore, by bravely giving up my life now, I will show myself worthy of my old age and leave to the young a noble example of how to die a good death willingly and nobly for the revered and holy laws' (2 Macc. 6.26–28). The young martyrs in chapter 7, however, do not simply accept death like Eleazar, but express hope that they will receive their destroyed bodies – each organ and each limb – back again in the resurrection. The first mention of this hope can be found in the last words of the second brother: 'You accursed wretch, you dismiss us from this present life, but the King of the universe will raise us up to an everlasting renewal of life, because we have died for his laws' (2 Macc. 7.9). The third brother expresses the same hope, but with greater specificity: 'When it was demanded, he quickly put out his tongue and courageously stretched forth his hands, and said nobly, "I got these from Heaven, and because of his laws I disdain them, and from him I hope to get them back again"' (2 Macc. 7.10–11). The fourth brother further clarifies that resurrection is reserved only for the martyrs: 'One cannot but choose to die at the hands of mortals and to cherish the hope God gives of being raised again by him. But for you there will be no resurrection to life!' (2 Macc. 7.14).

Each of these speeches expresses hope not only that God will bring back to life the young martyrs who were denied the pleasure of a bodily existence because of their premature death, but also that their restored bodies will be the exact replicas of their earthly bodies. The idea that destroyed bodily organs will be restored by God through resurrection is also found in the account of the death of Razis, one of the elders of Jerusalem (2 Macc. 14.37–46). When the Syrian troops sent to capture him surrounded his tower, he tried to commit suicide, but failed to do so swiftly. The narrator ends this story with a gruesome description of a dying Razis, who 'tore out his entrails, took them in both hands and hurled them at the crowd, calling upon the Lord of life and spirit to give them back to him again' (2 Macc. 14.46). In all these texts, the expected vindication operates according to the principle of *quid pro quo*. 'What has been destroyed must be restored.'[9]

The concept of resurrection in 2 Maccabees 7 includes another extraordinary feature. Unlike any other text discussed above, the account of the martyrdom of seven brothers and their mother suggests that the resurrected bodies of the righteous sufferers will not be restored from their earthly remains, however scanty, but will be recreated from nothing. God's power to resurrect is here compared to God's power to create. The analogy between the resurrection and the creation is most distinctly formulated in the poignant speeches of the mother who encourages her sons to persevere because, just as God created their bodies in her womb, he will recreate them in the future.

> I do not know how you came into being in my womb. It was not I who gave you life and breath, nor I who set in order the elements within each of you. Therefore the Creator of the world, who shaped the beginning of humankind and devised the origin of all things, will in his mercy give life and breath back to you again, since you now forget yourselves for the sake of his laws. (2 Macc. 7.22–23)

> I beg you, my child, to look at the heaven and the earth and see everything that is in them, and recognize that God did not make them out of things that existed. And in the same way the human race came into being. Do not fear this butcher, but prove worthy of your brothers. Accept death, so that in God's mercy I may get you back again along with your brothers. (2 Macc. 7.28–29)

The declaration that 'God did not make [the heaven and the earth and everything that is in them] out of things that existed' (2 Macc. 7.28) is usually regarded as the earliest formulation of the idea of *creatio ex nihilo*. Segal alleges that 'this passage shows that the motivation for developing a notion of *creatio ex nihilo* is actually the necessity of clarifying what bodily resurrection means ... Previously, the creation testified to God's power and the Sabbath was the ritual celebration of His power. Now, the creation is also the demonstration of God's power to resurrect. That was a total innovation in Jewish thought.'[10] The idea that bodily resurrection is analogous to the creation from nothing also suggests that the personal identity of the resurrected martyrs is not preserved through any kind of continuity between their mortal and resurrected bodies but by God alone.

The concept of resurrection in 2 Maccabees thus includes two distinctive, albeit paradoxical, features. On the one hand, the relevant texts emphasize the bodily, even fleshly, character of the resurrected bodies. On the other hand, the same texts indicate that God does not need the earthly bodies to restore the bodies of faithful Jews who have persevered in Torah obedience. Rather, the new bodies will be recreated *ex nihilo* after the pattern of God's original creation of the world from nothing.

2.7. Qumran Literature

The Dead Sea Scrolls contain various allusions to afterlife, such as the promise of 'eternal enjoyment with endless life, and a crown of glory with majestic raiment in eternal light' (1QS 4.7–8), the expectation that 'those who lie in the dust will hoist the flag, and the worm of the dead will raise the banner' (1QH^a 14.34), or the claim that purification of a person leads to union with 'your holy ones, to raise the worms of the dead from the dust' (1QH^a 19.12).[11] It is, however, controversial whether these references should be understood literally or merely as poetic descriptions of spiritual experiences of the members of the community. Explicit references to the resurrection of the dead in the Qumran literature are in fact quite rare. Two compositions that offer the clearest evidence of a belief in resurrection – the so-called *Messianic Apocalypse* and *Pseudo-Ezekiel* – are usually not regarded as sectarian documents, i.e. as documents composed by the members of the Qumran community. All of this suggests that resurrection hope belonged to the spectrum of various conceptions of afterlife held by the Qumranites, but may not have been their dominant belief.[12]

The *Messianic Apocalypse* (4Q521) was probably composed in the first century BCE. The second column of frg. 2 of this document contains the following description of the end-time events:

10 And the fru[it of a] good [wor]k will not be delayed for anyone,
11 and the glorious things that have not taken place the Lord will do as he s[aid],
12 for he will heal the wounded and give life to the dead, he will preach good news to the poor
13 and [sat]isfy the [weak], he will lead those who have been cast out and enrich the hungry[13]

Giving life to the dead in line 12 most likely refers to literal resurrection. The text unfortunately offers no information regarding the character of this event, such as the description of the resurrected bodies or the manner of preservation of personal identity. Even though grammatically (and theologically) God is the subject of this and other activities mentioned in this passage, the author(s) may envision these things occurring through the agency of the Messiah who is mentioned in line 1 of this column ('[... for hea]ven and earth will listen to his Messiah'). More significant, however, is the observation that the resurrection of the dead belongs to the glorious events that will be experienced by the righteous at the end of days. The reassurance in line 10 that the reward for righteous living ('the fruit of a good work') will not be delayed probably indicates that the resurrection functions as an act of divine justice. Since the text mentions only the resurrection of the pious, it seems that the resurrection of the wicked is not expected.

The document known as *Pseudo-Ezekiel* (4Q385–4Q388, 4Q391), which is usually dated to the second century BCE, offers one of the earliest interpretations of Ezekiel's vision of the valley of dry bones (Ezekiel 37) as a literal interpretation of the dead. 4Q385 frg. 2 lines 2–9 is the best-preserved copy of this text:

2 [And I said, 'O Lord!] I have seen many (men) from Israel who have loved your Name and have walked
3 in the ways of [your heart. And th]ese things when will they come to be and how will they be recompensed for their piety?' And the Lord said
4 to me, 'I will make (it) manifest[ ]to the children of Israel and they shall know that I am the Lord.'
5 [And he said,] 'Son of man, prophesy over the bones and let them be j[oi]ned bone to its bone and joint
6 [to its joint.' And it wa]s so. And He said a second time, 'Prophesy and let arteries come upon them and let skin cover them
7 [from above.' And it was so.] And He said, 'Prophesy once again over the four winds of heaven and let them blow breath
8 [into the slain.' And it was so,] and a large crowd of people came [to li]fe and blessed the Lord Sebaoth wh[o]
9 [had given them life ... and] I said, 'O Lord! When shall these things come to be?' And the Lord said to m[e, 'Until ...]¹⁴

In *Pseudo-Ezekiel*, Ezekiel's prophecy of the national restoration of Israel as a whole is presented as a prophecy of the future resurrection of righteous individuals. An introductory dialogue between Ezekiel and God clarifies that the prophecy is applicable to individual Israelites who have led pious lives but have not been rewarded for their righteous living during their lifetime. The actual description of the revivification of dry bones is significantly abbreviated with the help of a simple fulfilment formula, 'And it was so', which links the resurrection of the dead to the creation account in Genesis 1. Finally, the commentary from Ezekiel 37.11–14, which applies the vision of dry bones to national restoration of Israel, is omitted and replaced with a question about the time of the fulfilment of these prophecies which, despite the fragmentary character of the extant text, points to the eschatological future. With the help of these interpretative strategies, the physicality of the resurrected bodies, conveyed through a vivid description of a staged revitalization of dry bones, becomes the dominant aspect of resurrection hope.

2.8. Testaments of the Twelve Patriarchs

The *Testaments of the Twelve Patriarchs* is a Jewish composition from the second century BCE, which has undergone significant editing by a later Christian scribe. While separating editorial layers of this document is a challenging task, it is nonetheless possible to isolate the contours of the pre-Christian content of four passages that mention the resurrection of the dead.

> Then I shall arise in gladness and I shall bless the Most High for his marvels. (*T. Sim.* 6.7)

> And after this Abraham, Isaac and Jacob will be resurrected to life and I and my brothers will be chiefs (wielding) our sceptre in Israel: Levi, the first; I, second; Joseph, third; Benjamin, fourth; Simeon, fifth; Issachar, sixth; and all the rest in their order ... And those who died in sorrow shall be raised in joy; and those who died in poverty for the Lord's sake shall be made rich; those who died on account of the Lord shall be wakened to life. (*T. Jud.* 25.1, 4)

> And now, my children, do not grieve because I am dying, nor be depressed because I am leaving you. I shall rise again in your midst as a leader among your sons, and I shall be glad in

the midst of my tribe – as many as keep the Law of the Lord and the commandments of Zebulon, their father. But the Lord shall bring down fire on the impious and will destroy them to all generations. I am now hurrying to my rest, like my fathers. (*T. Zeb.* 10.1–4)

And then you will see Enoch and Seth and Abraham and Isaac and Jacob being raised up at the right hand in great joy. Then shall we also be raised, each of us over our tribe, and we shall prostrate ourselves before the heavenly king. Then all shall be changed, some destined for glory, others for dishonour, for the Lord first judges Israel for the wrong she has committed and then he shall do the same for all the nations. Then he shall judge Israel by the chosen gentiles as he tested Esau by the Midianites who loved their brothers. You, therefore, my children, may your lot come to be with those who fear the Lord. (*T. Benj.* 10.6–10)

In each of these speeches, a dying patriarch expresses hope that he will rise again. The *Testament of Judah* and the *Testament of Benjamin* also mention the resurrection of other prominent figures from Israel's past: Enoch, Seth, Abraham, Isaac, Jacob and the brothers of the dying patriarch. The sequence of their resurrection typically follows the chronological order in which they lived. These two testaments also mention the resurrection of the righteous, who are portrayed as those who died in sorrow, in poverty or for the sake of the Lord. In each case, the resurrection brings about a reversal of fortunes: sorrow becomes joy, poverty wealth and violent death life. While all texts in the *Testament of Twelve Patriarchs* presume the resurrection of the righteous, the *Testament of Benjamin* also mentions those who will be raised for dishonour (*T. Benj.* 10.8).

Even though these texts envision bodily resurrection, they provide no specific information about the character of the resurrected body apart from a hint that it may involve a certain transformation (*T. Benj.* 10.8). Some assertions seem to suggest the earthly location of the post-resurrection existence and its association with national restoration (*T. Jud.* 25.1; *T. Benj.* 10.7; *T. Zeb.* 10.2), while other statements point to the heavenly setting of the resurrection (*T. Benj.* 10.6–7). Such a mixture of mundane and transcendent categories cannot be easily harmonized, which impedes making any definite conclusion about the character of the resurrected life in this document.

2.9. Psalms of Solomon

Psalms of Solomon is a collection of 18 hymns, which were composed sometime between 65 and 30 BCE. The resurrection of the dead is mentioned in Psalm 3:

> He adds sin upon sin in his life; he falls – his fall is serious – and he will not get up. The destruction of the sinner is forever, and he will not be remembered when (God) looks after the righteous. This is the share of sinners forever, but those who fear the Lord shall rise up to eternal life, and their life shall be in the Lord's light, and it shall never end. (*Pss. Sol.* 3.10–12)

The author of this psalm draws a sharp contrast between the ultimate fate of sinners and the righteous. Only the righteous can hope to be raised to eternal life, whereas sinners will be destroyed and permanently erased from memory. The text, however, provides no specific information about the character of the resurrected body, except for its eternal duration and association with the divine light. There is also no explanation why 'those who fear the Lord' will be raised. Since the author does not indicate that they have suffered injustices during their earthly lives, their resurrection probably functions as a reward for their righteous living rather than as a compensation for the losses they suffered because of their right conduct.

2.10. Josephus

The writings of Flavius Josephus, which he composed in the aftermath of the fall of Jerusalem in 70 CE, contain several elaborate passages that give us invaluable insights into Jewish beliefs about resurrection in the first century CE. These references can be divided into two groups: (1) passages that reveal Josephus' own beliefs, and (2) passages that describe the beliefs of his contemporaries.

Two texts belong to the first group. The first is Josephus' speech to his companions who wanted to commit suicide rather than surrender to the Romans on the occasion of the fall of Jotapata.

> Why set asunder such fond companions as soul and body? ... All of us, it is true, have mortal bodies, composed of perishable matter, but the soul lives for ever, immortal: it is a portion of the Deity housed in our bodies ... Know you not that they who depart this life in accordance with the law of nature and repay the loan which they received from God, when He who lent is pleased to reclaim it, win eternal renown; that their houses and families are secure; that their souls, remaining spotless and obedient, are allotted the most holy place in heaven, whence, in the revolution of the ages, they return to find in chaste bodies a new habitation? But as for those who have laid mad hands upon themselves, the darker regions of the nether world receive their souls, and God, their father, visits upon their posterity the outrageous acts of the parents. (*J.W.* 3.362, 372, 374–375 [Thackeray, LCL])

The second text is found in *Against Apion*:

> [E]ach individual, relying on the witness of his own conscience and the lawgiver's prophecy, confirmed by the sure testimony of God, is firmly persuaded that to those who observe the laws and, if they must needs die for them, willingly meet death, God has granted a renewed existence and in the revolution of the ages the gift of a better life. (*Ag. Ap.* 2.218 [Thackeray, LCL])

For the most part, Josephus' Jotapata speech sounds like a Hellenistic treatise of the immortality of the soul. Josephus makes a sharp distinction between mortal bodies that are composed of perishable matter and the immortal soul that lives forever. He portrays death as a separation of the body from the soul. He also claims that only the souls of those who die a natural death (who are portrayed as those whose souls will remain 'spotless and obedient') will be allotted 'the most holy place in heaven', while the souls of the wicked (who are limited here to those who commit suicide) will depart to 'the darker regions of the nether world'. Toward the end of his speech, however, Josephus explains that heaven is not the final destiny of the righteous. Rather, 'in the revolution of the ages', these souls will return to find a new habitation in 'chaste bodies'. Both aspects of this claim – 'the revolution of the ages' and 'a renewed existence' – are also found in *Ag. Ap.* 2.218. Some scholars interpret these expressions as indications of Josephus' belief in the transmigration of souls, i.e. metempsychosis. However, Josephus does not speak of reincarnation of the soul in a general sense, but of its reincarnation into a 'chaste' body, i.e. a body with special qualities. It is therefore more accurate to say that Josephus' assertions represent his translation of a Jewish belief in the resurrection of the body into philosophical concepts that would be intelligible to his educated Roman audience. Since most of his readers would have found the idea of bodily resurrection repulsive, he used the concepts of the immortality of the soul and metempsychosis to express his belief that at the end of the ages the righteous will be restored to a new bodily life.

On several occasions, Josephus describes the beliefs of three major Jewish sects: the Sadducees, the Pharisees and the Essenes. Like in the passages discussed above, he tries to explain Jewish ideas about afterlife with the help of Greco-Roman concepts that would be familiar to his readers. To this end, he associates the Sadducees with the Epicureans, the Pharisees with the Stoics and the Essenes with the Pythagoreans. He also makes a distinction between the Sadducees, who denied life after death (*Ant.* 18.16–17; *J.W.* 2.165), and the Pharisees and the Essenes, who believed in afterlife. He describes the beliefs of the Pharisees as follows:

> Every soul, they maintain, is imperishable, but the soul of the good alone passes into another body, while the souls of the wicked suffer eternal punishment. (*J.W.* 2.163 [Thackeray, LCL])

> They believe that souls have power to survive death and that there are rewards and punishments under the earth for those who have led lives of virtue or vice; eternal imprisonment is the lot of evil souls, while the good souls receive an easy passage to a new life. (*Ant.* 18.14 [Feldman, LCL])

It is clear that Josephus' own beliefs about afterlife are close to those of the Pharisees. The Pharisees affirm, he claims, the immortality of the souls of all human beings, but they believe that only the souls of the righteous will pass 'into another body' or 'receive an easy passage to a new life'. These expressions are usually interpreted as references to bodily resurrection. Josephus thus portrays the Pharisaic concept of resurrection as a two-stage process: a separation of immortal soul from the body at death and a resurrection of the body at the turn of the ages. Yet he insists that the soul will not return to the same body from which it departed but will pass into 'another body'. It would be erroneous, however, to conclude from this that the Pharisees believed that the earthly bodies of the righteous would remain in their graves while their immortal souls would unite with the new bodies in resurrection. Josephus probably wanted to avoid offending the sensibilities of his Roman audience, who would have found the return of the soul to the same body, i.e. revivification of a decomposed corpse, absurd. His hesitance to affirm any continuity between the earthly body and the new body therefore does not mean that no continuity is presumed. But his silence on this subject also prevents us from turning this possibility into a probability and concluding that, in his view, the Pharisees did in fact expect a transformation of a mortal body into a different kind of body. Given Josephus' hermeneutical constraints, then, his claim pertaining to the resurrected body merely indicates that the new bodies of the righteous will be different from the perishable bodies they now possess.

Josephus' presentation of the beliefs of the Essenes is somewhat different from his presentation of the beliefs of the Pharisees.

> For it is a fixed belief of theirs that the body is corruptible and its constituent matter impermanent, but that the soul is immortal and imperishable. Emanating from the finest ether, these souls become entangled, as it were, in the prison-house of the body, to which they are dragged down by a sort of natural spell; but when once they are released from the bonds of the flesh, then, as though liberated from a long servitude, they rejoice and are borne aloft. Sharing the belief of the sons of Greece, they maintain that for virtuous souls there is reserved an abode beyond the ocean, a place which is not oppressed by rain or snow or heat, but is refreshed by the ever gentle breath of the west wind coming in from ocean; while they relegate base souls to a murky and tempestuous dungeon, big with never-ending punishments. (*J.W.* 2.154–155 [Thackeray, LCL])

They regard the souls as immortal and believe that they ought to strive especially to draw near to righteousness. (*Ant.* 18.18 [Feldman, LCL])

As in the passages that reveal Josephus' own beliefs and in his descriptions of the Pharisees, Josephus ascribes to the Essenes belief in the immortality of the soul. Another similarity is the motif of the body as a prison-house from which the soul is liberated at death, which is also found in his Jotapata speech. These ideas are not surprising, given a thoroughly Hellenistic character of Josephus' reports. What is different, however, is the absence of any idea of re-embodiment, such as the soul's entry to another body or a passage to a new life, which would indicate belief in bodily resurrection. Given Josephus' ability to Hellenize Jewish ideas of embodied afterlife, his failure to do so here probably means he did not find in his sources any reference to the Essenes' belief in the resurrection. Since the Dead Sea Scrolls demonstrate that resurrection hope was one of the beliefs of the Qumran community, it appears that neither Josephus nor his sources had a comprehensive knowledge of the sectarian literature. His presentation of the Essenes' notions of life after death is, thus, incomplete.

This conclusion remains valid even if we consider Josephus' account of the martyrdom of the Essenes who refused to 'blaspheme their lawgiver or to eat some forbidden thing' (*J.W.* 2.152), which precedes his description of their ideas about afterlife. Josephus' report includes one assertion that, according to some scholars, could point to some form of resurrection hope: 'Smiling in their agonies and mildly deriding their tormentors, they cheerfully resigned their souls, confident that they would receive them back again' (*J.W.* 2.153). Since, however, the explanation that follows in 2.154–155 contains no allusion to the bodily resurrection, the question of whether the idea of receiving back one's soul really implies the expectation of the resurrection of the body remains controversial.

2.11. Pseudo-Philo

Pseudo-Philo's *Liber Antiquitatum Biblicarum* is a rewritten scriptural narrative that is usually dated to the end of the first century

CE, which starts with the creation of the world and ends with the death of Saul. This work has many affinities with two apocalypses, 4 *Ezra* and 2 *Baruch*, although they do not belong to the same literary genre. All three compositions were written in the aftermath of the destruction of Jerusalem in 70 CE, all three were originally written in Hebrew and all three are of Palestinian provenance. They also share a common interest in the resurrection of the dead, even though their conceptions of life after death are not completely identical.

The author of *Liber Antiquitatum Biblicarum* proffers a two-stage scenario of afterlife. The first stage begins with a separation of the soul from the body at death, while the second stage begins with the resurrection of the dead. His descriptions of these two stages, however, include many assertions that only insinuate certain possibilities. For example, Pseudo-Philo clams that 'when the soul is separated from the body, then they will say, "Let us not mourn over these things that we suffer; but because whatever we ourselves have devised, these will we receive"' (*L.A.B.* 44.10). It seems that this depiction of the intermediate state of the wicked suggests that they will experience some kind of judgement right after death. If so, this could only be a partial judgement, because the last judgement will take place only after the resurrection. Another passage, found in Deborah's farewell speech, claims that souls in the intermediate state can neither repent of the sins committed during their lifetime nor continue sinning: 'For even if you seek to do evil in hell after your death, you cannot, because the desire for sinning will cease and the evil impulse will lose its power' (*L.A.B.* 33.3). The souls of the righteous, on the other hand, are stored in peace as they await the resurrection: 'But also at the end the lot of each one of you will be life eternal, for you and your seed, and I will take your souls and store them in peace until the time allotted the world be complete' (*L.A.B.* 23.13).

Pseudo-Philo portrays the resurrection of the dead as an event that will take place at the end of the world. The fullest description of this event is found in God's speech to Noah after the flood.

> But when the years appointed for the world have been fulfilled, then the light will cease and the darkness will fade away. And I will bring the dead to life and raise up those who are sleeping from the earth. And hell will pay back its debt, and the place

of perdition will return its deposit so that I may render to each according to his works and according to the fruits of his own devices, until I judge between soul and flesh. And the world will cease, and death will be abolished, and hell will shut its mouth. And the earth will not be without progeny or sterile for those inhabiting it; and no one who has been pardoned by me will be tainted. And there will be another earth and another heaven and everlasting dwelling place. (*L.A.B.* 3.10)

The author uses two synonymous formulations – bringing the dead to life and raising those who are sleeping – to describe the future resurrection. The use of the metaphor of sleep for death is fairly traditional, as we have seen in Daniel 12.1–3. The resurrection of the dead probably entails a reunion of soul and body, but this is only a deduction based on the references about the intermediate state of the souls after death and not a claim explicated in this text. What is clear, though, is that the purpose of the resurrection is to enable the implementation of the last judgement. Since both the wicked and the righteous will receive the final rendering 'according to his works and according to the fruits of his own devices', the expected resurrection has a universal scope. The reference to 'another earth and another heaven, an everlasting dwelling place' at the end of this passage probably indicates a radical transformation of the living conditions on earth and the abolishment of death.

God's speech to Moses before his death includes another reference to the resurrection of the dead that may shed additional light on Pseudo-Philo's notion of the resurrection.

And all the angels will mourn over you, and the heavenly hosts will be saddened. But neither angel nor man will know your tomb in which you are to be buried until I visit the world. And I will raise up you and your fathers from the land of Egypt in which you sleep and you will come together and dwell in the immortal dwelling place that is not subject to time … And when the time draws near to visit the world, I will command the years and order the times and they will be shortened, and the stars will hasten and the light of the sun will hurry to fall and the light of the moon will not remain; for I will hurry to raise up you who are sleeping in order that all who can live may dwell in the place of sanctification I showed you. (*L.A.B.* 19.12–13)

This text is admittedly ambiguous, so much so that some authors allege that two resurrections are envisioned, the first from the land of Egypt to the immortal dwelling place and the second at the end of time.[15] Such an unusual scenario, however, is not required by the text. There are, actually, some indications that the author uses two parallel descriptions of the same eschatological event, such as the analogous time references ('until I visit the world' and 'when the time draws near to visit the world') and the analogous descriptions of the post-resurrection habitations ('the immortal dwelling place that is not subject to time' and 'the place of sanctification'). If so, this passage compares the resurrection to the raising up from sleep. This metaphor suggests a restoration of embodied life that characterizes one's earthly existence. The text unfortunately does not provide any specific information about the nature of the restored life, except for the notion that it will transpire in the immortal and sanctified dwelling place. Since there is no suggestion that this locale is heaven, the author probably envisions the new life on a transformed earth.

2.12. Fourth Ezra

Like Pseudo-Philo, the author of this late first-century CE apocalypse envisions life after death in two stages: an intermediate state that begins with death and a restored life that begins with the resurrection. An angelic interpreter explains to Ezra that when a person dies, 'as the spirit leaves the body to return again to him who gave it, first of all it adores the glory of the Most High. And if it is one of those who have shown scorn and have not kept the way of the Most High, and who have despised his Law, and who have hated those who fear God – such spirits shall not enter into habitations, but shall immediately wander about in torments, even grieving and sad, in seven ways' (*4 Ezra* 7.78–80). In contrast, the souls of the righteous 'shall see with great joy of him who receives them, for they shall have rest in seven orders' (*4 Ezra* 7.91). After seven days, they will be 'gathered in their habitations' (*4 Ezra* 7.101). The souls will remain in this intermediate state until the number of the righteous is completed (*4 Ezra* 4.36).

The unique feature of the eschatological scenario described in *4 Ezra* 7.26–44 is the expectation of a temporary messianic kingdom lasting 400 years, which will be concluded with the death of the Messiah along with all human beings and followed by seven days of primeval silence. After that, 'the earth shall give up those who are asleep in it; and the chambers shall give up the souls which have been committed to them' (7.32). These assertions, which employ traditional vocabulary for the dead and their coming back to life, most likely refer to the resurrection of the dead. This assumption is confirmed in the description of the last judgement, which starts with the statement: 'Then the Most High will say to the nations that have been raised from the dead' (7.37). The resurrection of the dead probably involves a reunification of body and soul but this is nowhere explicated. The text also does not clarify whether the Messiah will be among those who will be brought back to life. As a matter of fact, the Messiah has no function in this passage. The author merely states that he will be revealed at the beginning of 400 joyful years and that he will die when this blessed period comes to an end. The resurrection of the dead, which is most likely universal in scope, will be followed by the last judgement of all nations. At the final reckoning of humanity, God will reward the righteous with delight and rest and punish the wicked with fire and torments (7.37–38).

The author of *4 Ezra* nowhere describes the resurrected bodies, but some of their qualities could probably be deduced from the passage that describes the age to come.

> But think of your own case, and enquire concerning the glory of those who are like yourself, because it is for you that Paradise is opened, the tree of life is planted, the age to come is prepared, plenty is provided, a city is built, rest is appointed, goodness is established and wisdom perfected beforehand. The root of evil is sealed up from you, illness is banished from you, and death is hidden; hell has fled and corruption has been forgotten; sorrows have passed away, and in the end the treasure of immortality is made manifest. (*4 Ezra* 8.51–54)

The references to the banishment of illness, hiddenness of death, disappearance of corruption and the treasure of immortality are readily applicable to the resurrected bodies. If so, the resurrection envisaged in *4 Ezra* involves a transformation of the earthly bodies that will restore them to their created glory before death and corruption became the toll of humanity.

2.13. Second Baruch

The composition known as *2 Baruch* shares many similarities with *4 Ezra*, but its theological concepts are usually better developed, including the notion of afterlife. For example, the author of this work offers an elaborate explanation of why there must be life after death.

> For if only this life exists which everyone possesses here, nothing could be more bitter than this. For of what help is strength which changes into weakness, or food in abundance which changes into famine, or beauty which changes into ugliness? For the nature of men is always changeable ... For if an end of all things had not been prepared, their beginning would have been senseless. (*2 Bar.* 21.13–15, 17)

Life after death is here, like in *4 Ezra*, presented as a two-stage process: an intermediate state (which is portrayed as 'the realm of death' and the 'treasuries of the souls' [*2 Bar.* 21.23]) and a restored life that begins with the resurrection of the dead. The resurrection of the dead begins with the appearance of the Messiah.

> And it will happen after these things when the time of the appearance of the Anointed One has been fulfilled and he returns with glory, that then all who sleep in hope of him will rise. And it will happen at that time that those treasuries will be opened in which the number of the souls of the righteous were kept, and they will go out and the multitudes of souls will appear together, in one assemblage, of one mind. And the first ones will enjoy themselves and the last ones will not be sad. For they know that the time has come of which it is said that it is the end of times. But the souls of the wicked will the more waste away, when they shall see all these things. For they know that their torment has come and that their perditions have arrived. (*2 Bar.* 30.1–5)

The resurrection of the dead is compared to arising from sleep, which, like in other texts that employ this conventional metaphor, suggests the idea of corporeal revivification. The author of this work probably envisions the resurrection as a reunion of body and soul; however, this fusion is not actually described but only hinted at with the reference to the opening of the treasuries in which the souls of the righteous are kept. The text is somewhat unclear with regard to the scope of the resurrection. It seems that it describes only the resurrection of the righteous, whereas the destiny of the wicked includes only descriptions of what their souls will experience as they apprehend their impending torment. Other passages in *2 Baruch*, however, clarify that the resurrection of the wicked is also in view, because the resurrection functions as a prerequisite of the final judgement.

What distinguishes this work from other Jewish documents that mention the resurrection of the dead is a unique, and quite elaborate, description of the resurrected body.

> But further, I ask you, O Mighty One; and I shall ask grace from him who created all things. In which shape will the living live in your day? Or how will remain their splendour which will be after that? Will they, perhaps, take again this present form, and will they put on the chained members which are in evil and by which evils are accomplished? Or will you perhaps change these things which have been in the world, as also the world itself?
>
> And he answered and said to me: 'Listen, Baruch, to this word and write down in the memory of your heart all that you shall learn. For the earth will surely give back the dead at that time; it receives them now in order to keep them, not changing anything in their form. But as it has received them so it will give them back. And as I have delivered them to it so it will raise them. For then it will be necessary to show those who live that the dead are living again, and that those who went away have come back. And it will be that when they have recognized each other, those who know each other at this moment, then my judgement will be strong, and those things which have been spoken of before will come.
>
> And it will happen after this day which he appointed is over that both the shape of those who are found to be guilty as also the glory of those who have proved to be righteous will be changed. For the shape of those who now act wickedly will be made more evil than it is (now) so that they shall suffer torment. Also, as for the glory of those who proved to be righteous on account of my Law, those who possessed intelligence in their

life, and those who planted the root of wisdom in their heart – their splendour will then be glorified by transformations, and the shape of their face will be changed into the light of their beauty so that they may acquire and receive the undying world which is promised to them. Therefore, especially they who will then come will be sad, because they despised my Law and stopped their ears lest they hear wisdom and receive intelligence. When they, therefore, will see that those over whom they are exalted now will then be more exalted and glorified than they, then both these and those will be changed, these into the splendour of angels and those into startling visions and horrible shapes; and they will waste away even more. For they will first see and then they will go away to be tormented. (*2 Bar.* 49.1–51.6)

The uniqueness of this description of the raised bodies lies not in their superior qualities, such as their beauty, incorruptibility or splendour. Other Jewish documents regularly presume that bodily resurrection involves a certain transformation of the earthly body, even if they do not always clarify what kinds of changes are envisioned. The uniqueness of this description lies in the idea that the dead will be raised in the same form which they had before death, but only for the purpose of their mutual recognition. Once the identification of the resurrected individuals has been achieved, their bodies will be subjected to gradual transformation. The shapes of the wicked will become uglier and uglier, while the shapes of the righteous will become more and more beautiful until they are changed into the splendour of angels. The author adds that 'time will no longer make them older. For they will live in the heights of that world and they will be like angels and be equal to the stars. And they will be changed into any shape which they wished, from beauty to loveliness, and from light to the splendor of glory' (*2 Bar.* 51.9–10). The idea that the resurrected righteous will become like angels and be equal to stars betrays the influence of Daniel 12.3. Unlike the Book of Daniel, however, *2 Baruch* promotes the idea of a progressive transformation of the resurrected body until its appearance becomes angelic and luminous.

2.14. Sibylline Oracles

The resurrection of the dead described in book 4 of this Hellenized Jewish writing of the late first century CE is, like in *4 Ezra 7*, preceded by a universal destruction of life.

> But when everything is already dusty ashes, and God puts to sleep the unspeakable fire, even as he kindled it, God himself will again fashion the bones and ashes of men and he will raise up mortals again as they were before. And then there will be a judgement over which God himself will preside, judging the world again. As many as sinned by impiety, these will a mound of earth cover, and broad Tartarus and the repulsive recesses of Gehenna. But as many as are pious, they will live on earth again when God gives spirit and life and favour to these pious ones. Then they will all see themselves beholding the delightful and pleasant light of the sun. (*Sib. Or.* 4.179–191)

The resurrection is in this passage presented as a creative act of God that resembles the creation of the first human beings in Genesis 2. The author puts emphasis on both the continuity and similarity of the earthly and the resurrected bodies. The material from which God will fashion the new bodies is 'the bones and ashes of men', and the raised bodies will look 'as they were before'. The scope of the resurrection, however, remains controversial. While the text envisions the resurrection of both the pious and the sinners, it is not clear whether these two groups comprise the entirety of humanity or only the last generation, which is to be destroyed by fire.

2.15. Pseudo-Phocylides

The author of this pseudonymous Jewish poem of Alexandrian provenance, which was composed around the turn of the era, juxtaposes two different concepts of afterlife – the resurrection of the body and the immortality of the soul.

> Do not dig up the grave of the deceased, nor expose to the sun what may not be seen, lest you stir up the divine anger. It is not good to dissolve the human frame; for we hope that the

remains of the departed will soon come to the light (again) out of the earth; and afterward they will become gods. For the souls remain unharmed among the deceased. For the spirit is a loan of God to mortals, and (his) image. For we have a body out of earth, and when afterward we are resolved again into earth we are but dust; and then the air has received our spirit ... Hades is (our) common eternal home and fatherland, a common place for all, poor and kings. We humans live not a long time but for a season. But (our) soul is immortal and lives ageless forever. (Ps.-Phoc. 100–108, 112–115)

Belief in bodily resurrection, which is put forward in the first part of this passage, and belief in the immortality of the soul, which is advanced in the second part, seem to be completely unrelated. In the first half of the text, the author issues a warning against disturbing the dead, either through digging up their corpses or dissecting their bodily parts, because such activities will interfere with the ultimate destiny of the deceased – their bodily resurrection. Such a literalistic notion of the resurrection of the dead is quite unique in the extant Jewish literature. It is also characterized by a lack of sophistication, because the author fails to consider the effects of the process of decay on the human body. In the second half, however, he not only affirms the immortality of the soul but also seems to deny any hope of resurrection. He also makes no distinction between the fate of the righteous and the fate of the wicked. Inconsistencies such as these frequently characterize the ideas about life after death held by philosophically untrained people.

3. Summary and Conclusions

The survey of the passages that articulate resurrection hope in the extant early Jewish literature offered in this chapter is by no means exhaustive but is nonetheless representative. A fully developed belief in the resurrection of the body emerged in the Maccabean period as a response to the suffering of the pious Jews who were punished not because of their disobedience but precisely because of their obedience to the Torah. This extraordinary set of circumstances, which seemingly contradicted the traditional understanding of God's rewards and punishments, called for a new assessment of God's justice. The answer was found in the hope of bodily resurrection. Even if in this life the wrongdoers – be they foreign oppressors, persecutors of the just, exploiters of the poor or just plain sinners – may have the upper hand, God will reward the righteous and punish the wicked in the life to come. The resurrection is regularly part of this eschatological scenario, although its specific function varies. In the passage that is usually regarded as the clearest expression of belief in bodily resurrection in the Hebrew Scriptures (Dan. 12.1–3), the resurrection functions as a means by which the exceptionally righteous and the exceptionally wicked will receive their respective vindication or condemnation. In the writings that envision general resurrection (*Testament of Benjamin*, L.A.B., *4 Ezra*, *2 Baruch*, *Sibylline Oracles*, Pseudo-Phocylides), the resurrection is typically presented as a prerequisite of the last judgement. Still in other writings (the Enochic literature, 2 Maccabees, 4Q521, *Pseudo-Ezekiel*, *Testament of Judah*, *Psalms of Solomon*, Josephus' description of the Pharisees), the resurrection itself is a reward for just living so that only the resurrection of the righteous is envisaged. Regardless of the actual scope of the resurrection, however, it is always imagined as a corporate event that will happen at the end of time. There is not a single text that envisions the resurrection of a single individual ahead of the general resurrection, however holy and righteous that person may be, and there is not a single text that envisions the resurrection of the Messiah.

What the available evidence also demonstrates is that resurrection hope, which became a dominant form of belief in the afterlife among Jews in the first century CE (although some Jews, such as the Sadducees, rejected it) was by no means uniform. The bodily character of the resurrection is clearly articulated in only some writings, such as the Similitudes of Enoch, 2 Maccabees, 4Q521, *Pseudo-Ezekiel*, Josephus, *4 Ezra*, *2 Baruch*, *Sibylline Oracles* and Pseudo-Phocylides. In other instances, the bodily character of the restored life is a deduction based on the metaphor of awakening/ raising up from sleep (Dan. 12.2; L.A.B.) or merely a possibility suggested by the text (Book of the Watchers, Animal Apocalypse, *Testaments of the Twelve Patriarchs*, *Psalms of Solomon*). Some texts even speak of the revival of the spirits of the dead, without clarifying whether some kind of embodiment is also presumed (Epistle of Enoch, *Jubilees*).

The available evidence is also not uniform with regard to the question of the continuity between earthly and resurrected bodies. Although it may sound counterintuitive, the concept of bodily resurrection in Jewish literature does not necessarily entail the idea that God will use the earthly bodies (or their physical remains) to fashion the new bodies. The clearest example of a disconnection between these two entities is 2 Maccabees 7, which, paradoxically, contains one of the most physical notions of bodily resurrection. Yet, the author of this text declares that mortal bodies are not really needed because God can recreate them *ex nihilo*. The author of *Jubilees* even asserts that the bones of the righteous will remain in the earth.

Jewish authors also disagree on the question of particular characteristics of the resurrected bodies. All of them seem to presume that the new bodies will possess superior qualities in comparison to the earthly bodies, such as immortality, splendour and beauty. But these qualities are only occasionally explicated; more often, the texts merely presume a certain transformation that is appropriate to the eschatological age in which the resurrection will take place. The extent of this transformation, however, can be very different. In 2 Maccabees 7, for example, the restored bodies of the martyrs seem to be the exact replicas of their earthly bodies that have been prematurely destroyed. Daniel 12.3 and *2 Bar.* 51.10, on the other hand, claim that the resurrected righteous will become like the angels and the stars. Moreover, the author of *2 Baruch* envisages a gradual transformation of the resurrected bodies, starting with the same form they had before death and ending with the beauty and splendour of angels. Related to this is the question of the location of the restored life. Several passages envision the post-resurrection life on earth (Book of the Watchers, 4Q521, *Pseudo-Ezekiel, Testament of Judah*), while others locate it in the heavenly realm (Similitudes of Enoch, Epistle of Enoch, *Testament of Benjamin*).

The lack of uniformity in various expressions of resurrection hope should not be regarded as a confounding factor when we start reading the New Testament accounts of Jesus' resurrection. Rather, they could assist us in creating a plausible interpretative framework within which various New Testament claims might be evaluated. A common error in a number of studies is the presumption that Christian sources offer a relatively coherent picture of what the followers of Jesus meant when they declared that he had been raised from the dead. Such uniformity is unlikely, given the variety of ideas and imageries that are used in Jewish documents to describe the expected resurrection from which Christian notions of resurrection took shape. Which of these notions were most instrumental for articulating the Christian claim that a corporate eschatological hope has been realized in one particular individual within the realm of history can be answered only after a careful analysis of each particular text. The next three chapters will be devoted to this task.

Notes

1 N. T. Wright, *The Resurrection of the Son of God* (vol. 3 of *Christian Origins and the Question of God*; Minneapolis: Fortress, 2003), 31.
2 See Dale B. Martin, *The Corinthian Body* (New Haven: Yale University Press, 1995), 108–17.
3 There are many excellent studies of this topic. Notable publications include Hans C. C. Cavallin, *Life After Death: Paul's Argument for the Resurrection of the Dead in 1 Cor 15, Part I: An Enquiry into the Jewish Background* (ConBNT 7; Lund: Gleerup, 1974); Alan J. Avery-Peck and Jacob Neusner, eds, *Death, Life-After-Death, Resurrection and the World-to-Come in the Judaisms of Antiquity* (part 4 of *Judaism in Late Antiquity*; HO I/49; Leiden: Brill, 2000); Wright, *The Resurrection of the Son of God*, 85–206; Alan F. Segal, *Life After Death: A History of the Afterlife in the Religions of the West* (ABRL; New York: Doubleday, 2004); James H. Charlesworth et al., *Resurrection: The Origin and Future of a Biblical Doctrine* (FSC; London: T&T Clark, 2006); George W. E. Nickelsburg, *Resurrection, Immortality, and Eternal Life in Intertestamental Judaism and Early Christianity* (expanded ed.; HTS 56; Cambridge, MA: Harvard University Press, 2006); Adela Yarbro Collins, *Mark: A Commentary* (Hermeneia; Minneapolis: Fortress, 2007), 782–94.
4 Nickelsburg, *Resurrection, Immortality, and Eternal Life*, 32.
5 Following the suggestions of Harold L. Ginsberg ('The Oldest Interpretation of the Suffering Servant', *VT* 3 [1953]: 400–4), who noticed a similarity between the description of the wise who lead many to righteousness in Dan. 12.3 and the servant who makes many righteous in Isa. 53.11, many scholars interpret the former in

light of the latter. On this reading, the author of Daniel identified the servant of Isa. 52.13–53.12 with 'the wise' of his own time and portrayed them as martyrs who led many to righteousness through their own suffering. The main weakness of this proposal is that the Book of Daniel never ascribes the propitiatory function to the martyrdom of 'the wise'. It is therefore more plausible to interpret Dan. 12.3 in light of Dan. 11.33 and conclude that although the leaders unjustly suffer because of their obedience to the Torah, 'instruction rather than martyrdom is the means of justification' (John J. Collins, *Daniel: A Commentary on the Book of Daniel* [Hermeneia; Minneapolis: Fortress, 1993], 393).

6 English translations of the quotations from *1 Enoch* are taken from George W. E. Nickelsburg and James C. VanderKam, *1 Enoch: A New Translation* (Minneapolis: Fortress, 2004). All other citations of the pseudepigraphical works are taken from James H. Charlesworth, ed., *The Old Testament Pseudepigrapha* (2 vols; New York: Doubleday, 1983–5).

7 George W. E. Nickelsburg, *1 Enoch 1: A Commentary on the Book of 1 Enoch, Chapters 1–36; 81–108* (Hermeneia; Minneapolis: Fortress, 2001), 304.

8 See Wright, *The Resurrection of the Son of God*, 144.

9 George W. E. Nickelsburg, 'Judgment, Life-After-Death, and Resurrection in the Apocrypha and the Non-Apocalyptic Pseudepigrapha', in *Death, Life-After-Death, Resurrection and the World-to-Come in the Judaisms of Antiquity* (part 4 of *Judaism in Late Antiquity*; eds. Alan J. Avery-Peck and Jacob Neusner; HO I/49; Leiden: Brill, 2000), 149.

10 Segal, *Life after Death*, 270–1.

11 Unless indicated otherwise, all translations of the Qumran documents are taken from Florentino García Martínez and Eibert J. C. Tigchelaar, *The Dead Sea Scrolls: Study Edition* (2 vols; Leiden: Brill, 1997–8).

12 For the view that the expectation of the resurrection was a major belief of the Qumran community, see Émile Puech, *La croyance des Esséniens en la vie future: Immortalité, résurrection, vie éternelle? Histoire d'une croyance dans le Judaïsme ancien* (EtB 21–22; 2 vols; Paris: Gabalda, 1993).

13 My translation.

14 Trans. Dimant, DJD 30:24. This text is also partially preserved in 4Q386 frg. 1 1.1–10 and 4Q388 frg. 7 lines 2–7.

15 Daniel J. Harrington, 'Afterlife Expectations in Pseudo-Philo, 4 Ezra, and 2 Baruch, and Their Implications for the New Testament', in *Resurrection in the New Testament* (eds. Reimund Bieringer, Veronica Koperski and Bianca Lataire; BETL 165; Leuven: Peeters, 2002), 29–30.

2

Non-Narrative Traditions about Jesus' Resurrection

The declaration that Jesus has been raised from the dead is arguably the central claim of the New Testament. The Apostle Paul alleges that 'if Christ has not been raised, then our proclamation has been in vain and your faith has been in vain … If Christ has not been raised, your faith is futile and you are still in your sins. Then those also who have died in Christ have perished' (1 Cor. 15.14, 17–18). Each of the four gospel narratives ends with the account of Jesus' resurrection. Resurrection not only reverses the tragic events of the first Good Friday but also sheds a new light on Jesus' entire ministry. Scholars frequently make a distinction between 'the historical Jesus' and 'the Christ of faith', or between 'the pre-Easter Jesus' and 'the post-Easter Jesus'. While the primary function of this differentiation is to enhance methodological clarity in the Jesus studies, this distinction is rooted in the New Testament itself, which indicates that a new understanding of Jesus' person and message came about after the resurrection. For example, the author of the Gospel of Luke emphasizes that Jesus' disciples could not understand the events that had just transpired in Jerusalem until the risen Jesus 'opened their minds to understand the scriptures … that the Messiah is to suffer and to rise from the dead on the third day' (Lk. 24.45–46). Similarly, the fourth evangelist points out that only 'after he was raised from the dead, his disciples … believed the scripture and the word that Jesus had spoken' (Jn 2.22).

The significance of Jesus' resurrection notwithstanding, what needs to be clarified is the question of what the followers of Jesus meant when they proclaimed that he has been raised from the dead. Did they mean that Jesus has been raised 'in very flesh and very bone' from the tomb, i.e. that his corpse was reanimated after remaining three days in the grave? Did they mean that he was spiritually raised regardless of what happened to his dead body? Or did they mean something else? Before addressing these questions through an analysis of individual texts, I wish to clarify the character of the New Testament evidence. It may come as a surprise to some readers, but the New Testament does not contain any eyewitness account of Jesus' resurrection. What is more, it does not contain any account of Jesus' resurrection at all. There is not a single New Testament report by or about a bystander who saw the actual transformation of Jesus' dead body into a living body. The only document that tries to provide, however unsuccessfully, an account of the actual resurrection is the *Gospel of Peter*, a non-canonical document from the second century CE, which narrates how the guard at the tomb saw the descent of two men from heaven who entered the sepulchre and, after a while, exited it with a third man (*Gos. Pet.* 34–49). Even this account, however, leaves in the dark what transpired in the tomb.

If we do not have any description of Jesus' resurrection, what, then, do we have? The New Testament evidence could be classified into two major groups of texts: the non-narrative traditions and the narrative traditions about Jesus' resurrection. The first group of texts includes traditional formulaic assertions about Jesus' resurrection and the interpretation of the resurrection provided by an eyewitness of Jesus' appearance – the Apostle Paul. The second group of texts includes the narratives about the discovery of the empty tomb and the narratives about the appearances of the risen Jesus. In this chapter, we will discuss the non-narrative traditions about Jesus' resurrection. The next two chapters will be devoted to the narratives about the discovery of the empty tomb and the narratives about the appearances of the risen Jesus.

1. Formulaic Statements

The declaration that God raised Jesus from the dead is frequently found in the earliest layers of the New Testament. This claim, which could be regarded as one of the oldest and most pivotal expressions of early Christian proclamation, appears in two basic forms: (1) in active formulations that have God as the subject of the sentence, and (2) in passive formulations that typically presume divine agency.

(1) The first group of formulations includes the following statements:

> But God raised him up, having freed him from death, because it was impossible for him to be held in its power. (Acts 2.24)

> But you rejected the Holy and Righteous One and asked to have a murderer given to you, and you killed the Author of life, whom God raised from the dead. (Acts 3.14–15)

> When God raised up his servant, he sent him first to you, to bless you by turning each of you from your wicked ways. (Acts 3.26)

> But God raised him on the third day and allowed him to appear … (Acts 10.40)

> And we bring you the good news that what God promised to our ancestors he has fulfilled for us, their children, by raising Jesus. (Acts 13.32–33)

> It will be reckoned to us who believe in him who raised Jesus our Lord from the dead. (Rom. 4.24)

> If the Spirit of him who raised Jesus from the dead dwells in you, he who raised Christ from the dead will give life to your mortal bodies also through his Spirit that dwells in you. (Rom. 8.11)

> If you confess with your lips that Jesus is Lord and believe in your heart that God raised him from the dead, you will be saved. (Rom. 10.9)

> Paul an apostle – sent neither by human commission nor from human authorities, but through Jesus Christ and God the Father, who raised him from the dead. (Gal. 1.1)

> And God raised the Lord and will also raise us by his power. (1 Cor. 6.14)

Because we know that the one who raised the Lord Jesus will raise us also with Jesus, and will bring us with you into his presence. (2 Cor. 4.14)

God put this power to work in Christ when he raised him from the dead and seated him at his right hand in the heavenly places. (Eph. 1.20)

When you were buried with him in baptism, you were also raised with him through faith in the power of God, who raised him from the dead. (Col. 2.12)

... and to wait for his Son from heaven, whom he raised from the dead – Jesus, who rescues us from the wrath that is coming. (1 Thess. 1.10)

Through him you have come to trust in God, who raised him from the dead and gave him glory, so that your faith and hope are set on God. (1 Pet. 1.21)

(2) The second group of formulations includes the following statements:

He has been raised from the dead ... (Mt. 28.7)

He has been raised; he is not here. (Mk 16.6)

After he was raised from the dead, his disciples remembered this. (Jn 2.22)

This was now the third time that Jesus appeared to the disciples after he was raised from the dead. (Jn 21.14)

... who was handed over to death for our trespasses and was raised for our justification. (Rom. 4.25)

Therefore we have been buried with him by baptism into death, so that, just as Christ was raised from the dead by the glory of the Father, so we too might walk in newness of life. (Rom. 6.4)

... so that you may belong to another, to him who has been raised from the dead ... (Rom. 7.4)

It is Christ Jesus, who died, yes, who was raised, who is at the right hand of God, who indeed intercedes for us. (Rom. 8.34)

... and that he was buried, and that he was raised on the third day in accordance with the scriptures ... (1 Cor. 15.4)

But in fact Christ has been raised from the dead ... (1 Cor. 15.20)

The closest Jewish parallel to early Christian confession that God raised Jesus from the dead is the concluding line of the second benediction of the *Amidah* (the *Shemoneh Esreh*): 'Blessed are you, O Lord, who raises the dead.' This liturgical invocation, which most likely antedates 70 CE, corroborates what the Second Temple literature consistently affirms: God, the Creator of the universe, is the only one who gives life to the dead. The Christian declaration that God raised Jesus from the dead has a similar taxonomy: it is a confession of faith that God is the ultimate source of life. But it is more than that. It is also a confession that God's ability to restore life was manifest in raising one specific individual – Jesus Christ. This assertion, however, is not a straightforward description of an experience. No one had seen God raising Jesus from the dead. Rather, this assertion is a hermeneutical conclusion that was probably reached on the basis of Jesus' appearances after his crucifixion, which convinced his followers that the Crucified One was no longer dead but was alive again.[1] The fact that the language used to describe this event is the same language that Jewish authors use to describe the end-time corporate resurrection of the dead indicates that Jesus' return to life was not interpreted as a simple revivification of his corpse but as an eschatological event that has been set in motion in the midst of human history.

There is another assertion that appears in some formulaic statements pertaining to Jesus' resurrection – the claim that Jesus was raised from the dead on the third day. Its earliest expression is found in the pre-Pauline confession preserved in 1 Corinthians 15.3–4: 'For I handed on to you as of first importance what I in turn had received: that Christ died for our sins in accordance with the scriptures, and that he was buried, and that he was raised on the third day in accordance with the scriptures.' The third-day motif also appears in the passion predictions in Matthew (16.21, 17.23, 20.19) and Luke (9.22, 18.33), as well as in several additional passages in Luke–Acts (Lk. 24.6–7, 46; Acts 10.40). The passion predictions in Mark consistently employ a variant expression, 'after three days' (8.31, 9.31, 10.34). Matthew's Gospel contains two additional references to three days: the formulation 'three days and three nights' in the analogy between the length of Jonah's sojourn in the belly of the sea monster and the length of the Son of Man's sojourn in the heart of the earth (12.40) and a peculiar combination of the phrases 'after three days' and 'until the third day' in the request of the Pharisees to Pilate (27.63–64).

How can we explain the development and meaning of the third-day tradition? One possibility is to say that the statements about Jesus' resurrection on the third day refer to the discovery of the empty tomb on the first day of the week (Mk 16.2; Mt. 28.1; Lk. 24.1; Jn 20.1). In favour of this interpretation speaks the fact that, given the customary Jewish reckoning that counts a part of a day as a whole day, both time references – the third day (after the crucifixion) and the first day of the week – are consistent with each other. The congruence of two traditions, however, does not necessarily mean that one derived from the other. The main weakness of the hypothesis that the empty tomb tradition gave rise to the third-day motif is that the former does not supply the language that so consistently appears in the latter. Put differently, it is difficult to explain how the references to the first day of the week generated the references to the third day (after the resurrection) because there is no linguistic overlap between these two traditions. Even more difficult is to explain the development of the variant 'after three days', which is consistently used in the Gospel of Mark.

Another possibility is to relate the third-day motif to the appearances of Jesus. This hypothesis is even more tenuous. The early tradition about Jesus' appearances in 1 Corinthians 15.5–7 contains only vague temporal references, such as 'then' and 'thereupon'. Given the geographic distance between Jerusalem and Galilee, only the traditions about Jesus' appearances in Jerusalem are relevant for the notion of his resurrection on the third day. Yet, temporal references in the gospel narratives about these encounters typically relate them to the discovery of the empty tomb (Lk. 24.13; Jn

20.19; 20.26). The only account that includes the third-day motif is Luke's story of Jesus' appearance to two disciples on the road to Emmaus (Lk. 24.21), but this is most likely a later development that betrays Luke's desire to harmonize various references to the third day.

In search for a plausible explanation of the emergence and meaning of the third-day motif, we must take into consideration the fact that this adverbial phrase always qualifies the verbs 'raise' or 'rise'. If this designation functions as a time reference, as it is frequently assumed, the declaration that God raised Jesus on the third day would be quite peculiar because it would suggest that Jesus' followers tried to assign a date to an act of God for which there were no eyewitnesses and which the early Christian interpreters refused to describe. If, then, no one knew exactly when God raised Jesus from the dead, how can we explain such a rapid development of the conviction that the resurrection took place on the third day? The best answer to this question is, in my view, the one that does not regard the third-day motif as a chronological but as a theological designation. This expression does not try to fix in time a hidden act of God; rather, it tries to explain its theological significance.

A clue to the meaning of the third-day slogan could be found in the earliest passage that employs the third-day motif – the pre-Pauline confession in 1 Corinthians 15.4. This text declares that Christ 'was raised on the third day in accordance with the scriptures'.[2] The adverbial expression 'in accordance with the scriptures' indicates that the phrase 'on the third day' is derived from scripture. The problem is, as every commentator on this text notes, that there are no obvious scriptural passages that speak about the resurrection on the third day. For some interpreters, the solution can be found in the conventional meaning of the phrase 'on the third day', which typically functions as a figure of speech for a short period of time (Gen. 1.13; 22.4; 31.22; 34.25; 40.20; 42.18; Exod. 19.11, 15, 16; Lev. 7.17, 18; 19.6, 7; Num. 7.24; 19.12, 19; 29.20; Josh. 3.2; 9.17; Judg. 20.30; 1 Sam. 20.12; 30.1; 2 Sam. 1.2; 1 Kgs 3.18; 12.12; 2 Kgs 20.5, 8; 2 Chron. 10.12; Ezra 6.15; Est. 5.1; Hos. 6.2; Jon. 2.1). On this reading, the third-day motif in 1 Corinthians 15.4 conveys the idea that Jesus was raised from the dead a short time after his death.

For other interpreters, the solution can be found in the rabbinic interpretation of Hosea 6.2. Even though in its original literary and historical context, Hosea 6.2 uses resurrection language to convey hope of God's quick intervention on behalf of Israel, rabbis routinely interpret this scriptural text as a prophecy of the resurrection of the dead at the turn of the ages. For example, Hosea 6.2-3 is invoked in *y. Ber.* 5.2 in support of an association of the resurrection from the dead that brings life without end and the descent of rain that should also bring life without end. In *Gen. Rab.* 56.1, the quotation of Hosea 6.2 is introduced with the phrase 'on the third day of resurrection'. In *Esth. Rab.* 9.2, the citation of Hosea 6.2 functions as a scriptural justification of the assertion that 'the dead also will come to life only after three days'. A saying attributed to Rabbi Gamaliel in *Pirqe R. El.* 51 (73b–74a) quotes Hosea 6.2 to validate the claim that on the third day God will revive the dead. The same understanding of Hosea 6.2 is documented in the Targum of Jonathan, which replaces the formulation 'on the third day' with 'on the day of the resurrection of the dead'.

In these and other related texts, the slogan 'on the third day' is sometimes used to support the claim that God does not leave Israel (or the righteous one) in distress more than three days (*Esth. Rab.* 9.2, *Gen. Rab.* 91.7, *Midr. Pss.* 22.5). If this exegetical tradition provides the interpretative framework of 1 Corinthians 15.4, the reference to the third day could be understood as a reference to the day of salvation. The theological import of this phrase would then be that God's salvific intervention on behalf of the righteous is realized through the concrete salvific event of the resurrection of Christ.[3] But another, more specific, exegetical tradition related to Hosea 6.2 is also plausible. The interpretation of the third day in Hosea 6.2 as the day of the resurrection of the dead is documented not only in the Targum of Jonathan but also in many rabbinic passages. Even though these documents postdate the New Testament, this interpretative tradition may already have been current in the first century CE. If early Christian interpreters were familiar with this interpretation of Hosea 6.2, their employment of the third-day motif could have allowed them to express their central conviction that with Jesus' resurrection the general resurrection of the dead had already begun. Thus, by declaring that Jesus was raised on the third day, they would have proclaimed that the resurrection of Jesus marks the inauguration of the eschatological age.

The usual objection to this interpretation of the third-day motif is the late date of the rabbinic documents that corroborate the conventional use of this phrase as a reference to the resurrection of the dead. However, substantiating evidence for this interpretation of Jesus' resurrection can be found in the New Testament documents themselves. One such passage is Matthew 27.50–53.

> Then Jesus cried again with a loud voice and breathed his last. At that moment the curtain of the temple was torn in two, from top to bottom. The earth shook, and the rocks were split. The tombs also were opened, and many bodies of the saints who had fallen asleep were raised. After his resurrection they came out of the tombs and entered the holy city and appeared to many.

The function of this peculiar account is not to describe some strange events that took place in the vicinity of Jerusalem on the occasion of Jesus' death and resurrection, but to provide an interpretation of their significance. This odd story about the resurrected saints who were raised when Jesus died on the cross but came out of the tombs after his resurrection seeks to demonstrate that the resurrection of the righteous, expected in the future, has already been set in motion. The text uses the imagery of the opening of graves from Ezekiel 37.12 and of rising of the dead from Isaiah 26.19 and Daniel 12.2 to convey the message that with Jesus' resurrection the general resurrection has already begun.

A similar idea is detectable in the early Christian confession, preserved in Romans 1.3–4, which speaks of 'the gospel concerning his Son, who was descended from David according to the flesh and was declared to be Son of God with power according to the spirit of holiness by resurrection from the dead'. The NRSV translation of the last phrase is not entirely accurate. A better translation of the Greek original is 'since the resurrection of the dead'. This text will be analysed at greater length in Chapter 6 of this book, but at this point suffice it to say that although it portrays Jesus' resurrection as a singular event that affected his status before God, it nonetheless portrays it as an inauguration of the general resurrection.

Support for the interpretation of the third-day motif as a shortcut for the universal resurrection of the dead also comes from Paul's own discussion of the resurrection in 1 Corinthians 15. In this chapter, he argues that Jesus' resurrection and the general resurrection are logically and theologically inseparable (15.12–19). Even more telling is his triumphant declaration that Christ is 'the first fruits of those who have fallen asleep' (15.20). The notion that Jesus was the first to be raised from the dead entails the idea that the resurrection of others will follow. The concept of Jesus' 'firstness' appears not only in the letters of Paul, but also in other New Testament documents, which describe Jesus as 'the firstborn within a large family' (Rom. 8.29), 'the firstborn from the dead' (Col. 1.18), 'the first to rise from the dead' (Acts 26.23) or 'the firstborn of the dead' (Rev. 1.5). In these passages, Jesus is consistently portrayed as the 'firstborn' or simply the 'first' to rise from the dead.

We can thus conclude that the confession that Jesus was raised on the third day most likely conveys the idea that Jesus' resurrection marked the beginning of the general resurrection of the dead. This notion enabled Christian interpreters, such as Paul, to speak about God's inauguration of the new age that has not yet been completed or to speak about God's kingdom as already present but not yet fully realized.

2. Paul's Understanding of the Resurrection

We will discuss Paul's understanding of the resurrection before the gospels for two reasons. First, Paul is the only eyewitness of Jesus' post-resurrection appearances who wrote about his experience. Second, Paul's letters were not only written before the gospels but also contain the pre-Pauline material that could give us a glimpse into the traditions about Jesus' resurrection that were articulated in the first decade of the Christian movement. Paul's letters are replete with various references to the resurrection of Jesus, but 1 Corinthians 15 is the only chapter in his corpus that is entirely devoted to this topic. Since this material is most pertinent for the questions of how Paul understands Jesus' resurrection and how he interprets its significance for others, the analysis below will focus on Paul's claims in this chapter.

2.1. 1 Corinthians 15.3–8

Paul begins his discussion in 1 Corinthians 15 by reciting the earliest Christian tradition about Jesus' death, burial and resurrection and providing the list of those who experienced his post-resurrection appearances, to which he adds his own encounter with the risen Christ.

> For I handed on to you as of first importance what I in turn had received: that Christ died for our sins in accordance with the scriptures, and that he was buried, and that he was raised on the third day in accordance with the scriptures, and that he appeared to Cephas, then to the twelve. Then he appeared to more than five hundred brothers and sisters at one time, most of whom are still alive, though some have died. Then he appeared to James, then to all the apostles. Last of all, as to one untimely born, he appeared also to me. (1 Cor. 15.3–8)

The exact content of the pre-Pauline formula, which is usually dated to the first half of the 30s CE, is debatable. The introductory clause, 'I handed on to you as of first importance what I in turn had received', clearly marks the beginning of the traditional material, but its ending remains controversial. The only thing that is generally agreed upon is that the last sentence, in which Paul refers to his own experience of the risen Christ, represents his own addition to the traditional formula. Even if we cannot be certain whether the pre-Pauline material included all of or only a part of vv. 3–7, we can at least assume that what Paul reports here agrees with the earliest Christian proclamation.

Some aspects of the first part of the formula have already been discussed in the previous section. Before we move to the second part – the list of the recipients of Jesus' post-resurrection appearances – we have to address one question that is regularly raised by the interpreters of this text. Does the early Christian confession of Jesus' death, burial and resurrection presume the knowledge of the empty tomb? Or, more specifically, did Paul himself know of the empty tomb? Those who believe that he did typically allege that the sequence burial–resurrection presumes the emptiness of the tomb. Indeed, it would be inconceivable that someone like Paul, a former Pharisee, could speak of the resurrection of Jesus without also believing that the tomb in which his body was buried was empty. The claim that Christ was raised entails the idea that a previously recumbent corpse has been raised to the standing position of a living body. Neither tradition nor Paul had to mention the empty tomb explicitly because their goal was to list the relevant events, rather than narrate the whole sequence. The emptiness of the tomb was clearly presumed; it did not have to be amplified.[4]

These are certainly valid arguments. However, saying that Paul could not have proclaimed Jesus' resurrection without imagining the empty tomb is not the same as saying that he knew that the tomb was found to be empty. The former refers to Paul's religious conviction while the latter refers to his knowledge. He could have believed that Jesus' corpse was no longer in the grave without actually knowing the tradition of the discovery of the empty tomb. Nothing conclusive can be inferred from his silence. Neither can we conclude anything definitive from Paul's failure to mention any of the women who were the primary witnesses of the discovery of the empty tomb. This could be an indication that the discovery of the empty tomb was not a widespread knowledge in the emerging Christian movement. It, however, could also be a consequence of a conscious effort to eliminate the legally unreliable female testimony (Josephus, *Ant.* 4.219; *m. Šebu.* 4.1; *m. Roš Haš.* 1.8) in order to bolster the credibility of the Christian message.

What the tradition handed down to Paul does include is the list consisting of two individuals and several groups to whom the risen Christ appeared: Cephas, the twelve, five hundred brothers and sisters, James, and all the apostles. The fact that each witness after Cephas (Peter) is preceded by a temporal conjunction 'then' indicates that they are listed in their relative chronological order. The primacy of Peter with regard to Jesus' appearances is asserted not only in this traditional formula but also in Luke 24.34. What is surprising, though, is that these two terse statements – that he appeared to Cephas (1 Cor. 15.5) and 'The Lord has risen indeed, and he has appeared to Simon!' (Lk. 24.34) – are the only evidence for the claim that Peter was the first to see the risen Jesus. The New Testament does not contain any narrative, not even a brief report, of this event.[5] The same applies to the second named individual in the traditional list – Jesus' brother James. Jesus' appearance to James is mentioned only in 1 Corinthians 15.7, but, like in Peter's case, it is conveyed only through a terse statement: 'Then he appeared to James.' There is no report of this occurrence and there is no narrative of it in the New Testament.

The traditional formula mentions three groups that witnessed the appearances of Jesus: the twelve, five hundred brothers and sisters, and all the apostles. Jesus' appearance to the twelve is consistent with the gospel narratives, which mention Jesus' appearances to the eleven, i.e. the twelve without Judas Iscariot (Mt. 28.16–20; Lk. 24.36–49; Jn 20.19-23 [without Thomas]; 20.24–29 [with Thomas]). The timing and location of these appearances varies, though. Mark and Matthew speak of Jesus' appearances in Galilee, while Luke and John locate them in Jerusalem. It is possible that all variants go back to one foundational event – Jesus' appearance to the twelve/eleven – regardless of its actual location. But it is also possible that there were multiple appearances to the twelve/eleven, especially if they took place in both Galilee and Jerusalem. Jesus' appearance to the five hundred is not attested anywhere else in the New Testament. Attempts to associate this event with Luke's account of Pentecost are not persuasive. Paul refers to this group as a known entity, consisting of individuals who were still alive at the time when he was writing 1 Corinthians, and who could therefore be interrogated. The last group mentioned – all the apostles – is difficult to identify. This is probably a reference to the entire group that came to be known as the apostles that included all who have seen the risen Jesus, but its identity and size remain vague.

Many scholars find it puzzling that the tradition handed down to Paul does not include any appearance of Jesus to Mary Magdalene and/or other women that are mentioned in the gospel narratives (Mt. 28.9–10; Jn 20.11–18). This tradition could have been suppressed because of a patriarchal prejudice that devalued the testimony of women or in order to preserve Peter's status as the first to have seen the risen Jesus. The second explanation has been especially advanced by Ann Graham Brock, who argues that the rivalry between Peter and Mary Magdalene, which is a recurring theme in the Gnostic writings (*Gos. Thom.* 114; *Gos. Mary* 9.16–18; 10.7–17.7; 17.18–22; *Pistis Sophia* 1–3), goes back to the earliest period of the early church.[6]

The verb 'appeared to' most likely refers to a visual experience. The active voice of the English translation conceals the fact that in Greek, this is the aorist passive of the verb 'to see', whose literal translation is 'was seen by'. Paul uses the perfect active of the same verb in 1 Corinthians 9.1 to declare that he has 'seen Jesus our Lord'. The aorist passive of this verb is frequently used in the Septuagint to describe the appearances of God or his messengers (Gen. 12.7; 17.1; 18.1; 26.2; Exod. 3.2; Judg. 6.12; 1 Kgs 3.5; 9.2; 2 Chron. 3.1). These references regularly emphasize the visual component of the appearances. While in some cases divine appearances to prominent persons may have been told to legitimate their authority, such a function is not detectable in 1 Corinthians 15.3–8, which mentions five hundred nameless individuals along with Peter, James and Paul. It should also be stressed that the use of the aorist passive of the verb 'to see' to describe Jesus' post-resurrection appearances highlights their visual aspect but says nothing about their other properties, such as their tangibility or their corporeality. The question of whether Jesus' appearances were subjective apparitions or objective occurrences within the normal space–time universe cannot be solved on the basis of the mere usage of the verb 'appeared to'.

Finally, there is Paul's own testimony. Given the fact that this is the only eyewitness account of an encounter with the risen Jesus, its significance cannot be overrated. At the same time, Paul does not say more about his own experience than what he says about the experiences of others: 'Last of all, as to one untimely born, he appeared also to me' (1 Cor. 15.8). Earlier in 1 Corinthians, he referred to his vision of Jesus with similar brevity: 'Have I not seen Jesus our Lord?' (1 Cor. 9.1) The only other place in the Pauline corpus where he refers to this experience is Galatians 1.15–16, but again he says next to nothing about the actual event and focuses rather on its significance – God's commission to preach the gospel among the Gentiles: 'But when God, who had set me apart before I was born and called me through his grace, was pleased to reveal his Son to me, so that I might proclaim him among the Gentiles, I did not confer with any human being.'

Two significant conclusions can nonetheless be made on the basis of 1 Corinthians 15.8. First, Paul believed that a series of Jesus' appearances came to an end. He was the last one to whom the risen Jesus appeared. Second, Paul put his own experience alongside the experiences of the earlier witnesses. He apparently believed that Jesus appeared to him in the same way as he appeared to others. For him, the only thing that was different was timing. His experience took place approximately three years later, which prompted him to describe it with a paradoxical metaphor, 'as to one untimely born'. The metaphor of untimely birth probably refers to Paul's unpreparedness to encounter the risen Christ and the surprising character of this experience, but it may also refer to the fact that it happened after a significant period had lapsed when no appearances of Jesus were reported. Yet even though Paul regarded Jesus' appearance to him as an exception with regard to its timing, he did not regard it as an exception with regard to its character.

We do not know to what extent Paul's assessment of his own experience was shared by others. We do know, for example, that at least one person held a different view. In Acts 9.1–9, Luke provides an elaborate account of Paul's encounter with the risen Jesus, but his description of Paul's vision is devoid of physicality that characterizes Luke's narratives about Jesus' appearances (Lk. 24.13–35, 36–49; Acts 10.40–41). The only thing that Paul saw, according to Luke, was a light from heaven flashing around him and the only thing that he heard was a voice speaking to him. Luke also stresses that Paul's entourage only heard the voice but saw no one (Acts 9.7). This tendency to de-objectivize Paul's experience is also apparent in Luke's report of Paul's recount of this event in his speech to the Jewish leaders in Jerusalem (Acts 22.6–11). Similar to the third-person account in Acts 9, the Lukan Paul speaks of a great light from heaven and a voice addressing him, but his entourage is again portrayed as having only a partial experience. This time, however, they only saw the light but did not hear the voice speaking to Paul (Acts 22.9). While these variations most likely reflect standard rhetorical conventions of avoiding repetitions and provoking the audience's interest, Luke's effort to differentiate Paul's experience from the experience of his companions remains, as does his persistent use of dream–vision terminology, such as the references to the heavenly light and the voice. They are also mentioned in Paul's second recounting of this event in Acts 26.12–19, where he explicitly calls it 'the heavenly vision' (v. 19). There is also an increased emphasis on the aspect of light, from 'a light from heaven' (Acts 9.3), via 'a great light from heaven' (Acts 22.6), to 'a light from heaven, brighter than the sun' (Acts 26.13). This portrayal of Paul's experience is consistent with Luke's chronological framework, which limits Jesus' appearances to a forty-day period that is concluded with Jesus' ascension (Acts 1.6–11). Paul apparently shared Luke's conviction that Jesus' appearances were limited to a fixed period, but unlike Luke he believed that what happened to him was an exception to the rule. To what extent Luke's description of light that flashed around Paul mirrors what Paul himself saw is difficult to say. Since Paul never met the historical Jesus, how he was able to recognize him remains an open question.

2.2. 1 Corinthians 15.12–28

Paul devotes the rest of 1 Corinthians 15 to a discussion of the resurrection of the believers. He insists, however, that the resurrection of Jesus and the resurrection of 'those who belong to Christ' (1 Cor. 15.23) are inseparable. A person cannot affirm that Christ has been raised without also affirming the general resurrection of the dead. He develops this argument immediately after his reiteration of the traditional material along with his personal testimony of the encounter with the risen Christ and his transformation from a persecutor of the church to an apostle (1 Cor. 15.1–11).

> Now if Christ is proclaimed as raised from the dead, how can some of you say there is no resurrection of the dead? If there is no resurrection of the dead, then Christ has not been raised; and if Christ has not been raised, then our proclamation has been in vain and your faith has been in vain. We are even found to be misrepresenting God, because we testified of God that he raised Christ – whom he did not raise if it is true that the dead are not raised. For if the dead are not raised, then Christ has not been raised. If Christ has not been raised, your faith is futile and you are still in your sins. Then those also who have died in Christ have perished. If for this life only we have hoped in Christ, we are of all people most to be pitied. (1 Cor. 15.12–19)

In this section, Paul addresses those members of the Corinthian church who, notwithstanding the proclamation of Jesus' resurrection, denied the resurrection of the dead. Paul's recurring references to 'the dead' (literally 'corpses') indicate that they rejected the idea that human corpses could be brought back to life. Their disbelief reflects the standard Greco-Roman attitude toward afterlife, which is so eloquently illustrated in Plutarch's claim that 'to mix heaven with earth is foolish ... We must not, therefore, violate nature by sending the bodies of good men with their souls to heaven' (*Rom.* 28.6, 8).[7] Paul's rebuttal of the Corinthian position is deeply informed by his Jewish heritage, which is able to envisage embodied afterlife.

Paul's argument in vv. 12–19, however, is not directed – at least not on the surface – against the notion that postulates a separation of body and soul but against the notion that postulates a separation of Jesus' resurrection and general resurrection, which raises a difficult interpretative issue. How could the Corinthians have accepted the proclamation of the resurrection of Jesus and yet denied the general resurrection of the dead? Would not the former have been as equally objectionable as the latter to an audience who believed that mixing heaven with earth was foolish? Many commentators assume that those who denied the general resurrection of the dead belonged to the intellectual elite who found the whole idea of bodily resurrection, including the resurrection of Jesus, repulsive. On this reading, some members of the Corinthian church rejected both the literal interpretation of Jesus' resurrection and the expectation of the general resurrection at the end of the age.[8]

If this were the case, however, why does Paul encourage the Corinthians to hold firmly to the message that he proclaimed to them (v. 2) or say that regardless of who proclaims Jesus' resurrection they 'have come to believe' (v. 11)? One way of approaching the apparent inconsistency of the Corinthian view (i.e. believing in Jesus' resurrection but rejecting the general resurrection of the dead) is to take into consideration various stories about Greek superheroes who were 'translated' to immortality, which were popular among lower classes. Plutarch, for example, recounts a tradition about a sudden disappearance of Romulus, the mythical founder of Rome, and compares it to other similar fables, such as the disappearance of the bodies of Aristeas, Cleomedes and Alcmene, which were popular among the Greeks (*Rom.* 27.3–28.6). He concludes his reports by noticing that 'many such fables are told by writers who improbably ascribe divinity to the mortal features in human nature, as well as to the divine' (*Rom.* 28.6). If some members of the Corinthian church held some of these popular beliefs, they could have interpreted the resurrection of Jesus as the bodily translation to immortality of some kind of superhero. For such individuals, believing in Jesus' resurrection would have been acceptable, but believing that this could happen to ordinary humans and their decaying corpses would have been deplorable.[9]

Even if none of the reconstructions of the 'deniers of the resurrection' in Corinth fully satisfies,[10] Paul's argument shows that some members of the church, for whatever reason, readily embraced Jesus' resurrection but rejected the idea that the long-dead bodies of the deceased will be raised to new life. In response, Paul creates a *reductio ad absurdum* argument that enables him to declare that Jesus' resurrection cannot be proclaimed without the belief that the dead are raised, i.e. without the belief in the general resurrection. Paul's rhetorical skills are here beautifully displayed, but his line of reasoning is not completely transparent. He does not explain, for example, why the (false) premise 'if there is no resurrection of the dead' leads to the (false) conclusion 'then Christ has not been raised' (1 Cor. 15.13). Closer scrutiny, however, reveals that the underlying principle of Paul's argument is that Jesus' resurrection is not an isolated event in history but the first occurrence of the general resurrection of the dead. Or, to use Paul's own declaration in the opening verse of the next section, Jesus' resurrection is 'the first fruits of those who have died' (1 Cor. 15.20). Only under this provision does the argument in vv. 12–19 make sense.

In vv. 20–28, Paul offers a scriptural reflection about the imagery of Christ as the first fruits of those who have died. Paul uses the metaphor of the first fruits, which is derived from the Jewish custom of consecrating the first sheaf of the grain harvest, to convince his Corinthian audience that the full harvest – the general resurrection of the dead – will surely follow. The primary function of this metaphor is to demonstrate that Jesus' resurrection functions as a pledge or a guarantee of the future resurrection of those who belong to him. Paul further elaborates this issue by juxtaposing Adam and Christ, through whom two radically different conditions – death and the resurrection of the dead – affect humanity. The emphasis falls not on a simple contrast between life and death, but on the reversibility of death through the resurrection of the dead. Paul thus proclaims the eschatological reversal of the human predicament yet simultaneously acknowledges the finitude that continues to characterize human existence. He also articulates the incorporative implications of the Adam–Christ typology by juxtaposing the expressions 'in Adam' and 'in Christ'. The former includes the entirety of humanity, because 'all die in Adam' (1 Cor. 15.22a). The latter, however, includes only 'those who belong to Christ' (1 Cor. 15.23). This view is consonant with Jewish traditions envisaging the resurrection of the righteous, which were integral to Paul's pharisaic worldview. While all people, including Jesus himself, have to die by virtue of their descent from Adam, only those who are 'in Christ' will be made alive at the general resurrection of the dead.

The metaphor of the first fruits also serves another purpose: to clarify the implications of the division of a single eschatological event into two separate occurrences – the resurrection of Christ that had already occurred and the resurrection of believers that is still in the future. In 1 Corinthians 15.23–28 Paul offers an outline of the future that has been put in motion with the resurrection of Jesus. He identifies three principal events that will take place in an orderly fashion. The first is Jesus' resurrection, which Paul describes with the metaphor of the first fruits. The second event is the resurrection of those who belong to Christ, which will take place at his coming. The third event is the end, when Christ 'hands over the kingdom to God the Father, after he has destroyed every ruler and every authority and power' (1 Cor. 15.24). In v. 26 Paul explains that 'the last enemy to be destroyed is death'. Despite certain ambiguities in his formulations, the destruction of death most likely refers to the resurrection of the dead at Christ's *parousia*. Here again Paul acknowledges the finitude that continues to characterize human existence despite Christ's initial defeat of death through his resurrection, but he also envisions the completion of this victory when those who belong to Christ will be raised from the dead.

2.3. 1 Corinthians 15.35–58

Paul begins this section with two questions: 'How are the dead raised?' and 'With what kind of body do they come?' Both questions clearly pertain to the general resurrection of the dead, but, given Paul's fervent insistence up to this point that the resurrection of Jesus and the resurrection of believers are inseparable, everything that Paul says about the future resurrection body is also applicable to the resurrection of Jesus.

Paul's answer to the first question is relatively short: 'What you sow does not come to life unless it dies. And as for what you sow, you do not sow the body that is to be, but a bare seed, perhaps of wheat or of some other grain. But God gives it a body as he has chosen, and to each kind of seed its own body' (1 Cor. 15.36–38). Paul uses an analogy from agriculture – the planting of a seed and the growth of a plant from that seed – to explain that the restoration of life only comes through God's agency. He neither argues that each kind of seed must grow into a particular kind of plant nor mentions human soul as a potential link between the earthly body and the resurrected body. The NRSV translation of the verb 'come to life' in v. 36 gives a false impression that the seed has an inherent ability to grow into a new plant. But the Greek verb 'to make alive', which is in the New Testament regularly used as a reference for bringing the dead to life, is in the passive voice, indicating divine action. When the seed dies, only God can make it alive again.

Paul also emphasizes a distinction between the earthly body and the risen body. He vehemently insists on this differentiation by asserting, on the one hand, that the earthly body is 'not ... the body that is to be' and, on the other hand, that the new body is the body that 'God gives ... as he has chosen'. Since Paul uses the term 'body' to describe both pre-mortem and post-mortem existence, it can certainly be assumed that the idea of embodied life functions as a conceptual link between these two stages separated by death. But in this section Paul is not interested in the continuity but in the discontinuity between these two forms of embodied life, even to the point of almost erasing any connection between them. His argument is focused so much on God's freedom to choose the new body that the only continuity that surfaces in the text is the continuity guaranteed by God. It would be erroneous, however, to take Paul's rhetorical emphasis as an indication that he believed that God would create the new body *ex nihilo*, i.e. without any involvement of the earthly body, just as it would be erroneous to take Josephus' description of the Pharisees composed for the Roman audience as an indication that the Pharisees believed that the earthly bodies would remain in the graves while the souls of the righteous unite with the new bodies in resurrection.

Paul's answer to the second question starts in v. 39, which reminds the audience that there are different kinds of flesh, such as human flesh, flesh of animal, flesh of birds and flesh of fishes. This line of argumentation is continued in vv. 40–41, which first call attention to the difference between heavenly and earthly bodies and then focus on one aspect of their dissimilarity – their different glories. Paul's argument here reflects the standard Hellenistic cosmology that presumes the polarity between heaven and earth, but his emphasis falls on different categories within each group of heavenly and earthly bodies. It is also important to note that Paul uses the category of 'flesh' only when he describes earthly beings (v. 39); heavenly beings do not have 'flesh' but only 'bodies'. This distinction is fundamental for Paul's understanding of the resurrected bodies, which are never described as 'fleshly'.

In v. 42 Paul finally returns to the central question of this section by explaining that his remarks about different kinds of bodies serve as analogies for the resurrection of the dead. He now offers a series of contrasting pairs set forth to illustrate the difference between earthly bodies ('what is sown') and resurrected bodies ('what is raised'): perishable–imperishable, in dishonour–in glory, in weakness–in power and physical body–spiritual body. While Paul provides no justification for the other pairs, he does so for the last one: 'If there is a physical body, there is also a spiritual body' (v. 44b). This assertion is based on the assumption that the existence of one opposite demands the existence of its counterpart.

The origin and the meaning of the expressions 'physical body' and 'spiritual body' are controversial. Many scholars prefer the formulations 'the body animated by the soul' and 'the body animated by the spirit' because they better convey the meaning of the Greek terms, which do not describe 'what something is *composed of*, but what it is *animated by*'.[11] Speaking about the body animated by the soul versus the body animated by the spirit also prevents the modern misconception that Paul's concept of 'spiritual body' refers to the non-physical (non-material) body. In order to explain these terms, Paul uses scriptural imagery to juxtapose the first Adam, who exemplifies the body animated by the soul, and the last Adam, who exemplifies the body animated by the spirit.

> Thus it is written, 'The first man, Adam, became a living being'; the last Adam became a life-giving spirit. But it is not the spiritual that is first, but the physical, and then the spiritual. The first man was from the earth, a man of dust; the second man is from heaven. As was the man of dust, so are those who are of the dust; and as is the man of heaven, so are those who are of

heaven. Just as we have borne the image of the man of dust, we will also bear the image of the man of heaven. (1 Cor. 15.45–49)

Paul's assertions about the first Adam are pretty straightforward. He starts with the quotation of Genesis 2.7c, which explains how the man, whom God formed from the dust of the ground, became a living being after God breathed into his nostrils the breath of life. The literal meaning of the phrase that is rendered in the NRSV as 'living being' is 'living soul'. Only when the Greek terms are translated with precision can the English reader recognize the linguistic and conceptual links between the expression 'the body animated by the soul' and Paul's reference to the first Adam as a 'living soul'. All Paul's remarks about the first Adam, however, deal not with his identity as a living soul but with his identity as a creature from the dust. No less than three times in this short section is Adam called 'the man of dust'. Paul's focus on this aspect of human identity indicates that for him, the expression 'the body animated by the soul' primarily points to its transient character, i.e. to its mortality.

Paul's assertions about the last Adam are more complex. Paul begins his explanation of the spiritual body with the declaration that 'the last Adam became a life-giving spirit'. The introductory clause in v. 45, 'Thus it is written', seems to suggest that this statement, like the previous citation of Genesis 2.7c, also comes from scripture, but such a quote is nowhere to be found. Reconstructing the text(s) to which Paul alludes is not easy. The declaration that 'the last Adam became a life-giving spirit' is usually regarded as Paul's free rendering based on Genesis 2.7b: 'and [God] breathed into his nostrils the breath of life'. This explanation, however, raises both terminological and conceptual questions. Why does Paul change the term 'breath of life' to 'life-giving spirit'? Moreover, if Paul associates the last Adam with the breath of God that gave life to the lifeless body of the first human, how can he say in the next verse that the spiritual (which is presumably a reference to the spiritual body) does not precede but follows the physical (literally 'the soulish' – which is presumably a reference to the physical body, i.e. the body animated by the soul)? If only Genesis 2.7 provides the interpretative framework for Paul's claims, it is difficult, if not impossible, to explain why Paul's sequence (first the physical, then the spiritual) completely reverses the Genesis pattern (first the spiritual, then the physical). There is no doubt that Paul's understanding of the chronological sequence of the two types of bodies reflects the sequence in which the first Adam and the last Adam (the risen Jesus) appeared in human history. But how can we explain Paul's exegetical reasoning that provides the primary justification for his claims?

Paul's exegetical activity makes sense only if we locate it within the stream of Jewish tradition that understands the resurrection of the dead as a new creation. The correlation of *Urzeit* (primeval time) and *Endzeit* (end time) is a common tenet of Jewish eschatological hope, but the conceptualization of the resurrection of the dead in terms of the Genesis creation accounts is most prominent in 2 Maccabees 7.22–23; 14.46, *Pseudo-Ezekiel* and *Gen. Rab.* 14.5. The authors of these texts regularly refer (explicitly or implicitly) to Ezekiel's vision of the dry bones, which they interpret as a literal description of bodily resurrection. These passages from Jewish literature are relevant to 1 Corinthians 15.45b because the participle 'life-giving' comes from the Greek verb that in the New Testament writings typically refers to the restoration of life that has been terminated by death (e.g. Jn 5.21; Rom. 4.17; 8.11; 1 Cor. 15.21-22; 1 Pet. 3.18). In view of these considerations, Paul's declaration that the last Adam became a life-giving spirit most likely refers to the revival of the dead by the spirit of life in Ezekiel 37.5–14 rather than to the breath of life that animated the creature from the dust in Genesis 2.7. The tendency of the NRSV and other English translations to render almost all references to the spirit in Ezekiel 37 (called the 'spirit of life' in v. 5) with the term 'breath' (vv. 5, 6, 8, 9, 10) supports the interpretation of the resurrection of the dead as a new creation but obscures the difference between the initial giving of life and the restoration of life that has been terminated by death, which informs Paul's discussion of the first Adam and the last Adam. Paul's exegesis presumes that with the resurrection of Jesus the eschatological resurrection of the dead has begun. Christ as the last Adam became life-giving spirit because through him those who have died will be brought back to life.

In the discussion that follows (1 Cor. 15.47–49), Paul continues to use the imagery of Genesis 1–2 to articulate the difference between Adam and Christ. They are here called either 'the first man' and 'the second man' or 'the man of dust' and 'the man of heaven'. The most difficult question in this subsection is the meaning of the expression 'the man of heaven'. Does the term 'heaven' denote the 'stuff' out of which the body of the risen Christ was made, his heavenly origin/dwelling, or something else? Many scholars prefer the second option because it is consistent with Paul's description of the current dwelling place of the risen Christ who 'must reign until he has put all his enemies under his feet' (1 Cor. 15.27), as well as Paul's claim in Philippians 3.20–21 that 'our citizenship is in heaven, and it is from there that we are expecting a Saviour, the Lord Jesus Christ. He will transform the body of our humiliation that it may be conformed to the body of his glory, by the power that also enables him to make all things subject to himself.' Paul's main objective here, as elsewhere, is to express the impact Adam and Christ have on others, which is clearly articulated in the last verse of this paragraph: 'Just as we have borne the image of the man of dust, we will also bear the image of the man of heaven' (1 Cor. 15.49). Paul claims, in other words, that just as we all have mortal bodies, we will also, in due time, get immortal bodies that will be modelled after Christ's resurrected body.

Paul concludes his discussion in vv. 35–49 by emphatically declaring that 'flesh and blood cannot inherit the kingdom of God, nor does the perishable inherit the imperishable' (1 Cor. 15.50). This assertion confirms Paul's general agreement with the standard Hellenistic cosmology, but his discussion shows that he used the distinction between the earthly and heavenly entities to defend a very Jewish concept of afterlife – bodily resurrection. Paul's closing remarks in vv. 51–57 do not introduce any new argument but clarify a few points from the previous discussion and declare the ultimate victory over death.

> Listen, I will tell you a mystery! We will not all die, but we will all be changed, in a moment, in the twinkling of an eye, at the last trumpet. For the trumpet will sound, and the dead will be raised imperishable, and we will be changed. For this perishable body must put on imperishability, and this mortal body must put on immortality. When this perishable body puts on imperishability, and this mortal body puts on immortality, then the saying that is written will be fulfilled: 'Death has been swallowed up in victory.'
>
> 'Where, O death, is your victory? Where, O death, is your sting?' The sting of death is sin, and the power of sin is the law.

But thanks be to God, who gives us the victory through our Lord Jesus Christ. (1 Cor. 15.51–57)

One thing that was not so clear up to this point was the relation between the earthly and the resurrected body. Paul was so focused on explaining the difference between them that his readers may have got the impression that there was no connection between these two forms of embodied life. He now clarifies that his arguments, which are summed up in his claim that 'flesh and blood cannot inherit the kingdom of God' (v. 50), do not mean that the mortal body will be left behind, but that it will be transformed into an immortal body. He envisions two groups that will undergo this change at the end-time: (1) the dead who will be raised imperishable and (2) the living who will be rapidly ('in a moment, in the twinkling of an eye') transformed. Paul uses the imagery of 'putting on' to describe this transformation, but the character of this alteration is less clear. For example, does Paul imagine that the perishable elements of human body, such as flesh and blood, will be transformed into imperishable elements or that they will be removed and replaced by imperishable elements? Either option is consistent with Paul's overall description of the resurrected body. He is not interested in the mechanics of this transformation but only in the fact that when it takes place – i.e. 'when this perishable body puts on imperishability, and this mortal body puts on immortality' (v. 54a) – death will be finally defeated.

3. Summary and Conclusions

The earliest New Testament references pertaining to Jesus' resurrection are short formulaic statements that either declare that God raised Jesus from the dead (active formulations) or assert that Jesus was raised from the dead (passive formulations that presume divine agency). These declarations are not experiential statements. Rather, they are faith statements that express the Christian conviction that God's ability to create and restore life was manifest in raising Jesus from the dead. Some of these early formulas also include a reference to the third day. The confession that Jesus was raised on the third day, however, is not a chronological but theological statement. Its purpose is not to locate in time a hidden act of God but to assert that Jesus' resurrection represents the beginning of the general resurrection. This conclusion is based on the interpretation of Hosea 6.2 in the rabbinic and targumic writings, which routinely use the phrase 'on the third day' as a reference to the resurrection of the dead at the turn of the ages.

This basic conviction is further elaborated in the letters of Paul. His main claim in 1 Corinthians 15 is that the resurrection is a two-stage process: first Jesus, then the believers. It could probably be said that this division of a single corporate eschatological event into two occurrences – the one that had already happened when Jesus was raised from the dead and the one that still lies in the future when all those who are in Christ will be raised – is Paul's major modification of the traditional resurrection hope. The earliest Christian confessional formulas indicate that from the very beginning Jesus' resurrection was conceived as a commencement of the general resurrection of the dead. But it was Paul who further developed and consolidated this idea through theological reflection informed by the Christological interpretation of scripture. Paul's interpretation of the resurrected body as a body animated by the spirit stands in continuity with his Pharisaic heritage, but given the paucity of the first-century evidence about the beliefs of the Pharisees it is difficult to say to what extent he modified their understanding of the link between the pre-mortem and post-mortem bodies. What he clearly shared with them was the belief that the resurrection represents God's reward for the righteous, although in his view the righteous are those who belong to Christ. Yet, Paul's eschatological vision, though focused on the believers, is universal: the expected resurrection at the end of times will mean the ultimate defeat of death that has already begun with the resurrection of Jesus.

Notes

1 Dale C. Allison Jr notes that these confessional formulas do not mention the appearance and concludes from this that 'the phrase "God raised Jesus from the dead" has no epistemological prop and

in itself does not serve an apologetic end' (*Resurrecting Jesus: The Earliest Christian Tradition and its Interpreters* [London: T&T Clark, 2005], 230). The confession that God raised Jesus from the dead, however, must have been preceded by some kind of experience. One possible, and in my view quite plausible, reconstruction of the unspoken premises of this confession has been proposed by Ingolf U. Dalferth, who argues that the followers of Jesus witnessed the death of Jesus on the one hand and his post-resurrection appearances on the other hand. These two certainties – that Jesus died and that he was seen alive – created the cognitive *aporia* which had to be solved. Theoretically, one could either say '(1) that Jesus was not really dead; or (2) that he is not really alive; or (3) that the one who died and the one who is experienced as alive are not really the same. Christians rejected all three of them ... by confessing: Christ was raised from the dead by God' (Ingolf U. Dalferth, 'The Resurrection: The Grammar of "Raised"', in *Biblical Concepts and Our World* [eds D. Z. Phillips and Mario von der Ruhr; Claremont Studies in the Philosophy of Religion; New York: Palgrave Macmillan, 2004], 204 [original emphasis removed]).

2 The resurrection of Jesus on the third day is also linked to the testimony of scripture in three gospel passages: Lk. 18.31–33; 24.46; Mt. 12.40.

3 Karl Lehmann, *Auferweckt am dritten Tag nach der Schrift: Früheste Christologie, Bekenntnisbildung und Schriftauslegung im Lichte von 1 Kor. 15,3–5* (QD 38; Freiburg: Herder, 1968), 262–80.

4 Wright, *The Resurrection of the Son of God*, 321; Robert H. Gundry, 'Trimming the Debate', in *Jesus' Resurrection: Fact or Figment* (eds. Paul Copan and Ronald K. Tacelli; Downers Grove, IL: InterVarsity Press, 2000), 118.

5 It is sometimes argued that one or more gospel narratives reflect Jesus' initial appearance to Peter: Peter's confession of Jesus' messiahship and his recognition as the rock on which Jesus will build his church (Mt. 16.13–19), the miraculous catch of fish and the calling of the first disciples (Lk. 5.1–11), or the miraculous catch of fish and the commissioning of Peter to feed Jesus' sheep (Jn 21.1–19); see, for example, Allison, *Resurrecting Jesus*, 254–9, who offers a strong argument for the claim that 'Luke 5 and John 21 are descendants of a story purporting to recount Jesus' first postresurrection appearance to Peter'. However, even if a reasonable case can be made for such a reconstruction, it still remains puzzling why the tradition developed in this way, rather than preserving a foundational memory of Peter's solitary encounter with the risen Jesus.

6 Ann Graham Brock, *Mary Magdalene, the First Apostle: The Struggle for Authority* (HTS 51; Cambridge, MA: Harvard University Press, 2003).

7 See Martin, *Corinthian Body*, 112–17; Jeffrey R. Asher, *Polarity and Change in 1 Corinthians 15: A Study of Metaphysics, Rhetoric, and Resurrection* (HUT 42; Tübingen: Mohr Siebeck, 2000), 92.

8 Richard B. Hays, for example, offers the following imaginative paraphrase of the Corinthian position: 'The resurrection of Jesus is a wonderful metaphor for the spiritual change that God works in the lives of those who possess knowledge of the truth. "Resurrection" symbolizes the power of the Spirit that we experience in our wisdom and our spiritual gifts. But the image of resuscitated corpses (*anastasis nekrōn*) is only for childish fundamentalists. Those of us who are spiritual find it repugnant' (*First Corinthians* [Interpretation; Louisville: John Knox Press, 1997], 260).

9 For this reconstruction of the Corinthian view, see Dag Øistein Endsjø, 'Immortal Bodies Before Christ: Bodily Continuity in Ancient Greece and 1 Corinthians', *JSNT* 30 (2008): 417–36.

10 The precise nature of the Corinthian denial of the resurrection remains a controversial issue; see, for example, A. J. M. Wedderburn, 'The Problem of the Denial of the Resurrection in 1 Corinthians XV', *NovT* 23 (1981): 229–41; Karl A. Plank, 'Resurrection Theology: The Corinthian Controversy Reexamined', *PRSt* 8 (1981): 41–54; Gerhard Sellin, *Der Streit um die Auferstehung der Toten* (FRLANT 138; Göttingen: Vandenhoeck & Ruprecht, 1986), 17–37; Christopher M. Tuckett, 'The Corinthians Who Say "There Is No Resurrection of the Dead" (1 Cor. 15,12)', in *The Corinthian Correspondence* (ed. R. Bieringer; BETL 125; Leuven: Peeters, 1996), 247–75; Joël Delobel, 'The Corinthians' (Un)Belief in the Resurrection', in *Resurrection in the New Testament* (eds. Reimund Bieringer, Veronica Koperski and Bianca Lataire; BETL 165; Leuven: Peeters, 2002), 343–55.

11 Wright, *The Resurrection of the Son of God*, 352 (original emphasis).

3

Narratives about the Discovery of the Empty Tomb

The reports about the discovery of the empty tomb are found in all four gospels. In each case, the empty tomb story follows the report of Jesus' death on the cross and his burial. The author of the Gospel of Mark, our earliest gospel, narrates that Joseph of Arimathea, a respected member of the Sanhedrin, obtained permission from Pilate to bury the dead Jesus. He wrapped his body in a linen cloth, laid it in a tomb that had been hewn out of the rock and rolled a stone against its door. Mark also adds that Jesus' burial was witnessed by the women who came to the tomb two days later and found it empty, perhaps in order to indicate that they knew exactly where it was (Mk 15.42–47). The basic contours of this account are also found in other gospels, but they betray a tendency toward embellishment of the burial rite. Matthew adds that the linen cloth into which Jesus' body was wrapped was clean, that the tomb was new and belonged to Joseph, and that the stone he rolled to the door was great (Mt. 27.59–61). Luke clarifies that no one had ever been laid into the tomb where Jesus' body was buried (Lk. 23.53). While all three synoptic gospels indicate that Jesus was buried in a hurry without having been properly anointed with spices (which explains why the women came to the tomb after the Sabbath was over), the author of the Fourth Gospel narrates that two secret disciples of Jesus – Joseph of Arimathea and Nicodemus – jointly prepared a burial for Jesus worthy of a royal dignitary. They brought a mixture of myrrh and aloes, about a hundred pounds' weight, they bound the body of Jesus in linen cloths with the spices, and they laid him in a new tomb in a nearby garden where no one had ever been laid (Jn 19.38–42).

In Matthew, Luke and John, the accounts of the discovery of the empty tomb are followed by the stories of Jesus' appearances. Even in Mark, which stops short of providing such a report, Jesus' post-resurrection appearance in Galilee is announced by a young man in a white robe whom the women saw in the tomb (Mk 16.7). This narrative sequence (Jesus' burial–the discovery of the empty tomb–Jesus' post-resurrection appearances) compellingly suggests that the body that disappeared from the tomb and then appeared outside of the tomb (be it in the vicinity of Jerusalem or in Galilee) is the same body. Without this narrative sequence, however, the meaning of the empty tomb narratives remains ambiguous and puzzling. This ambiguity and puzzlement is especially evident in the earliest account of the discovery of the empty tomb that is preserved in the Gospel of Mark.

1. The Gospel of Mark

Mark is the only evangelist that closes his gospel with a report of how three women – Mary Magdalene, Mary the mother of James, and Salome – came to the tomb on the first day of the week and found it empty. There is no story of how Jesus appeared to Peter and other disciples, even though such an appearance is announced. Notwithstanding the joyful news from a young man in a white robe that Jesus has been raised from the dead, the women fled from the tomb utterly terrified and amazed. And notwithstanding the command to tell Jesus' disciples and Peter that Jesus would meet them in Galilee, the women said nothing to anyone because they were afraid. This is how the extant text of the Gospel of Mark ends – with a reference to the women's fear and silence in v. 8. The fact that the earliest manuscripts of Mark, without exception, break at the end of the explanatory clause 'for they were afraid' and not in the middle of it decreases the likelihood of a lost ending. The so-called longer ending of Mark (16.9–19), which is not found in our earliest and most reliable copies of this gospel, is a later scribal addition to supplement and harmonize Mark's strange ending with the appearance narratives in other gospels.

> When the sabbath was over, Mary Magdalene, and Mary the mother of James, and Salome bought spices, so that they might go and anoint him. And very early on the first day of the week, when the sun had risen, they went to the tomb. They had been saying to one another, 'Who will roll away the stone for us from the entrance to the tomb?' When they looked up, they saw that the stone, which was very large, had already been rolled back. As they entered the tomb, they saw a young man, dressed in a white robe, sitting on the right side; and they were alarmed. But he said to them, 'Do not be alarmed; you are looking for Jesus of Nazareth, who was crucified. He has been raised; he is not here. Look, there is the place they laid him. But go, tell his disciples and Peter that he is going ahead of you to Galilee; there you will see him, just as he told you.' So they went out and fled from the tomb, for terror and amazement had seized them; and they said nothing to anyone, for they were afraid. (Mk 16.1–8)

In Mark's account of the discovery of the empty tomb the women who came to Jesus' burial place on the first day of the week were the same three women who observed the crucifixion from afar (15.40). Two of them – Mary Magdalene and Mary, the mother of James and Joses – also watched Jesus' burial (15.47). When they arrived at the tomb, the stone (about which they were concerned on the way to their destination) was already rolled back. The position of the stone immediately suggested that the body was no longer there. The absence of the corpse, however, is not explicated by the Markan narrator, but by a young man dressed in a white robe whom the women saw when they entered the tomb. Although Mark does not identify him as an angel, he provides several clues that point to his function as a heavenly messenger. In Jewish literature, angels are sometimes presented as young men splendidly dressed (2 Macc. 3.26, 33–34; Dan. 8.15–16; Tob. 5.9; Josephus, *Ant.* 5.277, 279). The women's apprehension at the sight of the young man in white indicates that they recognized him as a heavenly envoy. Most importantly, his message conveyed divine revelation, which consisted of two major assertions. First, Jesus of Nazareth, the Crucified One, has been raised. Second, the risen

Jesus is going ahead of his disciples and Peter to Galilee, where he will meet them, just as he told them.

The first assertion – that Jesus has been raised from the dead – functions as a proclamation of the meaning of the empty tomb. By identifying the Risen One as 'Jesus of Nazareth, who was crucified', the divine envoy establishes the continuity between Jesus' crucifixion and Jesus' resurrection. The use of the passive voice, 'he has been raised', suggests that the resurrection was an act of God. The assertion 'he is not here' clarifies that Jesus' corpse has been brought back to life. This interpretation of a disappearance of a body, however, was one that was least expected in antiquity. The most common explanations of such a phenomenon were a revival of an apparently dead person, a theft of a body by grave robbers or a relocation of a corpse to another tomb. Some of these possibilities are, in fact, considered and then refuted in the gospels (theft by the disciples [Mt. 28.11–15]; theft by grave robbers [Jn 20.2, 13]; removal to another tomb [Jn 20.15]). If a disappearance of a body was ascribed to a divine intervention, the most likely explanation in the Greco-Roman world was a translation of a person into a heavenly realm. One of the most telling examples is found in the first-century CE novel *Chaereas and Callirhoe*, written by Chariton of Aphrodisias. When Chaereas' bride Callirhoe died, she was lavishly buried. During the night, the tomb robbers opened the tomb with the intention of taking the treasure that was buried with the dead girl, but since she revived as they were breaking in (because she was not really dead) they took her along. When her grieving husband came to her tomb next morning, he found it open and empty. Yet his first thought was not that Callirhoe came back to life or that she was taken by grave robbers, but that she was taken away by the gods.

> Then Chaereas himself decided to go in, eager to see Callirhoe once more even though she was dead, but on searching the tomb he could find nothing. Many others entered incredulously after him. All were baffled, and one of those inside said, 'The funeral offerings have been stolen! This is the work of tomb robbers. But where is the corpse?' Many different speculations were entertained by the crowd. But Chaereas, looking up to heaven, stretched forth his hands and said, 'Which of the gods has become my rival and carried off Callirhoe and now keeps her with him, against her will but compelled by a mightier fate?

... Or can it be that I had a goddess as my wife and did not know it, and she was above our human lot?' (Chariton, *Chaer.* 3.3.3–5; Goold, LCL)

Such an interpretation would not be intuitive for a first-century Jew, of course, nor would the idea that a missing body has been raised from the dead. The reason for this lies not in the oddness of bodily resurrection, given the popularity of this belief in afterlife, but in its singularity and in its timing. The resurrection of the dead was never conceived as a solitary event that could happen during the ordinary course of events; it was always conceived as a corporate event that would happen at the end of the age. We could therefore assume that for both the women in Mark's narrative and the readers/hearers of his gospel the discovery of the empty tomb could have meant many things, but the least likely among them would have been the idea that Jesus has been raised from the dead. Mark's version of this story accentuates the unlikelihood of this conclusion more pointedly than any other gospel. Even after hearing the good news about Jesus' resurrection from the heavenly messenger, the women left the tomb in bewilderment, 'for terror and amazement had seized them' (v. 8). These considerations notwithstanding, the angel's message serves to remove the ambiguity of the empty tomb and give it one specific, however unlikely, meaning: Jesus' corpse is not there because he has been raised from the dead. His body is no longer in the tomb but outside of it.

The second assertion – that the risen Jesus will meet his disciples in Galilee – includes the promise of Jesus' post-resurrection appearance and the command to communicate this news to Jesus' disciples. Some scholars regard the first part of v. 7 ('But go, tell his disciples and Peter that he is going ahead of you to Galilee') as Mark's editorial addition to a primitive version of the empty tomb narrative to conform it to Jesus' prediction in Mk 14.28 ('But after I am raised up, I will go before you to Galilee').[1] In its present setting, the promise that the disciples will see the risen Jesus in Galilee points toward the experiential proof of Jesus' resurrection – his post-resurrection appearances. The materialization of this proof, however, is not found in Mark. Jesus' appearance to his followers is merely announced but not reported.

The greatest oddity of Mark's ending, however, is his closing statement about the women's silence. For some scholars, this reference provides an explanation of the limited knowledge of the empty tomb tradition. Others regard it as an apology for the proclamation of the resurrection based on Jesus' appearances rather than on the empty tomb reports that depended upon female testimony. Still others insist that the women's silence was only temporary, because the news about the discovery of the empty tomb clearly did not remain a secret forever. On the other end of the spectrum are those who ascribe the entire story of the empty tomb to Mark's creativity. In Mark's narrative, however, the women's silence is not directly related to the proclamation of the empty tomb but to the angelic command to tell the disciples that Jesus is going to meet them in Galilee. Their failure to speak is therefore more limited in scope than it is usually assumed. It also fits the recurrent theme in Mark's Gospel, which repeatedly shows how various characters fail to obey Jesus. Just as Jesus' command to silence was met with disobedience during his earthly ministry, the angelic command to speak was met with silence after the discovery of the empty tomb.

2. The Gospel of Matthew

The Matthean version of the discovery of the empty tomb by the women is sandwiched in between a story of the Roman guard that was placed at Jesus' tomb at the request of the Jewish leaders and a report of the guard back to the Jewish authorities, who in turn bribe them to tell a lie about a theft of Jesus' body by his disciples.

> The next day, that is, after the day of Preparation, the chief priests and the Pharisees gathered before Pilate and said, 'Sir, we remember what that impostor said while he was still alive, "After three days I will rise again." Therefore command the tomb to be made secure until the third day; otherwise his disciples may go and steal him away, and tell the people, "He has been raised from the dead," and the last deception would be worse than the first.' Pilate said to them, 'You have a guard of soldiers; go, make it as secure as you can.' So they went with the guard and made the tomb secure by sealing the stone. (Mt. 27.62–66)

After the sabbath, as the first day of the week was dawning, Mary Magdalene and the other Mary went to see the tomb. And suddenly there was a great earthquake; for an angel of the Lord, descending from heaven, came and rolled back the stone and sat on it. His appearance was like lightning, and his clothing white as snow. For fear of him the guards shook and became like dead men. But the angel said to the women, 'Do not be afraid; I know that you are looking for Jesus who was crucified. He is not here; for he has been raised, as he said. Come, see the place where he lay. Then go quickly and tell his disciples, "He has been raised from the dead, and indeed he is going ahead of you to Galilee; there you will see him." This is my message for you.' So they left the tomb quickly with fear and great joy, and ran to tell his disciples. Suddenly Jesus met them and said, 'Greetings!' And they came to him, took hold of his feet, and worshiped him. Then Jesus said to them, 'Do not be afraid; go and tell my brothers to go to Galilee; there they will see me.' (Mt. 28.1–10)

While they were going, some of the guard went into the city and told the chief priests everything that had happened. After the priests had assembled with the elders, they devised a plan to give a large sum of money to the soldiers, telling them, 'You must say, "His disciples came by night and stole him away while we were asleep." If this comes to the governor's ears, we will satisfy him and keep you out of trouble.' So they took the money and did as they were directed. And this story is still told among the Jews to this day. (Mt. 28.11–15)

Many scholars question the historicity of the story of the Roman guard at the tomb. Even if one accepts N. T. Wright's suggestion that a short-term collaboration between the Jewish leaders and Pilate forged on a Sabbath is 'not beyond possibility',[2] the likelihood that a Roman guard would be placed at a tomb of a crucified criminal is extraordinarily slim. This impression is reinforced by the fact that no other evangelist mentions the guard at the tomb. It is also not very likely that Jesus' opponents would have known his predictions of rising after three days, which are in Matthew always relayed to Jesus' disciples in private (Mt. 16.21; 17.23; 20.19). Even more improbable is the Jewish leaders' anticipation of the proclamation of Jesus' resurrection.

It is therefore best to regard this account as a later apologetic development to counteract the accusation that Jesus' body was stolen.[3] It suggests that by the time of the writing of the Gospel of Matthew (which is usually dated to the period between 80–90 CE) knowledge of the empty tomb was widespread, probably because the Christians made use of the empty tomb in their proclamation of Jesus' resurrection. The purpose of this tale is to show that the Jewish opponents of Christianity did not dispute the historicity of the empty tomb but rather promulgated a different interpretation: the disciples stole Jesus' dead body while the soldiers were asleep. This story represents a Christian answer to this slander. In this way, Matthew emphasizes the deliberate character of Jewish unbelief and their malicious intent to deceive others. It also portrays the Roman soldiers as complicit in the Jewish plot of deliberate deception. The story is deeply ironic. The soldiers are bribed to propagate a lie that the Jewish leaders originally presented to Pilate as the plan of Jesus' disciples (27.64).

Matthew's account of the discovery of the empty tomb follows Mark's, but it nonetheless contains several significant modifications. Matthew mentions only two women, Mary Magdalene and the other Mary, coming to the tomb at dawn on the first day of the week. He reports that on their way there they witness a great earthquake and a descent of an angel from heaven, who rolls back the stone from the entrance of the tomb. It is clear from the narrative logic of this account that the stone is removed to enable the women to enter the tomb (even though their actual entry is not described) rather than to enable the risen Jesus to exit the tomb. An earthquake is an apocalyptic motif that signifies the beginning of the eschatological age (see Mt. 24.7). This impression is reinforced by the story of the resurrection of the saints in Matthew 27.51–53 (which also includes a reference to an earthquake) whose purpose is to show that Jesus' resurrection marks the beginning of the general resurrection. The Matthean version leaves no doubt that what the women witnessed was an angelophany. The mention of the guard at the tomb links this story to its framing narrative. The narrator emphasizes that the descent of the angel and the opening of Jesus' tomb was witnessed not only by the women but also by the Roman guard.

Like in Mark, the angel interprets the meaning of the empty tomb, not just once but twice: first by declaring to the women

'He has been raised' (v. 6), and then by repeating this declaration as part of the message for the disciples: 'He has been raised from the dead' (v. 7). The angel's message is similar to the kerygmatic announcement in Mark: Jesus, the Crucified One, has been raised. The angel does not single out Peter when he mentions the disciples, but this declaration corresponds to Matthew's description of Jesus' appearance to the eleven disciples in Galilee, where Peter is just one of the group (Mt. 28.16–20). Like in Mark, Jesus has already prophesied in Matthew 26.32 that he will go before the disciples to Galilee. Unlike Mark, the message to the women ends with the reference to the angel's (not Jesus') message. This resembles the prophetic formula and reinforces the idea that the angel is conveying the words of God himself.

Matthew's description of the reaction of the women is very different from Mark's. He added the motif of joy, he removed any reference to the women's silence, and he added a note that the women ran to tell the angel's message to Jesus' disciples. Matthew also attached a brief report about Jesus' appearance to the women as they were leaving the tomb. We will discuss the gospel narratives about the appearances of the risen Jesus in the next chapter, but at this point it is important to note that Jesus' message to the women ('Do not be afraid; go and tell my brothers to go to Galilee; there they will see me' [Mt. 28.1–10]) is merely a repetition of the words of the angel in the tomb ('Do not be afraid ... Then go quickly and tell his disciples, "He has been raised from the dead, and indeed he is going ahead of you to Galilee; there you will see him"' [28.5a, 7]). The only differences are Jesus' use of the address 'my brothers' for his disciples and the omission of the message of his resurrection, which was no longer necessary in light of the women's encounter with the risen Jesus. In this way, Jesus' appearance outside the tomb provides the strongest validation of the meaning of the empty tomb and establishes a direct link between the missing body and the resurrected body, i.e. between Jesus' disappearance and Jesus' re-appearance. Even this narrative association of two different experiences of Jesus, however, stops short of describing the event that connects them – the actual resurrection of Jesus. Like in the earliest formulaic statements preserved in various New Testament writings, Jesus' resurrection in Matthew is merely proclaimed but not described.

3. The Gospel of Luke

Luke's version of the discovery of the empty tomb is augmented by a description of the male disciples' reaction to the women's testimony and Peter's subsequent authentication of its veracity.

> But on the first day of the week, at early dawn, they came to the tomb, taking the spices that they had prepared. They found the stone rolled away from the tomb, but when they went in, they did not find the body. While they were perplexed about this, suddenly two men in dazzling clothes stood beside them. The women were terrified and bowed their faces to the ground, but the men said to them, 'Why do you look for the living among the dead? He is not here, but has risen. Remember how he told you, while he was still in Galilee, that the Son of Man must be handed over to sinners, and be crucified, and on the third day rise again.' Then they remembered his words, and returning from the tomb, they told all this to the eleven and to all the rest. Now it was Mary Magdalene, Joanna, Mary the mother of James and the other women with them who told this to the apostles. But these words seemed to them an idle tale, and they did not believe them. But Peter got up and ran to the tomb; stooping and looking in, he saw the linen cloths by themselves; then he went home, amazed at what had happened. (Lk. 24.1–12)

In Luke's account, the group of women who came to the tomb at early dawn on the first day of the week includes Mary Magdalene, Joanna, Mary the mother of James and several others. Their motive for coming to the tomb is the same as in Mark – to anoint Jesus' body. Like in Mark, the stone was already rolled away when they arrived at Jesus' burial place (Lk. 24.2). Unlike in Mark, Luke first describes the interior of the tomb when the women entered it by explicitly stating that 'they did not find the body' (Lk. 24.3). Only then does he describe the angelophany. Instead of Mark's young man in a white robe, however, Luke has 'two men in dazzling clothes' (Lk. 24.4). The assumption that Luke uses a conventional description of angels is confirmed by the reaction of the women, who 'were terrified and bowed their faces to the ground' (24.5). The motif of fear is also prominent in Luke's description of

Zechariah's and Mary's reactions to the appearances of the angel Gabriel (Lk. 1.12–13, 29–30) and the shepherds' reaction to the appearance of an angel of the Lord (Lk. 2.9–10). This conclusion is further corroborated by the recapitulation of this event in the Emmaus narrative: 'Moreover, some women of our group astounded us. They were at the tomb early this morning, and when they did not find his body there, they came back and told us that they had indeed seen a vision of angels who said that he was alive' (Lk. 24.22–23).

Luke has considerably modified the angelic words. The initial question of the angels, 'Why do you look for the living among the dead?' (Lk. 24.5), replaces the assurance that the angel gives to the women in Mk 16.6 ('Do not be alarmed; you are looking for Jesus of Nazareth, who was crucified'). The rhetorical question in Luke is theologically charged because it emphasizes Jesus' triumph over death. The authenticity of the declaration, 'He is not here, but has risen', is somewhat uncertain because it is not found in the otherwise expansionistic Western text-type copies of the Gospel of Luke (hence the technical term 'Western non-interpolations').[4] The appearance of this text in the papyrus manuscript P^{75} (which is dated to the early third century CE) alongside its occurrence in major codices, such as Sinaiticus, Alexandrinus and Vaticanus, strengthens the assumption that it belongs to Luke's original text.[5]

The most interesting change is Luke's replacement of Mark's reference to Galilee as the place where Jesus will appear to his disciples with the reference to Galilee as the place where Jesus predicted his crucifixion and resurrection (Lk. 9.22, 44; 18.31–33). This change is coherent with Luke's accounts of the appearances of the risen Jesus, none of which take place in Galilee. It should be noted, however, that the message of the angels contains no announcement of Jesus' appearances. The emphasis falls solely on the necessity of Jesus being handed over to sinners, his crucifixion, and his resurrection on the third day, i.e. on the divine plan that came to fulfilment in these events. Luke's account of the empty tomb is the only one that employs a third-day motif, but this motif is associated with Jesus' passion predictions and not with the discovery of the empty tomb. While the presence of the women in the scenes where Jesus made his passion and resurrection predictions (Lk. 9.22, 44; 18.31–33) is not explicitly noted, it is certainly implied given the remark in Lk. 8.1–3 that several Galilean women, including Mary Magdalene and Joanna, accompanied Jesus and his disciples during Jesus' earthly ministry.

Another distinctive feature of Luke's editorial activity is his removal of any commission to the women to deliver the message of Jesus' resurrection to the disciples. Consequently, the women in Luke are not charged to proclaim the good news that Jesus has been raised from the dead. They are asked to remember Jesus' predictions of this event, but they are not asked to declare their fulfilment (Lk. 24.6). Even if one hesitates to ascribe this editorial change to Luke's deliberate attempt to decrease the role of women as the primary witnesses of Jesus' resurrection, as some scholars allege,[6] it is difficult to deny a diminished role of the women in Luke's account. Although they promptly inform the disciples of everything that transpired at the tomb, despite not being asked to do so, the men do not take them seriously. The narrator stresses that the male disciples did not believe the women's report because they regarded it as 'idle tale' (literally 'nonsense'). At the same time, however, Luke's narrative clearly shows that the women, not the men, got it right. It is certainly true that their understanding of the empty tomb was facilitated by the heavenly message, but the fact remains that it was they and not the men who received this insight into the meaning of the empty tomb. Luke also emphasizes their recollection of Jesus' words, which helps them interpret the otherwise ambiguous disappearance of Jesus' body within the framework of the overall purpose of God.

The next verse, which describes Peter's visit to the empty tomb, is another example of a Western non-interpolation, but its authenticity is corroborated by the recapitulation of this event in Lk. 24.24: 'Some of those who were with us went to the tomb and found it just as the women had said; but they did not see him.' Although this reiteration mentions several men rather than Peter alone, it nevertheless confirms the main objective of Lk. 24.12. The testimony of women had to be validated by the testimony of men. Another reason could be Luke's apologetic intent to keep 'the official witness of the resurrection independent of the women's story'.[7] Yet, it is important to note that Peter's visit to the empty tomb confirms the accuracy of the women's report that the tomb was empty but remains inconclusive with regard to its meaning. He saw the linen cloths by themselves; there was no body. While the presence of the cloths excluded the possibility that the body was stolen (because grave robbers would have taken the body along with the grave cloths), it did not offer any alternative suggestion of where the body really was. Not surprisingly, then, Peter went home, 'amazed at what had happened'. Without an interpreting angel or an encounter with the risen Jesus, the mere sight of the empty tomb could not convince Peter that Jesus has been raised from the dead.

4. The Gospel of John

The story of the discovery of the empty tomb in the Fourth Gospel is quite different from the synoptic reports, although the parts that describe Mary Magdalene are roughly parallel to the synoptic versions.

> Early on the first day of the week, while it was still dark, Mary Magdalene came to the tomb and saw that the stone had been removed from the tomb. So she ran and went to Simon Peter and the other disciple, the one whom Jesus loved, and said to them, 'They have taken the Lord out of the tomb, and we do not know where they have laid him.' Then Peter and the other disciple set out and went toward the tomb. The two were running together, but the other disciple outran Peter and reached the tomb first. He bent down to look in and saw the linen wrappings lying there, but he did not go in. Then Simon Peter came, following him, and went into the tomb. He saw the linen wrappings lying there, and the cloth that had been on Jesus' head, not lying with the linen wrappings but rolled up in a place by itself. Then the other disciple, who reached the tomb first, also went in, and he saw and believed; for as yet they did not understand the scripture, that he must rise from the dead. Then the disciples returned to their homes. But Mary stood weeping outside the tomb. As she wept, she bent over to look into the tomb; and she saw two angels in white, sitting where the body of Jesus had been lying, one at the head and the other at the feet. They said to her, 'Woman, why are you weeping?' She said to them, 'They have taken away my Lord, and I do not know where they have laid him.' (Jn 20.1–13)

Mary Magdalene, who is, in the synoptic accounts, always mentioned first among other women, appears in John alone. However, her report to Peter and the beloved disciple is constructed as a corporate statement: 'They have taken the Lord out of the tomb, and we do not know where they have laid him' (20.3). This unexpected use of the first-person plural could be a reminiscence of an original story that mentioned several women, but it could also be an indication that Mary Magdalene functions as a representative character. Like in the synoptic accounts, Mary Magdalene is the first person to discover the empty tomb. The reason for her coming is not given. At her arrival, she only saw that the stone had been removed from the entrance, but she did not enter the tomb to make sure that it was empty. At this point the similarities with the synoptic accounts come to an end. During her initial visit to the tomb, Mary did not experience an angelophany. Her behaviour shows what would be the most natural reaction in antiquity to a sight of an open tomb. Her assumption, which she repeats two more times (to the angels at her second visit to the tomb and to the risen Jesus before she recognized him), is that the body has been taken away, probably by grave robbers.

After Mary voices this concern, which is not immediately refuted, she disappears from the scene, which now focuses on Peter and the beloved disciple. Mary will not appear again until we hear about the men's experience of the empty tomb. When the male disciples return home, Mary Magdalene reappears (v. 11). She is now portrayed as weeping outside the tomb. The narrator gives no explanation of how and when she arrived there. These narrative gaps are frequently regarded as signs of the editorial integration of two independent stories, one about Mary Magdalene and one about Peter and the beloved disciple. Indeed, without vv. 2–10, the account of Mary Magdalene's experience at the empty tomb runs much more smoothly. Her weeping outside the tomb and her worries about the whereabouts of the body appear to have been caused by the perplexing sight of an open tomb. Her anguish is suddenly interrupted by an angelophany. As she bends over to look into the tomb, she sees two angels sitting on either side of the burial shelf. Despite the obvious parallels with the synoptic accounts, there is no angelic interpretation of the empty tomb. The only words that the angels utter is a question: 'Woman, why are you weeping?' Mary's answer is a repetition of the explanation that she initially gave to Peter and the beloved disciple, the only difference being the use of the first-person singular: 'They have taken away my Lord, and I do not know where they have laid him.' Before the angels can respond to Mary's persistent and clearly inaccurate interpretation of the empty tomb, she sees the risen Jesus standing there, whom she initially identifies as a gardener. Her dramatic encounter with the resurrected Jesus will be examined in more detail in the next chapter. What is important to note at this point is that the fourth evangelist shifts the interpretation of the empty tomb from an angelophany to the Christophany.[8] Like Matthew, who also provides a report of Jesus' appearance to the women near the tomb, John connects the disappearance of the body from the tomb to the appearance of the risen Jesus outside the tomb. Unlike Matthew, John does not mention the angelic message of Jesus' resurrection so that the meaning of the empty tomb remains a mystery until Jesus appears to Mary Magdalene.

The central section of John's narrative is devoted to the male experience of the empty tomb. The only other gospel that mentions this subject is the Gospel of Luke, which contains a brief description of how Peter went to the tomb to verify the women's testimony (Lk. 24.12) and an equally brief reference to the visit of the tomb by several male disciples in the reminiscences of the two disciples on the Emmaus road (Lk. 24.24). The fourth evangelist, however, devotes nine verses (Jn 20.2–10) to this topic. As soon as Peter and the beloved disciple hear Mary's report, they head toward Jesus' grave. Their motives are not explained, but male verification of the women's testimony is probably one of them. In John's account, the men's reaction is more plausible, because Mary did not come to them with the joyful message of Jesus' resurrection but with the alarming message of the body's disappearance and a suspicion that this was the result of a grave robbery. The narrator describes a competition between Peter and the beloved disciple as running toward the tomb. The beloved disciple ran faster and arrived at the tomb first, but Peter was more courageous and entered the tomb first. He saw the linen wrappings for the body and the cloth neatly rolled up. Like in Luke 24.12, Peter did not see any angel inside the tomb. The narrator does not explain what Peter concluded from the sight of the body wrappings; he points out, however, that when the beloved disciple entered the tomb, 'he saw and believed'.

This description of the beloved disciple's belief in response to the sight of the empty tomb is quite unique. Apart from John 20.8, there is no character in the gospel accounts – not even the women who witness an angelophany – who is portrayed as coming to faith on the basis of the empty tomb. The content of the beloved disciple's belief, however, is not clarified in the text. Many interpreters find the idea, originally proposed by Augustine (*Cons.* 3.24.69), that this verse refers to the beloved disciple's endorsement of Mary's report that Jesus' body was no longer in the tomb, though plausible, nonetheless trivial. Moreover, if only such a mundane confirmation is in view, why did the author single out the beloved disciple? Wouldn't Peter also come to the same obvious conclusion? In search for a more satisfying solution, scholars usually assume that the beloved disciple came to believe that Jesus has been raised from the dead. This explanation is frequently supported by the observation that in all cases in which John uses the verb 'believe' in an absolute sense, i.e. without an object, it always refers to religious faith.[9] In the context of the discovery of the empty tomb, this religious faith could only be the faith that Jesus has been raised from the dead. The usual explanation is that the linen wrappings lying there convinced him that Jesus' body was not stolen but passed through the burial clothes in some mysterious way. The fact that Peter did not come to the same conclusion despite seeing the same things is typically taken to mean that the beloved disciple possessed special discernment deriving from the bond of love that he shared with Jesus.

The biggest challenge for this interpretation is the apparent tension between the idea that the beloved disciple acquired the resurrection faith and the explanatory note in v. 9, 'for as yet they did not understand the scripture, that he must rise from the dead'. Verse 9 describes the situation not yet characterized by the proper understanding of scripture that could lead to the conclusion that Jesus must rise from the dead. The text does not indicate which passages are in view, but, since there is no obvious biblical text that envisions the resurrection of a single individual ahead of the general resurrection, the narrator probably refers to a specifically Christian – i.e. Christological – interpretation of the Jewish Scriptures. If so, John 20.8 agrees with Luke 24.25–27, 44–47 that the Torah and the prophets can be understood as pointers to Jesus' resurrection only after the encounters with the risen Christ. Such an interpretation requires a different mindset, which the disciples did not possess before seeing Jesus alive. Additional difficulty comes from the change from a third-person singular narration in v. 8 ('he saw and believed') to a third-person plural explanation in v. 9 ('for as yet they did not understand the scripture'). Finally, there is no information that the faith of the beloved disciple had any effect on Peter or Mary Magdalene, who was portrayed as standing nearby weeping.

Scholars who are interested in the redaction history of the text may be content with Raymond Brown's suggestion that v. 8 is a later addition to an older story of how Peter and another disciple (who was not yet identified as the one whom Jesus loved) came to the tomb and went away puzzled, like in Lk. 24.12, 24,[10] or with Rudolf Bultmann's proposal that v. 9 is a gloss added by a later redactor.[11] One of the most plausible solutions for those who seek to understand the text of John in its final form is to argue that although the beloved disciple reached the right conclusion, this faith was still based on seeing ('he saw and believed') and not the faith that Jesus commends in John 20.29: 'Blessed are those who have not seen and yet have come to believe.' The faith of the beloved disciple did not entail much comprehension, because he, like Peter, did not yet understand the scripture and the necessity of Jesus' resurrection.[12] This interpretation supports the conclusion that the Gospel of John, despite associating the initial belief of the beloved disciple with the sight of the empty tomb, does not differ from the main tenor of the synoptic gospels. The discovery of the empty tomb, in and of itself, does not produce faith. Only an encounter with the risen Jesus can generate the belief that Jesus has been raised from the dead.

5. Development of the Empty Tomb Tradition

The gospel accounts of the discovery of the empty tomb incorporate a relatively stable core story about a group of women who came to the place where Jesus was buried early on the first day of the week and found the tomb empty. While the names of these women vary, Mary Magdalene is mentioned in every gospel. The evangelists are also unanimous that during their visit to the tomb the women experienced an angelophany. Individual narratives that embody this core story, however, are marked by considerable diversity. The table below includes several constitutive elements where the gospel accounts differ, such as the number and the identity of the women who came to the tomb, the scenario outside and inside the tomb, the number of angels, the content of the angelic message, the reaction of the women to the experience of the empty tomb, the reaction of the men to the testimony of the women, and the reaction of the men to their own experience of the empty tomb.

	Mk 16.1–8	Mt. 28.1–8	Lk. 24.1–12	Jn 20.1–13
Time	Very early on the first day of the week, when the sun had risen	As the first day of the week was dawning	On the first day of the week, at early dawn	Early on the first day of the week, while it was still dark
Women	Mary Magdalene Mary, mother of James Salome	Mary Magdalene Other Mary	Mary Magdalene Mary, mother of James Joanna Other women	Mary Magdalene
Men			Peter Several disciples	Peter The beloved disciple
Scenario outside the tomb	Stone already rolled back	Earthquake An angel descended from heaven, rolled back the stone and sat on it	Stone already rolled away from the tomb	Stone already removed from the tomb
Scenario inside the tomb	A young man, dressed in white robe, sitting on the right side	The angel invites the women to see the place where the body was laid, but there is no report that they really entered the tomb	Two men in dazzling clothes appeared after the women entered the tomb. Peter saw the linen cloths by themselves	Peter and the beloved disciple saw the linen wrappings laying there and the face cloth rolled up in a place by itself. When, later, Mary entered the tomb, she saw two angels in white

Message of the angel(s)	'Do not be alarmed; you are looking for Jesus of Nazareth, who was crucified. He has been raised; he is not here. Look, there is the place they laid him. But go, tell his disciples and Peter that he is going ahead of you to Galilee; there you will see him, just as he told you.'	'Do not be afraid; I know that you are looking for Jesus who was crucified. He is not here; for he has been raised, as he said. Come, see the place where he lay. Then go quickly and tell his disciples, "He has been raised from the dead, and indeed he is going ahead of you to Galilee; there you will see him." This is my message for you.'	'Why do you look for the living among the dead? He is not here, but has risen. Remember how he told you, while he was still in Galilee, that the Son of Man must be handed over to sinners, and be crucified, and on the third day rise again.'	'Woman, why are you weeping?'
Reaction of the characters	Women fled from the tomb in terror and amazement; they said nothing to anyone because they were afraid.	Women left the tomb quickly with fear and great joy, and ran to tell the disciples.	Women left the tomb and told everything to the eleven and the rest. After Peter saw the empty tomb, he was amazed at what had happened.	Mary ran away from the tomb and went to Peter and the beloved disciple; she told them that the body had been taken. After Peter and the beloved disciple saw the empty tomb, they returned to their homes.

How should we explain this diversity? Is there a way to recreate what actually happened? The traditional solution, which was popular until the eighteenth century, was to create a composite account that removed all discrepancies among the gospel narratives. Augustine, for example, proposed the following sequence of events as part of one connected narrative (*Cons.* 3.24.69):

1. When a group of women came to the tomb in the early morning of the first day of the week, the events that are described only in Matthew had already happened, such as an earthquake, the rolling away of the stone, and the terror of the guards (Mt. 28.2, 4).

2. Then Mary Magdalene approached the tomb, leaving behind other women who came with her; when she saw that the stone was rolled away, she immediately reported this to Peter and John (whom Augustine identified as the disciple whom Jesus loved) (Jn 20.1–2).

3. Then Peter and John came to the tomb, entered it, and, after confirming that the body had been taken away, they returned home (Jn 20.3–10).

4. Thereafter Mary and other women saw an angel sitting upon the stone outside the tomb, who told them that the risen Jesus would meet the disciples in Galilee (Mt. 28.2–3, 5–8; Mk 16.1–8).

5. At these words, Mary, still weeping, looked into the tomb and saw two angels, who asked her why she was weeping; she responded by expressing her concern that the body had been taken away; the angels replied with the words from Luke's version of the angelophany (Jn 20.11–13; Lk. 24.4–7).

6. Thereupon Mary encountered the risen Jesus, whom she initially mistook for a gardener (Jn 20.14–18).

7. Then Mary, and along with her other women, departed from the tomb in fear and trembling and said nothing to anyone (Mk 16.8).

8. As they were leaving, Jesus appeared to them for the second time to strengthen them by a repeated experience of seeing him alive and to bring them out of the state of fear; he commissioned them again to inform the disciples that he would meet them in Galilee (Mt. 28.9–10).

9. Finally, Mary Magdalene told the disciples that she had seen the Lord; with her were other women mentioned in Luke; their words seemed to other disciples like madness and they did not believe them (Lk. 24.9–11).

Such a composite account that includes three, possibly even four, angels, several trips to the tomb and two appearances of Jesus to the women prior to their report to the eleven disciples is no longer acceptable in modern biblical scholarship, although in may still be popular in some circles. The artificial arrangement of events, though based on the gospel narratives, is not really supported by any of the gospel reports. By trying to harmonize discrepant events, the composite account creates new narrative gaps that are even more difficult to explain than the original ones. As the heirs of more than 200 years of critical scholarship, modern interpreters are aware that any reconstruction of the origin of the empty tomb traditions must take into consideration literary relationships among the gospels, their socio-historical settings and their theological tendencies.

Scholars are divided with regard to how many independent sources we have for the empty tomb tradition. Most interpreters uphold Matthew and Luke's dependence on Mark and ascribe their variations either to the influence of oral traditions or to the evangelists' theological tendencies. Many scholars also affirm the independence of the Fourth Gospel, but this question remains controversial, especially with regard to obvious similarities between John and the synoptic accounts. Indeed, some of the variations and embellishments in the gospel versions can only be explained if we assume a complex oral traditioning process that preceded and went along with the writing of the gospels.

Much of scholarly discussion has centred on the origin of the earliest version of the empty tomb tradition preserved in the Gospel of Mark. Some interpreters argue that this account has no historical basis but was created by Mark to bolster the belief in the bodily resurrection of Jesus.[13] The assumption that Mark 16.1–8 is a late legend is usually supported by the observation that the pre-Pauline tradition in 1 Corinthians 15.3–4 makes no mention of the empty tomb, which is taken to mean that there was no early knowledge of its discovery. The assertion in Mk 16.8 that the women 'said nothing to anyone' is interpreted as an indication that the story is a late invention. On this reading, Mark added a note about the women's silence to explain the fact that nobody had heard of this story before.

Many scholars, however, are unwilling to ascribe the empty tomb narrative to Mark's creativity. They rightly allege that nothing conclusive can be inferred from Paul's silence on the subject of the empty tomb. Interpreting Mark's reference to the women's silence as a literary device to justify the recent origin of the story fails to convince. Those who defend the historicity of the empty tomb regularly emphasize that all four evangelists credit the discovery of the empty tomb to the women. Had they wished to fabricate the story, they would not have attributed this discovery to women, whose testimony did not carry much legal weight in ancient Judaism. The most relevant evidence comes from Josephus, who asserts, 'From women let no evidence be accepted, because of the levity and temerity of their sex' (*Ant.* 4.219). Even though Josephus refers to women's testimony in a courtroom, his statement reflects general prejudice against women's trustworthiness that was prevalent in the first-century Jewish world. For example, in his rewritten scriptural narrative *Liber Antiquitatum Biblicarum*, Pseudo-Philo describes a dream of Miriam that predicted the birth of Moses and his future leadership of Israelites, which she was instructed to tell her parents. But 'when Miriam told of her dream, her parents did not believe her' (*L.A.B.* 9.10). Pseudo-Philo describes a similar reaction to a woman's message in his account of Samson's birth. When Manoah's wife told him about a vision of the angel of the Lord who announced the birth of her son, 'Manoah did not believe his wife' (*L.A.B.* 42.5).

One cannot help but recognize the similarities between Pseudo-Philo's descriptions of a typical male reaction to female testimony about divine revelation and the reaction of Jesus' male disciples to the women's reports about the discovery of the empty tomb. Luke informs his audience that when the Galilean women related to the apostles their discovery and the angelic message, 'these words seemed to them an idle tale, and they did not believe them' (Lk. 24.11). John does not provide such an explicit comment about Peter and the beloved disciple's reaction to the report of Mary Magdalene, but their immediate race to the tomb was most likely motivated by a desire to verify her testimony (Jn 20.2–3). The same applies to Luke's note about Peter's run to the tomb after hearing the report of the women (Lk. 24.12). Most scholars regard the men's visit of the tomb as a later addition to the original account of the women's discovery of the empty tomb. The reports about male verification of female testimony, which are found only in the late first-century gospels of Luke and John, serve a clear apologetic purpose. To say that an account exhibits apologetic tendencies does not exclude the possibility of its historicity, but it certainly diminishes its likelihood.

Finally, we should also discuss the function of the angelophany, i.e. the appearance of one or two angels to the women at the tomb. In all synoptic accounts, the main task of the angel(s) is to interpret the meaning of Jesus' missing body. Matthew and Mark also add a commission to the women to tell the disciples that Jesus will meet them in Galilee, but the interpretative task remains primary. The significance of the interpretative function of an angelophany becomes especially apparent when we consider John's account in which the angels do not have this role, because they do not tell Mary Magdalene what the empty tomb means. This is why she continues suggesting that Jesus' body had been taken away, even to the risen Jesus himself before she recognizes him. Without the angelic explanation, the empty tomb remains enigmatic and confusing, as John's narrative beautifully illustrates. This confusion is removed only when the risen Jesus appears to Mary Magdalene and she realizes that this is her Teacher who has been raised from the dead. In this account, Christophany has replaced angelophany.

The transfer of the interpretative function from the angels to the risen Jesus, which can be observed in John's narrative, raises the question of the relationship between angelophany and Christophany. In the Gospel of Matthew, Mary Magdalene and the other Mary also experience a Christophany near the empty tomb, but here the interpretative function associated with Christophany merely replicates the interpretative function associated with angelophany. One reconstruction, favoured by some scholars, is to claim that the original angelophany gave rise to a later the Christophany. On this reading, the primitive tradition about the vision of an angelic figure, who gave the women assurance that Jesus has been raised from the dead, later developed into a tradition about the vision of the risen Christ.[14] An alternative reconstruction is to affirm the genuineness of Mary Magdalene's Christophany and argue that it was later turned into an angelophany.[15] Given John's relative independence of the Synoptics, the tradition about Jesus' appearance to Mary Magdalene may be very old. A transfer from a Christophany to an angelophany seems to be more plausible given the patriarchal prejudice that was prevalent in the first century. As we have seen above, the traditional material in 1 Corinthians 15.3–7 makes no mention of women, either as witnesses of an angelophany or as witnesses of a Christophany. While nothing certain can be concluded from this silence, the omission of the women from the traditional formula increases the likelihood that Jesus' appearance to either Mary Magdalene alone or to a group of women in close proximity to the empty tomb was largely ignored or even deliberately suppressed. The fact that all gospel narratives associate the women at Jesus' tomb with a vision of one or two angels could be taken as further evidence that an earlier Christophany was later turned into an angelophany in order to downplay the women's significance in the Easter events.[16]

6. Summary and Conclusions

In many churches, the only text that is read during the Easter service is a story about the discovery of the empty tomb from one of the gospels, which creates the impression that this story alone conveys the message of Jesus' resurrection. Evidence from the gospels does not support such a conclusion. Each evangelist emphasizes that finding a tomb without a body was an ambiguous experience. Only when the story of the empty tomb functions as a prequel to the stories of Jesus' post-resurrection appearances does this ambiguity disappear. The beginning of this process can be seen in Mark, but what Mark only anticipates other evangelists fully narrate. By adding the accounts about the encounters with the risen Christ to the story of the discovery of the empty tomb, Matthew, Luke and John created narrative demonstrations that the body that disappeared from the tomb was the same body that appeared outside the tomb.

All four gospels agree that the empty tomb was discovered by a group of women. The name of Mary Magdalene appears on every list while the names of the other women vary. In the Gospel of John Mary appears alone, but she probably functions there as a representative character. This early tradition about the women's discovery of a missing body is, in the gospels of Luke and John, supplemented by the accounts about male verification of female testimony. The primary purpose of the tradition about the men's visit to the tomb is apologetic, i.e. to provide a reliable confirmation of the women's report.

All four gospels also link the women's discovery of the empty tomb to an angelophany. The primary function of the angel(s) at the tomb is to remove the ambiguity created by the discovery of a missing body and to convey the message of the resurrection. Only in the Gospel of John is the interpretation of the meaning of the empty tomb transferred from angelophany to Christophany. Moreover, in the Gospel of Matthew an angelophany is accompanied by a Christophany. In light of the patriarchal prejudice that was prevalent in antiquity, it is more likely that an original Christophany to the women was later turned into an angelophany than that an original angelophany was later turned into a Christophany. While all such reconstructions remain conjectural, the ambiguity created by the discovery of the empty tomb is not. This ambiguity is best visible in the reports about the trips to the tomb that are not linked to an angelophany. Without an interpreting angel, the discovery of a missing body can only generate questions (Lk. 24.12, 24) or speculations about the body's whereabouts (Jn 20.3, 13). But even a story that includes the angelic interpretation of the meaning of the empty tomb does not produce certainty that Jesus has been raised from the dead unless it is accompanied by an account about Jesus' post-resurrection appearance. The ending of the Gospel of Mark demonstrates this conclusion most vividly: 'So they went out and fled from the tomb, for terror and amazement had seized them; and they said nothing to anyone, for they were afraid' (Mk 16.8).

Notes

1 Rudolf Bultmann, *The History of the Synoptic Tradition* (trans. John Marsh; New York: Harper & Row, 1963), 285.
2 Wright, *The Resurrection of the Son of God*, 637.
3 Helmut Koester, *Ancient Christian Gospels: Their History and Development* (London/Philadelphia: SCM/Trinity Press International, 1990), 237; W. D. Davies and Dale C. Allison Jr, *A Critical and Exegetical Commentary on the Gospel according to Saint Matthew* (ICC; 3 vols; Edinburgh: T&T Clark, 1988–97), 3:652–3.
4 Brooke F. Westcott and Fenton J. A. Hort, *The New Testament in the Original Greek* (2 vols; Cambridge: Macmillan, 1881), 2:183.
5 Bruce M. Metzger, *A Textual Commentary on the Greek New Testament* (2nd edn; Stuttgart: Deutsche Bibelgesellschaft/United Bible Societies, 1994), 156–8, 160–6.

6 Barbara E. Reid, *Choosing the Better Part? Women in the Gospel of Luke* (Collegeville, MN: Liturgical Press, 1996), 200–2; Brock, *Mary Magdalene*, 35, 40, 51, 68.

7 Edward Lynn Bode, *The First Easter Morning: The Gospel Accounts of the Women's Visit to the Tomb of Jesus* (AnBib 45; Rome: Biblical Institute Press, 1970), 67.

8 In *Epistula Apostolorum* 10, a Christian document dated to the second century CE, the angelophany is entirely replaced by a Christophany.

9 See Jn 1.50; 4.48, 53; 5.44; 6.36, 47, 64; 9.38; 10.25, 26; 11.15, 40; 14.29; 19.35; 20.25, 29.

10 Raymond E. Brown, *The Gospel according to John (xiii–xxi)* (AB 29A; Garden City, NY: Doubleday, 1970), 1000–2.

11 Rudolf Bultmann, *The Gospel of John: A Commentary* (trans. G. R. Beasley-Murray et al.; Philadelphia: Westminster Press, 1971), 685.

12 Craig S. Keener, *The Gospel of John: A Commentary* (2 vols; Peabody, MA: Hendrickson, 2003), 2:1184; Craig R. Koester, 'Jesus' Resurrection, the Signs, and the Dynamics of Faith in the Gospel of John', in *The Resurrection of Jesus in the Gospel of John* (eds Craig R. Koester and Reimund Bieringer; WUNT 222; Tübingen: Mohr Siebeck, 2008), 69.

13 Adela Yarbro Collins, 'Apotheosis and Resurrection', in *The New Testament and Hellenistic Judaism* (eds. Peder Borgen and Søren Giversen; Peabody, MA: Hendrickson, 1995), 88–100; John Dominic Crossan, 'Empty Tomb and Absent Lord', in *The Passion in Mark: Studies on Mark 14–16* (ed. Werner H. Kelber; Philadelphia: Fortress, 1976), 134–52; Michael Goulder, 'The Baseless Fabric of a Vision', in *Resurrection Reconsidered* (ed. Gavin D'Costa; Oxford: Oneworld, 1996), 57–8.

14 Barnabas Lindars, *The Gospel of John* (NCB; London: Oliphants, 1972), 604.

15 Allison, *Resurrecting Jesus*, 249–53.

16 Cf. Allison's suggestion 'that the story of the women seeing an angel or angels at the tomb may well be a metamorphosis of the story of them seeing Jesus' (ibid., 253).

4

Narratives about the Appearances of the Risen Jesus

The accounts of Jesus' post-resurrection appearances are found in three gospels – Matthew, Luke and John. Each of these evangelists describes at least two appearances, which follow certain patterns. The recipients of the first appearance are always specific individuals (Mary Magdalene and the other Mary in Matthew, Cleopas and his companion in Luke, and Mary Magdalene in John), while the recipients of the second appearance are regularly Jesus' disciples. Matthew and Luke describe only one group Christophany, whereas John describes three collective experiences of the risen Jesus. In Acts 1.3, however, Luke provides an augmentation to his gospel report by noting that Jesus continued to appear to his disciples, apparently on multiple occasions, during the forty days before his ascension.

In the gospels, the narratives about Jesus' appearances follow the accounts of the discovery of the empty tomb. This narrative sequence is not only descriptive but also apologetic. It seeks to demonstrate that the body that disappeared from the tomb is the same body that appeared outside the tomb, regardless of whether this happened nearby the tomb, in Jerusalem or in Galilee. The narrative arrangement that is thereby created, however, includes a major gap that none of the evangelists tried to eliminate: the actual transformation of Jesus' dead body into a living body. The resurrection of Jesus was a hidden act of God for which the early Christian interpreters offer no description. This indescribable event functions as a presumed prequel to the narrated events. When the women arrive at the tomb, the body has already disappeared, but when and how this happened remains in the dark. The narrated events also include other gaps, especially with regard to the question of Jesus' whereabouts between his appearances. The only such comment is found in John 20.17, in which Jesus explained to Mary Magdalene that he was ascending to his Father. There are no similar explanations on other occasions. For example, the evangelists never clarify whether Jesus appeared from heaven or from some undisclosed terrestrial location.

Unlike the empty tomb narratives, the stories about Jesus' post-resurrection appearances are characterized by considerable diversity. In this chapter we will review the gospel accounts of Jesus' appearances with the purpose of identifying their distinctive features, such as the location and the timing of the appearances, the characters' ability to recognize the risen Jesus and the descriptions of Jesus' resurrected body.

1. The Gospel of Matthew

Matthew describes two appearances of the risen Jesus, one in Jerusalem and one in Galilee. Jesus first appears to Mary Magdalene and the other Mary in close proximity to the empty tomb as they hurry to deliver the message of the angel to the disciples.

> Suddenly Jesus met them and said, 'Greetings!' And they came to him, took hold of his feet, and worshipped him. Then Jesus said to them, 'Do not be afraid; go and tell my brothers to go to Galilee; there they will see me.' (Mt. 28.9–10)

Matthew's description of this encounter is quite brief, but several observations can nonetheless be made. It seems that Mary and her companion did not have any difficulty recognizing Jesus. While the text does not provide any description of the risen body, the fact that the women could hold Jesus' feet suggests that his body was tangible. The remark that they 'worshipped him' reveals a new, reverent attitude toward the risen Jesus. Finally, Jesus' message is a mere repetition of the message of the angel: to tell his disciples, whom he now calls 'brothers', to go to Galilee, where they will see him. In his classic study of the gospel accounts of the women's visit to the tomb of Jesus, Edward Lynn Bode gives several reasons that, in his view, speak against the historicity of this account: 'First, such an appearance would seem to nullify any utility with an angel – if Jesus was to repeat the message why bother with an angel? Second, it would seem strange that the first appearance would be to the women rather than to the official witnesses. Third, of what value would the appearance to the women be, whose report would have been suspect?'[1] However, exactly these reasons can be taken to support the historicity of this account. Why would someone invent an obvious doublet to the message of the angel or invoke a legally unreliable testimony of the women? 'The only obvious answer is,' as James D. G. Dunn rightly points out, 'that there was a persistent report within the communal memory of the earliest churches that the first witnesses had been women, a report which Matthew could not ignore, however less than satisfying his telling of it'.[2]

The second appearance of the risen Jesus that is described in Matthew's narrative took place in Galilee and its recipients were Jesus' disciples.

> Now the eleven disciples went to Galilee, to the mountain to which Jesus had directed them. When they saw him, they worshipped him; but some doubted. And Jesus came and said to them, 'All authority in heaven and on earth has been given to me. Go therefore and make disciples of all nations, baptizing them in the name of the Father and of the Son and of the Holy Spirit, and teaching them to obey everything that I have commanded you. And remember, I am with you always, to the end of the age.' (Mt. 28.16–20)

Like the account about Jesus' appearance to the women, the story of his appearance to the eleven disciples is characterized by brevity. Matthew points out that it took place on the mountain to which Jesus directed his disciples, even though such a reference is missing from the angel's commission to the women. Since mountains play a significant role in Matthew's narrative (Mt. 4.8; 5.1; 8.1; 14.23; 15.29; 17.1; 24.3), the reference to the mountain in 28.16

highlights its significance as a place of divine revelation. There is no indication about the timing of the appearance, but a certain time lapse is clearly presumed given the geographic distance between Jerusalem and Galilee. The event itself is described with three concise assertions: (1) the disciples saw Jesus; (2) they worshipped him; (3) some of them doubted. The first statement emphasizes the visual character of Jesus' appearance. The second statement explains that the risen Jesus becomes the object of worship, which relates the reaction of the disciples to the reaction of the women when Jesus appeared to them. The third statement introduces the element of doubt, but its cause is not explained. Unlike Luke and John, who describe a similar reaction of (some of) the disciples to the appearance of the risen Jesus (Lk. 24.41–43; Jn 20.24–29), the reference to doubt in Mt. 28.17 remains unresolved. Matthew offers no description of Jesus' resurrected body and provides no indication about the origin of Jesus' appearance, i.e. whether he appeared from heaven or on earth. The largest portion of the text is devoted to Jesus' speech to his disciples, which includes the claim to his universal authority, a commission to make disciples of all nations and a reassurance that Jesus will always remain with them.

2. The Gospel of Luke

Like Matthew, Luke describes two appearances of the risen Jesus, but neither of them corresponds to Matthew's accounts. The first appearance involves two disciples on their way from Jerusalem to a nearby village called Emmaus. The second appearance takes place in Jerusalem to the eleven disciples as a group. There is also a brief remark about Jesus' appearance to Peter, which is found at the end of the account of Jesus' appearance to the disciples on the Emmaus road (Lk. 24.35), but it is not clear whether Luke wanted to situate this event before or after the Emmaus appearance.

Luke's account of Jesus' appearance to two disciples on the Emmaus road is an extended and highly dramatic narrative about the disciples' inability to recognize the risen Jesus and Jesus' words and actions that led them to finally identify him as they gathered around the table in their home.

Now on that same day two of them were going to a village called Emmaus, about seven miles from Jerusalem, and talking with each other about all these things that had happened. While they were talking and discussing, Jesus himself came near and went with them, but their eyes were kept from recognizing him. And he said to them, 'What are you discussing with each other while you walk along?' They stood still, looking sad. Then one of them, whose name was Cleopas, answered him, 'Are you the only stranger in Jerusalem who does not know the things that have taken place there in these days?' He asked them, 'What things?' They replied, 'The things about Jesus of Nazareth, who was a prophet mighty in deed and word before God and all the people, and how our chief priests and leaders handed him over to be condemned to death and crucified him. But we had hoped that he was the one to redeem Israel. Yes, and besides all this, it is now the third day since these things took place. Moreover, some women of our group astounded us. They were at the tomb early this morning, and when they did not find his body there, they came back and told us that they had indeed seen a vision of angels who said that he was alive. Some of those who were with us went to the tomb and found it just as the women had said; but they did not see him.' Then he said to them, 'Oh, how foolish you are, and how slow of heart to believe all that the prophets have declared! Was it not necessary that the Messiah should suffer these things and then enter into his glory?' Then beginning with Moses and all the prophets, he interpreted to them the things about himself in all the scriptures.

As they came near the village to which they were going, he walked ahead as if he were going on. But they urged him strongly, saying, 'Stay with us, because it is almost evening and the day is now nearly over.' So he went in to stay with them. When he was at the table with them, he took bread, blessed and broke it, and gave it to them. Then their eyes were opened, and they recognized him; and he vanished from their sight. They said to each other, 'Were not our hearts burning within us while he was talking to us on the road, while he was opening the scriptures to us?' That same hour they got up and returned to Jerusalem; and they found the eleven and their companions gathered together. They were saying, 'The Lord has risen indeed, and he has appeared to Simon!' Then they told what had happened on the road, and how he had been made known to them in the breaking of the bread. (Lk. 24.13–35)

Luke's opening remarks place the narrated events on the same day when the women discovered the empty tomb. Only one of the two disciples is identified by name – Cleopas – while his companion remains unnamed. Jesus is described as joining them as they were on their way to Emmaus, discussing the events that transpired in Jerusalem during the last few days. Luke does not offer any explanation of why they could not recognize Jesus, but his use of the passive voice, 'their eyes were kept from recognizing him', indicates that their spiritual blindness was the result of divine activity. As the story unfolds, however, it becomes clear that their inability to recognize Jesus was, if not caused, then certainly reinforced by their erroneous perception of Jesus' mission and aims. They concluded their recapitulation of the tragic events that had taken place in Jerusalem in the previous days, of which the 'stranger' appeared to be strangely ignorant, with a pointed expression of their disappointed hope: 'But we had hoped that he was the one to redeem Israel' (v. 21). The first step toward the recognition of the risen Jesus was the Christological interpretation of the Jewish Scripture ('he interpreted to them the things about himself in all the scriptures' [v. 27]). Yet, the full recognition did not happen before they entered the house and gathered around the table to share a meal. When Jesus 'took bread, blessed and broke it, and gave it to them' (v. 30) they finally recognized him. At that moment, however, Jesus 'vanished from their sight' (v. 31).

Given a number of specifically Lukan features and motives, many scholars regard this account as Luke's composition. The question of the historicity of the story is thereby not settled. It would be very difficult to explain why Luke would attribute the first appearance of Jesus in his narrative to two obscure disciples unless he found it in the traditional material available to him. It is therefore conceivable, though not provable, that Luke 24.13–15 preserves historical memory, which Luke then embellished with various details to create a dramatic story that expresses his theological concerns. One of them is a reiteration that the women's report about the discovery of the empty tomb and the angelic message that Jesus was alive could not convince Jesus' male disciples that this was so, because despite the fact that they also found the tomb empty, 'they did not see him' (v. 24). This small detail also confirms the conclusion from the previous chapter that without the appearances of the risen Jesus, the empty tomb remains confusing. Another theme is a new understanding of the sacred texts that is possible only from a post-Easter perspective. Indeed, the risen Jesus rebukes the disciples for their slowness of heart to believe ancient prophecies, but they were not able to do that before Jesus opened the scriptures to them. Finally, the recognition of the risen Jesus in the breaking of the bread serves as a reminder of various meals during Jesus' earthly ministry, such as the miraculous feeding of the five thousand (Lk. 9.16) and the last supper (Lk. 22.19), and anticipates the future meals of the post-Easter community (Acts 2.42, 46; 20.7).

The second appearance of Jesus narrated in Luke's Gospel occurs as soon as Cleopas and his companion finish their report to other disciples, which ensures that it is still dated to the first day of the week. Jesus' solo appearance to Peter is briefly mentioned as part of the exchange between the two disciples from Emmaus and the group that stayed in Jerusalem, but its timing and locale are not specified.

> While they were talking about this, Jesus himself stood among them and said to them, 'Peace be with you.' They were startled and terrified, and thought that they were seeing a ghost. He said to them, 'Why are you frightened, and why do doubts arise in your hearts? Look at my hands and my feet; see that it is I myself. Touch me and see; for a ghost does not have flesh and bones as you see that I have.' And when he had said this, he showed them his hands and his feet. While in their joy they were disbelieving and still wondering, he said to them, 'Have you anything here to eat?' They gave him a piece of broiled fish, and he took it and ate in their presence. Then he said to them, 'These are my words that I spoke to you while I was still with you – that everything written about me in the law of Moses, the prophets, and the psalms must be fulfilled.' Then he opened their minds to understand the scriptures, and he said to them, 'Thus it is written, that the Messiah is to suffer and to rise from the dead on the third day, and that repentance and forgiveness of sins is to be proclaimed in his name to all nations, beginning from Jerusalem. You are witnesses of these things. And see, I am

sending upon you what my Father promised; so stay here in the city until you have been clothed with power from on high.' (Lk. 24.36–49)

It is usually assumed that the group to whom Jesus appeared included only eleven disciples. Such a conclusion seems plausible if we consider only this story. However, if we take into account its current literary context, those who 'were talking about this' before Jesus appeared to them (v. 36) were, according to v. 33, 'the eleven and their companions' along with two disciples from Emmaus. Jesus' appearance to this group resembles his disappearance from the table in the Emmaus narrative. Just as he vanished from the sight of Cleopas and his companion, he materialized out of nowhere in the midst of his disciples in Jerusalem. Luke, however, takes great pains to demonstrate that Jesus was a real human being consisting of flesh and bones. The narrator first describes the disciples' reaction to the sight of Jesus by stating that they were terrified and thought that they were seeing a ghost. The risen Jesus then responds to this concern by asking the disciples to look at his hands and his feet and to touch him to be assured that this was really him. He also points out that 'a ghost does not have flesh and bones as you see that I have' (v. 39) and shows them his hands and his feet. Finally, since they were still not fully convinced, he asked for food and ate a piece of broiled fish in their presence. Luke's contention that the risen Jesus could consume food is also evident in the recapitulation of the Easter events in Acts 10.40–41: 'but God raised him on the third day and allowed him to appear, not to all the people but to us who were chosen by God as witnesses, and who ate and drank with him after he rose from the dead'.

The second major theme in Luke's appearance narrative is the necessity of the Christological interpretation of scripture. This hermeneutical stance was also emphasized in the Emmaus narrative. Like in vv. 25–27, Jesus explains in vv. 44–47 that a proper understanding of the sacred texts can be achieved only if they are read with a conviction that they point to the Messiah. Luke describes this process as the opening of the disciples' minds to understand the scriptures. Since he, like all Christian interpreters, regards Jesus as the Messiah, he equates the messianic interpretation with the Christological interpretation of scripture. This is why the risen Jesus could say that 'everything written about me in the law of Moses, the prophets, and the psalms must be fulfilled' (v. 44). This statement is usually understood as a reference to the entire Jewish Scripture, but the phrase 'everything about me' indicates that only those passages that refer to the Messiah are in view, even if there is no indication what these passages are.

The third major theme in this account is Jesus' commission to his disciples to stay in the city until they have been clothed with power from on high (v. 49). Before Jesus gives them this task, he explains to them that the testimony of scripture about the necessity of the suffering and the resurrection of the Messiah also contains the obligation to proclaim repentance and forgiveness of sins to all nations, beginning with Jerusalem. By instructing his disciples to wait for divine empowerment Jesus includes them into God's salvific purpose for the world.

3. The Gospel of John

John describes four appearances of Jesus. The first three take place in Jerusalem, while the fourth is situated in Galilee. Only the first appearance is portrayed as an individual experience. The other three are presented as collective experiences of Jesus' disciples, but the number of the recipients is always different. The first appearance involves ten disciples (the twelve *sans* Judas and Thomas), the second involves all eleven disciples, while the fourth involves only seven of them.

The recipient of the first appearance of the risen Jesus in John's narrative is Mary Magdalene. The fourth evangelist leaves no doubt about the chronological priority of this event. He directly links it to the discovery of the empty tomb and Mary's vision of two angels inside it. Her encounter of the risen Jesus is preceded by a short conversation with the angels, which has no revelatory content. They merely ask her about the cause of her sorrow and she responds by repeating her initial idea that Jesus' corpse has been taken away.

> When she had said this, she turned around and saw Jesus standing there, but she did not know that it was Jesus. Jesus said to her, 'Woman, why are you weeping? Whom are you looking

for?' Supposing him to be the gardener, she said to him, 'Sir, if you have carried him away, tell me where you have laid him, and I will take him away.' Jesus said to her, 'Mary!' She turned and said to him in Hebrew, 'Rabbouni!' (which means Teacher). Jesus said to her, 'Do not hold on to me, because I have not yet ascended to the Father. But go to my brothers and say to them, "I am ascending to my Father and your Father, to my God and your God."' Mary Magdalene went and announced to the disciples, 'I have seen the Lord'; and she told them that he had said these things to her. (Jn 20.14–18)

The first part of this poignant story describes Mary's initial inability to recognize Jesus and her sudden perception of his identity when he pronounces her name. The narrative elaboration of this dramatic motif is similar to the Emmaus narrative in Luke 24.13–35. The complication is created by a mistaken identity of the protagonist. Like in the Emmaus narrative, in which two disciples regarded Jesus as a stranger, Mary supposes him to be a gardener. Moreover, the recognition of Jesus is triggered either by a familiar act (breaking of the bread) or a familiar word (pronouncement of Mary's name). Unlike the Emmaus narrative, however, the narrator does not offer any explanation – either theological or mundane – of Mary's initial failure to recognize Jesus. We are thus in the dark with regard to whether her misidentification of Jesus had an objective or a subjective cause.

The second part of this story consists of Jesus' discourse and Mary's report to the disciples. As soon as Mary recognizes him, Jesus replies with a command, 'Do not hold on to me, because I have not yet ascended to the Father' (v. 17). The KJV translation of this verse, 'Touch me not; for I am not yet ascended to my Father', while not impossible, is still misleading because the Greek text uses the present imperative with a negative particle, which typically refers to a prohibition of an action already in progress. It is also difficult to explain why Jesus would ask Mary not to touch him and then invite Thomas to touch his body later in this chapter. John, like Luke, assumes the tangibility of Jesus' resurrected body. Yet, Jesus' request to Mary to stop holding his body is not easy to explain. One of the most plausible suggestions is offered by Raymond E. Brown, who interprets Mary's clinging to Jesus as a clinging to his bodily presence that will not be permanent but will be replaced with the enduring presence of the Spirit.[3]

What seems to be clear, though, is that in John's narrative Jesus' ascension takes place after his appearance to Mary and before his appearances to his disciples. It would be erroneous, however, to infer from this narrative sequence that Jesus' appearance to Mary Magdalene had a different character from Jesus' appearances to his disciples. The fourth evangelist does not suggest that the narrative time lag between the resurrection and the ascension has theological implications. For him, Jesus' resurrection and ascension are two aspects of one unified event. This timeline differs from Luke–Acts, in which the ascension concludes the period of Jesus' resurrection appearances (Lk. 24.50–53; Acts 1.1–11). John's fusion of Jesus' resurrection and ascension is consistent with other New Testament references that associate these two events, such as Romans 8.34 ('Christ Jesus is the one who died – more than that, who was raised – who is at the right hand of God, who indeed is interceding for us'), Philippians 2.8–9 ('And being found in human form, he humbled himself by becoming obedient to the point of death, even death on a cross. Therefore God has highly exalted him and bestowed on him the name that is above every name') and 1 Peter 3.21b–22 ('through the resurrection of Jesus Christ, who has gone into heaven and is at the right hand of God, with angels, authorities, and powers having been subjected to him').

The risen Jesus commissions Mary to go to his 'brothers' – a new term for his disciples – and give them the message of his impending ascension. Yet, Mary prefaces her report with her own testimony of the encounter with the risen Jesus: 'I have seen the Lord'. The fact that Jesus' disciples make the same declaration after Jesus appeared to them, 'We have seen the Lord' (Jn 20.25), indicates that for the fourth evangelist there was no difference between Mary and the disciples' experiences of the risen Jesus.

John situates Jesus' first appearance to a group of his disciples on the evening of the same day when his tomb was found empty and he appeared to Mary Magdalene.

> When it was evening on that day, the first day of the week, and the doors of the house where the disciples had met were locked for fear of the Jews, Jesus came and stood among them and said, 'Peace be with you.' After he said this, he showed them his

hands and his side. Then the disciples rejoiced when they saw the Lord. Jesus said to them again, 'Peace be with you. As the Father has sent me, so I send you.' When he had said this, he breathed on them and said to them, 'Receive the Holy Spirit. If you forgive the sins of any, they are forgiven them; if you retain the sins of any, they are retained.' (Jn 20.19–23)

This passage does not indicate how many disciples were present, but v. 24 clarifies that Thomas was not with them. The group, then, included only ten disciples. Although the narrator does not explicitly say that Jesus passed through the locked doors, his sudden appearance in a locked room suggests such an entrance. While Jesus' ability to pass through solid objects points to the trans-physical character of his resurrected body, the very next scene seeks to establish its physicality – Jesus showed his disciples his hands and his side. The significance of these parts of Jesus' body is clarified in the conversation with Thomas in the subsequent episode (Jn 20.25). Jesus' hands bore the marks of the nails and his side was pierced after he died on the cross (Jn 19.31–37). These identity markers have the purpose of demonstrating that the Crucified One is the Risen One. This concept is akin to the description of the resurrected bodies in 2 Bar. 49.1–51.6, which promotes the idea that the dead will be raised in the same form they had before death for the purpose of their recognition. This is, however, the only similarity between the Gospel of John and 2 Baruch. The fourth evangelist does not suggest that Jesus' resurrected body started to transform once his identification was made. Just the opposite: the risen Jesus who appeared to Thomas and other disciples one week later bore the same marks of the crucifixion as the body that appeared to them on the day of the discovery of the empty tomb.

John's description of Jesus' first appearance to his disciples does not include an explicit statement about their difficulty in recognizing him, but this idea is nonetheless insinuated by the sequence of the narrated events. First Jesus stood among his disciples and greeted them, 'Peace be with you.' Then he showed them his hands and his side. Only after this the narrator reports that 'the disciples rejoiced when they saw the Lord' (Jn 20.20). The implied causality is suggestive: they were able to rejoice only after the risen Jesus identified himself through the marks of the crucifixion.

The second half of this passage is devoted to Jesus' commission of his disciples, which includes the sending formula, the reception of the Holy Spirit and the power to forgive sins. John's chronology again differs from Luke's, who locates the outpouring of the Spirit fifty days after the resurrection (Acts 2.1–4). It is neither possible nor necessary to reconcile the Johannine and Lukan chronologies because they reflect different theological interests. Both authors, however, agree that the reception of the Holy Spirit took place after Jesus' ascension and that the gift of the Spirit is related to the sending of the disciples into the world. In John, the disciples are sent to continue the mission of Jesus ('As the Father has sent me, so I send you' – v. 21b), and they immediately receive the empowerment of the Spirit to do so.

Jesus' second appearance to his disciples is prefaced by a short exchange between the disciples who witnessed the previous appearance and Thomas who was absent.

> But Thomas (who was called the Twin), one of the twelve, was not with them when Jesus came. So the other disciples told him, 'We have seen the Lord.' But he said to them, 'Unless I see the mark of the nails in his hands, and put my finger in the mark of the nails and my hand in his side, I will not believe.' A week later his disciples were again in the house, and Thomas was with them. Although the doors were shut, Jesus came and stood among them and said, 'Peace be with you.' Then he said to Thomas, 'Put your finger here and see my hands. Reach out your hand and put it in my side. Do not doubt but believe.' Thomas answered him, 'My Lord and my God!' Jesus said to him, 'Have you believed because you have seen me? Blessed are those who have not seen and yet have come to believe.' (Jn 20.24–29)

This memorable story portrays Thomas as a disciple who refused to believe that the risen Jesus was the same person as the earthly Jesus until he verified his identity by touching the marks of Jesus' crucifixion. When one week later Jesus appeared to his disciples for the second time, he invited Thomas to act upon his request. The narrator, however, does not report whether Thomas actually touched Jesus' hands and side but immediately relates Thomas' acknowledgement of Jesus' identity. Known as 'Doubting Thomas', this disciple embodies a person whose faith demands empirical verification. Thomas' universal significance is reinforced by Jesus' timeless pronouncement 'Blessed are those who have not seen and yet have come to believe' (v. 29). At the same time, however, Thomas also embodies a person who gives the most profound confession of Jesus' identity: 'My Lord and my God!' (v. 28). There is no character in John's narrative that gives a higher Christological acclamation than Thomas. It is also important to recognize that Jesus does not disdain Thomas' need for empirical verification but only clarifies that this is not the highest level of faith. 'Although seeing is not believing, there is not believing without seeing, that is, without somebody's having seen.'[4]

Most scholars regard chapter 21 as a later addition to the Gospel of John. This is why the story of Jesus' third appearance to his disciples, which is narrated in this chapter, stands in a certain tension with the previous appearances. Unlike the appearances recounted in chapter 20, all of which take place in Jerusalem, Jesus' appearance in chapter 21 takes place in Galilee. The account begins with a description of a group of seven disciples who follow Peter's lead to go fishing. This decision, which suggests that Peter and some of his fellow disciples returned to their previous occupation (although the fourth evangelist never expounds that they were fishermen by trade), is utterly baffling given their encounters with the risen Lord narrated in the previous chapter. Their decision is not so baffling, though, if we have here an independent account that was only later appended to John's narrative.

> After these things Jesus showed himself again to the disciples by the Sea of Tiberias; and he showed himself in this way. Gathered there together were Simon Peter, Thomas called the Twin, Nathanael of Cana in Galilee, the sons of Zebedee, and two others of his disciples. Simon Peter said to them, 'I am going fishing.' They said to him, 'We will go with you.' They went out and got into the boat, but that night they caught nothing.
>
> Just after daybreak, Jesus stood on the beach; but the disciples did not know that it was Jesus. Jesus said to them, 'Children, you have no fish, have you?' They answered him, 'No.' He said to them, 'Cast the net to the right side of the boat, and you will find some.' So they cast it, and now they were not able to haul it in because there were so many fish. That disciple whom Jesus loved said to Peter, 'It is the Lord!' When Simon Peter heard that

it was the Lord, he put on some clothes, for he was naked, and jumped into the sea. But the other disciples came in the boat, dragging the net full of fish, for they were not far from the land, only about a hundred yards off.

When they had gone ashore, they saw a charcoal fire there, with fish on it, and bread. Jesus said to them, 'Bring some of the fish that you have just caught.' So Simon Peter went aboard and hauled the net ashore, full of large fish, a hundred and fifty-three of them; and though there were so many, the net was not torn. Jesus said to them, 'Come and have breakfast.' Now none of the disciples dared to ask him, 'Who are you?' because they knew it was the Lord. Jesus came and took the bread and gave it to them, and did the same with the fish. This was now the third time that Jesus appeared to the disciples after he was raised from the dead. (Jn 21.1–14)

The story of Jesus' appearance by the Sea of Tiberias, also known as the Sea of Galilee (Jn 6.1), includes the motif that characterizes many appearance narratives: the characters' difficulties to recognize the risen Jesus. The narrator does not explain what caused this difficulty; he merely states that 'the disciples did not know that it was Jesus' (v. 4). Before the recognition of Jesus took place, Jesus advised his disciples to cast the net to the right side of the boat, which resulted in a miraculous catch of a large amount of fish. The beloved disciple was the first to recognize Jesus, but it seems that Peter and others were able to do so only after the beloved disciple verbally declared Jesus' identity. When the disciples came ashore, Jesus offered them breakfast. Although the narrator does not report that the risen Jesus actually participated in the meal that he prepared for his disciples, there is nothing in the whole scene that would point to Jesus' trans-physicality, such as passing through solid objects or suddenly disappearing. The hand responsible for appending this story to chapter 20 added a note in v. 14 that this was Jesus' third appearance to his disciples after he was raised from the dead. This note, whose purpose is to tie this account to the preceding narrative, disregards Jesus' appearance to Mary Magdalene, and hence betrays a similar preference for male testimony that is attested in the traditional material preserved in 1 Corinthians 15.5–7.

The similarity between this account and the ending of the *Gospel of Peter* has frequently been noted. In this document, the angelophany to Mary Magdalene and her women friends is followed by a description of how the disciples returned home after the Feast of Unleavened Bread had ended: 'But we, the twelve disciples of the Lord, wept and grieved; and each one returned to his home, grieving for what had happened. But I, Simon Peter, and my brother Andrew, took our nets and went off to the sea. And with us was Levi, the son of Alphaeus, whom the Lord ...' (*Gos. Pet.* 59–60).[5] Although the extant text ends at this point, it seems that what followed was a description of Jesus' appearance to Peter and his fellow disciples. The second-century CE date of the *Gospel of Peter* and its dependence on the synoptic tradition does not preclude the possibility that this particular story may derive from an independent oral tradition. In the literary context of the *Gospel of Peter*, however, the account about the grieving disciples resuming their previous occupation in Galilee appears more plausible than John's story about seven disciples who, despite having witnessed two appearances of the risen Jesus in Jerusalem, went fishing on the Sea of Tiberias.

4. Development of the Appearance Traditions

Jesus' appearances to his followers, which are narrated only in the Gospels of Matthew, Luke and John, are characterized by such diversity that an effective comparison of their common characteristics and a reconstruction of their chronological relationships are nearly impossible. Moreover, when we compare the gospel accounts to the traditional material preserved in 1 Corinthians 15.5–7, the only element they share is Jesus' appearance to the group of eleven disciples (marked in italics in the table below).

Even though every gospel either mentions (Mark) or narrates (Matthew, Luke and John) Jesus' appearance to the eleven, the locations of these appearances are different. While Mark 16.7 refers to and Matthew 28.16–20 describes Jesus' appearance to his disciples in Galilee, both Luke 24.36–49 and John 20.19–29 claim that Jesus first appeared to his disciples in Jerusalem. The situation in John is more complicated, though, because he describes two Christophanies in Jerusalem, the first to a group of ten disciples (Jn 20.19–23) and

1 Cor. 15.5-8	Matthew	Luke–Acts	John

1 Peter
2 *The twelve*
  (effectively eleven
  because Judas is
  not included)
3 500 brothers and
  sisters
4 James
5 All the apostles
5 Paul
	1 Mary
	  Magdalene and
	  the other Mary
	2 *Eleven disciples*
		1 Cleopas
		  and another
		  disciple
		2 Peter (not
		  described)
		3 *Eleven disciples*
			1 Mary
			  Magdalene
			2 Ten disciples
			3 *Eleven disciples*
			4 Seven disciples

the second to a group of eleven disciples (20.24–29); the main focus of the second Christophany, however, is not on the eleven but on Thomas. John also adds a third corporate Christophany (21.1–14), but this event includes only seven disciples and is located in Galilee. The timing of these appearances is also different. While Mark and Matthew do not provide any chronological designations, a certain time lapse is presupposed given the distance between Jerusalem and Galilee (the usual estimate for traveling on foot is at least four days). Luke and John locate Jesus' appearances in Jerusalem on the day of the discovery of the empty tomb, i.e. on the first day of the week. John dates the second collective Christophany in Jerusalem one week later. The Galilean Christophany is not accompanied with any specific time designation except the remark that it took place 'after these things' (Jn 21.1).

How should we assess these variations of the appearance narratives? Do they represent multiple versions of the same tradition or do they derive from the memories of different events? The earliest reference to Jesus' appearance to the Twelve in 1 Corinthians 15.5 is not of much help here because it is given without any geographic and chronological designations. The reconstruction that seeks to conflate all New Testament narratives into a series of Jesus' appearances – the first appearance in Jerusalem (Lk. 24.36–49; Jn 20.19–29), then another appearance in Galilee (Mk 16.7; Mt. 28.16–20; Jn 21.1–14), then additional appearances in Jerusalem upon the disciples' return to the city (Acts 1.3–9) – ends up doing more violence to the evidence than a critical evaluation of individual accounts. The Johannine chronology, which provides the main support for the above conflation, is problematic not only because of the obvious literary incongruities that betray a redactional hand but also because the Johannine sequence of events lacks plausibility. Why would the disciples who have seen the risen Jesus in Jerusalem and (if one considers Luke's version of these events) received the commission to wait there until they receive the empowerment by the Holy Spirit return to Galilee and resume their previous occupations? Moreover, why would the Galilean appearance convince them to go back to Jerusalem if the previous appearance in Jerusalem did not succeed in keeping them there?

A more constructive way forward is to assess the geographic and chronological elaborations provided in the gospel narrative in light of the theological interests of their authors. For example, Luke's location of all Christophanies in Jerusalem is clearly related to his desire to portray Jerusalem as the centre of the Christian movement (Lk. 24.47; Acts 1.8). While John does not exclude the Galilean appearance, his prioritizing of the appearances in Jerusalem seems to be also theologically motivated. For example, by locating the first appearance in Judea, John is able to underpin his negative portrayal of the Jews (Jn 20.19) and link the reception of the Holy Spirit to Jesus' ascension (Jn 20.17, 22). There are, therefore, good reasons to regard the Lukan and Johannine timetables as secondary. The chronological priority of the Galilean appearance is not only supported by the Markan and Matthean versions of the post-resurrection events but also has greater historical plausibility. In light of Jesus' crucifixion and their own fear of possible repercussions, the disciples' discouragement and swift return home seems realistic. If Jesus appeared to them for the first time in Galilee and commissioned them to preach the good news, we can better understand why they decided to return to Jerusalem. The historical priority of the Galilean appearance is also supported by the assumption that the early Christian movement centred in Jerusalem had no compelling reason to transfer the appearances to Galilee, while transferring them to Jerusalem appears much more likely.

The above evaluation of the plausibility of the alternative sequences of Jesus' appearances is based on the premise that Jesus appeared to his disciples more than once and that at least one of these appearances took place in Galilee and one in Jerusalem. This supposition, however, may not be the only conclusion that is warranted by the evidence. Only John describes three collective Christophanies. Matthew and Luke narrate only one, and Mark's angel announces only one. Moreover, the gospel Christophanies reported in Matthew 28.16–20, Luke 24.36–49 and John 20.19–23, despite their different geographic locations (Galilee in Matthew, Jerusalem in Luke and John) have similar structural elements. All three evangelists report Jesus' appearance, the disciples' reaction to the sight of the risen Jesus, Jesus' commission and the promise of assistance, be it in the form of Jesus' permanent presence (Matthew), the future empowerment from on high (Luke) or the immediate reception of the Holy Spirit (John).

	Mt. 28.16–20	Lk. 24.36–49	Jn 20.19–23
Jesus' appearance	28.17a	24.36	20.19–20a
Reaction of the disciples	28.17b	24.37–41	20.20b
Jesus' commission	28.18–20a	24.44–48	20.21, 23
Promise of assistance	28.20b	24.49	20.22

These common patterns may indicate that the gospel Christophanies represent variations of a core tradition that goes back to the primitive confession that Jesus appeared to the Twelve (1 Cor. 15.5).[6] This conclusion, however, does not rule out the possibility that Jesus' disciples may have experienced several Christophanies. If this was indeed the case, the variations of the locales and other specific features are probably the result of diverse traditions that developed out of the memories of these experiences.

Jesus' appearance to Peter, which establishes his primacy among the witnesses of the Christophanies listed in 1 Corinthians 15.5, is only stated in Luke 24.35, but the New Testament contains no story of how this actually happened. Some scholars, however, suggest that behind the account of Jesus' appearance to Peter and his fellow disciples at the Sea of Tiberias (Jn 21.1–14) stands an older and no longer recoverable story of Peter's Christophany.[7] The ensuing dialogue between Jesus and Peter (Jn 21.15–19), which functions as a rehabilitation of Peter after his threefold denial of Jesus, strengthens this hypothesis. On this reading, the parallel story in Luke 5.1–11 about the miraculous catch of the fish represents a variant of the same tradition, which Luke transposed to the pre-Easter period because his Jerusalem-centred theological framework did not allow him to incorporate Peter's Christophany in Galilee. Despite the plausibility of this hypothesis, it is still puzzling why no early account of Peter's encounter with the risen Christ has survived, especially in light of his primacy on the pre-Pauline list of witnesses preserved in 1 Corinthians 15.5–7.

The absence of a distinct account about Peter's Christophany is even more mystifying in light of the preservation of a specific account about Mary Magdalene's Christophany in John 20.14–18. A possible variant of the same tradition is the brief account of Jesus' appearance to Mary Magdalene and the other Mary in Matthew 28.8–10. Both evangelists portray Mary Magdalene as the first witness of a Christophany. It seems that Matthew and John included these accounts because of their familiarity with the reports based on the communal memory that Mary Magdalene was indeed the first person that had seen the risen Jesus. It is also conceivable, as we have seen in the previous chapter, that Mary's original Christophany was later transformed into an angelophany in order to downplay her significance in the Easter events.

The fragmentary character of other reports about Jesus' appearances hinders any plausible reconstruction of their developments. The Emmaus narrative, despite its remarkable literary embellishment, offers very little in terms of historical evidence, such as the identity of Cleopas and his companion or the location of Emmaus. Jesus' appearance to James, mentioned in 1 Corinthians 15.7, has left no traces in the canonical gospels. Finally, there is Paul's encounter of the risen Jesus, but he says very little about his own experience (1 Cor. 9.1; 15.8; Gal. 1.15–16).[8] The narrative versions of this event are found in Acts 9.1–9; 22.6–11; 26.12–19, but for Luke Paul's experience did not have the same character as the experiences of the disciples before Jesus' ascension to heaven.

5. Summary and Conclusions

Despite the diversity that characterizes the narratives about Jesus' appearances, almost all of them include a reference about the characters' difficulties in recognizing the risen Jesus. In some cases, such as the Emmaus narrative (Lk. 24.13–35), the disciples' assumption that Jesus was a ghost (Lk. 24.36–43), Mary Magdalene's belief that Jesus was a gardener (Jn 20.14–18) and Thomas' request to touch the marks of Jesus' crucifixion

(Jn 20.24–29), Jesus' initial unrecognizability is the central feature of the plot. In other cases, this motif appears as a brief note or an inference suggested by the sequence of events. For example, Mt. 28.17 remarks that after the disciples saw Jesus and worshipped him, 'some doubted'. In Jn 20.20, the narrator first explains that Jesus showed his hands and his side to the disciples and then adds that 'the disciples rejoiced when they saw the Lord'. In Jn 21.4, the narrator notes that when Jesus appeared on the beach of the Sea of Tiberias, 'the disciples did not know that it was Jesus'.

In light of the frequency of this motif, it is somewhat surprising that none of the evangelists provides an explanation of why the recipients of the Christophanies could not immediately identify Jesus. They merely offer circumstantial evidence, such as divine providence (Lk. 24.16), the disciples' disappointed hopes about Jesus' aims (Lk. 24.21), their slowness of heart to believe scriptural prophecies (Lk. 24.25–26, 45) or Mary's erroneous assumption that Jesus' body was taken away (Jn 20.13), but they never clarify what was different about Jesus' appearance that caused the initial confusion. The only explanation of this sort appears in the later scribal addition to the Gospel of Mark: 'After this he appeared in another form to two of them, as they were walking into the country' (Ps.-Mark 16.12). Whether the evangelists themselves presumed that Jesus appeared in 'another form' is much less certain. It seems, in fact, that their literary and theological aims were just the opposite: to establish the identity between the earthly Jesus and the risen Jesus. In each account, the emphasis falls on the continuity between the Crucified One and the Risen One. One of the functions of Jesus' mistaken identity is to create a narrative complication that finds its resolution in a demonstration that the risen Jesus is the same one who died on the cross and who was buried. While Paul emphasizes the discontinuity between the earthly body (the body animated by the soul) and the risen body (the body animated by the spirit), the evangelists seek to establish the continuity – even sameness – between the earthly Jesus and the risen Jesus.

The emphasis on the physicality of Jesus' resurrected body, which characterizes almost all gospel narratives, serves the same purpose. Luke is especially concerned to demonstrate that the risen Jesus possessed the same qualities as the earthly Jesus: his hands and feet could be touched (Lk. 24.39a); his body had flesh and bones (Lk. 24.39b); and he was able to consume food (Lk. 24.41–43; Acts 10.41). A similar concern can be detected in the Johannine appearance narratives: Jesus' risen body could be held (Jn 20.17); it bore the marks of crucifixion that could be seen and touched (Jn 20.20, 25, 27); and presumably it could consume food (Jn 21.12–13). Even Matthew, who is relatively silent on this subject, still mentions that the women took hold of Jesus' feet when he appeared to them (Mt. 28.9).

Such a stress on the physicality of the risen Jesus appears at odds with Paul's insistence that 'flesh and blood cannot inherit the kingdom of God' (1 Cor. 15.50). While their differences should not be exaggerated, neither should they be downplayed. It seems that Paul and the evangelists derive their conceptions of the resurrected body from different streams of Jewish traditions. Paul's description of the spiritual body conveys the idea of resurrection as a new creation, which he further elaborates with the help of scriptural imageries from Ezekiel 37 and other related passages. He also draws on the traditions that ascribe superior qualities to the resurrected bodies. The evangelists' emphasis of the physicality of Jesus' body is closer to the traditions that put emphasis on the corporeal character of the resurrected bodies, such as 2 Maccabees 7. Luke's portrayal of Jesus as an innocent victim of injustices (Lk. 23.4, 14–15, 41, 47) is also akin to the idea of unjust suffering for the sake of the Torah, which provides the theological basis of the concept of resurrection in 2 Maccabees.

Since the nineteenth century, many interpreters have argued that Luke and John's stress on the physicality of Jesus' risen body was a piece of anti-docetic polemic.[9] The main parallel here is Ignatius' letter to the Smyrnaeans, which is usually dated to the early second century CE, i.e. just a few decades after the gospels of Luke and John.

> For he [Jesus] suffered all these things for our sakes, in order that we might be saved; and he truly suffered just as he truly raised himself – not, as certain unbelievers say, that he suffered in appearance only (it is they who exist in appearance only!). Indeed, their fate will be determined by what they think: they will become disembodied and demonic.
>
> For I know and believe that he was in the flesh even after the resurrection; and when he came to Peter and those with him, he

said to them: 'Take hold of me; handle me and see that I am not a disembodied demon.' And immediately they touched him and believed, being closely united with his flesh and blood. For this reason they too despised death; indeed, they proved to be greater than death. And after his resurrection he ate and drank with them like one who is composed of flesh, although spiritually he was united with the Father. (Ignatius, *Smyrn.* 2.1–3.3)[10]

While Ignatius' description of his opponents provides enough information to reconstruct the polemical setting of his letter, the claim that Luke and John were combating docetic beliefs about Jesus cannot be conclusively demonstrated. Luke and John ascribe to Jesus' resurrected body not only physical but also trans-physical qualities, which undermine these gospels' supposed anti-docetic tendencies. For example, they claim that the risen Jesus was able to appear suddenly (Lk. 24.36; Jn 20.14), vanish (Lk. 24.31), or pass through the closed doors (Jn 20.19, 26). Yet, even if the anti-docetic tenor of Luke and John remains conjectural, it seems that the appearance narratives in these two gospels share more similarities with Ignatius' deliberations than they share with Paul's descriptions of the spiritual body in 1 Corinthians 15. It is therefore fair to conclude that, regardless of how we reconstruct the impetus toward the physicality of Jesus' resurrected body, this probably represents a later rather than an earlier development.

The New Testament evidence reviewed in this and the previous two chapters shows that the earliest non-narrative tradition about Jesus' appearances does not mention the empty tomb (1 Cor. 15.3–8), while the earliest narrative tradition about the discovery of the empty tomb is transmitted without the appearances (Mk 16.1–8). The three gospels – Matthew, Luke and John – that include both the narratives about the discovery of the empty tomb and the narratives about Jesus' appearances are usually dated to the last quarter of the first century CE. This literary evidence suggests that the tradition about the discovery of the empty tomb and the traditions about Jesus' appearances developed independently of each other. The literary evidence also suggests that these two independent traditions were joined together at a later date, probably for apologetic purposes, i.e. to demonstrate that Jesus was bodily raised from the dead.[11] Nevertheless, this inference from the textual data, which is admittedly speculative, does not yet explain how the resurrection belief developed. More specifically, why did the followers of Jesus conclude that Jesus was raised from the dead and not, for example, that he was translated to heaven? There is no doubt that multiple witnesses claimed to have seen Jesus alive, but what was the character of these visions? Were they objective experiences or mere apparitions? To what extent can we reconstruct the events that gave rise to the belief in Jesus' resurrection? These are historical questions to which we turn in the next chapter.

Notes

1 Bode, *The First Easter Morning*, 56.
2 James D. G. Dunn, *Jesus Remembered* (vol. 1 of *Christianity in the Making*; Grand Rapids, MI: Eerdmans, 2003), 843.
3 Brown, *The Gospel according to John (xiii–xxi)*, 1012, 1014.
4 D. Moody Smith, *John* (ANTC; Nashville: Abingdon, 1999), 384.
5 Trans. Bart D. Ehrman and Zlatko Pleše, *The Apocryphal Gospels: Texts and Translations* (Oxford: Oxford University Press, 2011), 387.
6 Brown, *The Gospel according to John (xiii–xxi)*, 972; Allison, *Resurrecting Jesus*, 245.
7 Brown, *The Gospel according to John (xiii–xxi)*, 1085–95; Allison, *Resurrecting Jesus*, 254–9.
8 See Chapter 2, section 2.1. of this book.
9 Daniel Schenkel, *A Sketch of the Character of Jesus: A Biblical Essay* (London: Longmans, Green, 1869), 318; Morton Scott Enslin, *Christian Beginnings* (New York: Harper & Brothers, 1938), 411–2; Charles H. Talbert, *Luke and the Gnostics: An Examination of Lucan Purpose* (Nashville: Abingdon, 1966), 31–2.
10 Trans. Michael W. Holmes, *The Apostolic Fathers: Greek Text and English Translations* (3rd edn; Grand Rapids, MI: Baker Academic, 2007), 251.
11 Daniel A. Smith, *Revisiting the Empty Tomb: The Early History of Easter* (Minneapolis: Fortress, 2010), 2–8.

5

Jesus' Resurrection and History

The question of whether the resurrection of Jesus is a historical event is probably one of the most contentious issues in modern biblical studies. The controversial character of this subject is a post-Enlightenment phenomenon. Before the eighteenth century, Christian scholars simply assumed the historical accuracy of the biblical accounts. With the rise of modernity, however, many of the old assumptions could no longer pass the test of rational enquiry. As a result, the historical character of Jesus' resurrection became, and has remained, a highly divisive issue. On the one side are the interpreters who passionately defend its historicity because they are convinced that this is the most effective way of proving the truth of Christianity. On the other side are the interpreters who deny the historicity of Jesus' resurrection and offer all kinds of naturalistic explanations for the emergence of the resurrection belief. The scholars who belong to the first group, mostly comprised of Christian apologists, regularly accuse scholars who belong to the second group, the so-called sceptics, of superimposing their naturalistic worldview upon biblical witnesses and thus excluding God from the picture from the outset of the discussion. The sceptics, in turn, accuse the apologists of letting their Christian beliefs influence their historical conclusions. The arguments for both positions have caught the spotlight through various public debates between some of the most prominent representatives of each camp. Many of these debates are available on YouTube[1] or through published transcripts, which typically include not only the views of the participants but also of several respondents who were asked by the editors to evaluate the strength of the presented arguments or shed additional light on the debated issues.[2] The literature on this subject is enormous. The most prominent publications over the past thirty years includes the books by William Lane Craig,[3] John Dominic Crossan,[4] Gerd Lüdemann,[5] N. T. Wright,[6] Dale C. Allison[7] and Michael R. Licona.[8]

The complexity of the arguments for or against the historicity of Jesus' resurrection can be quite perplexing for a non-specialist. The main difficulty, however, is not caused by the sheer volume of publications or by the level of sophistication of the presented arguments but by the lack of agreement of what is the task of historical research and to what extent can someone's faith convictions influence her evaluation of the available evidence. As a result, the adjective 'historical' can mean different things to different people. For some, the term 'historical' means that an event took place in time and space regardless of whether it is caused by natural or divine activity, while for others the term 'historical' is applicable only to the events whose occurrence can be demonstrated with historical arguments based on empirical evidence that are independent of someone's religious beliefs. It is therefore imperative that we first address the question of the nature of historical enquiry and only then proceed with a review of the evidence for the historicity of the resurrection. The latter involves two types of arguments: those that pertain to the historicity of the empty tomb and those that pertain to the objective character of Jesus' post-resurrection appearances. These two sets of data are usually regarded as the foundational evidence for two different, though related, types of historical judgement: (1) a reconstruction of the emergence of the resurrection belief, and (2) a demonstration of the historicity of the resurrection.

1. The Nature of Historical Enquiry

Modern understanding of history has been fundamentally shaped by three basic tenets of historical investigation articulated by Ernst Troeltsch. The first tenet is the principle of criticism. All historical judgements are open to revision; hence, they can only attain higher or lower degrees of probability. The second tenet is the principle of analogy. Historical judgements presuppose an essential similarity between our normal, customary experiences in the present and the past events. The third tenet is the principle of interconnectedness of all historical phenomena. A historian always looks for natural rather than divine causes of the events under investigation.[9]

The principle of criticism, which emphasizes the tentative character of all historical judgements, means that no conclusion reached through historical reasoning can provide absolute certainty about the past. Written records about past events do not give us 'the facts' but only someone's interpretations of the past. Moreover, the extant evidence is, in most cases, meagre or fragmentary. This fragmentary nature is all the more evident when we consider the available evidence about Jesus' resurrection. Our sources preserve fragmentary memories that do not provide enough information for a comprehensive historical reconstruction of the resurrection events. They not only mirror the worldview of ancient authors but also seek to express the extraordinary nature of the Easter experiences. Paul is the only person who offers an eyewitness account of Jesus' appearance, but, to our dismay, he says very little about this experience. Luke's narrative about Paul's encounter of the risen Jesus (Acts 9.1–9) reduces it to a visionary experience that was only partially accessible to the bystanders. All gospel narratives about the discovery of the empty tomb and Jesus' appearances are third-person accounts that reflect several decades of oral transmission and embellishment as well as the evangelists' socio-historical circumstances and theological tendencies. While the narratives of the discovery of the empty tomb are characterized by a relatively stable storyline, the narratives of Jesus' appearances display such diversity that a reconstruction of their commonalities and chronological development becomes very difficult. Given the fragmentary and tendentious character of the extant evidence, all our conclusions about the historicity of the events related to Jesus' resurrection are doomed to be not only tentative but also quite limited. Dale Allison's assessment of historical enterprise is therefore right on point: 'That something happened does not entail our ability to show that it happened, and that something did not happen does not entail our ability to show that it did not happen.'[10]

The principle of analogy is usually regarded as most problematic for the question of the historicity of the resurrection because the latter has no analogy in human history. Those who seek to demonstrate the historicity of Jesus' resurrection typically contend that all historical events are unrepeatable and thus unique. The uniqueness of Jesus' resurrection, however, is not a uniqueness that characterizes every historical event as such but uniqueness *par excellence*. Jesus' resurrection radically differs from all events in human history, past and present. The difficulty lies not primarily in its miraculous character but in its eschatological character. Saying that Jesus was raised from the dead is not just claiming that his dead body was revived, contrary to the laws of nature, but that it was transformed into a new kind of life that could only be imagined, or, as Paul calls it, into 'the body that is to be' (1 Cor. 15.37). The current discussion focuses too much on the questions of whether we can demonstrate that the body of Jesus emerged physically from the tomb, which gives the wrong impression that the only problem we have is the set of rigid natural laws that do not allow dead people to become live again. According to Paul, however, the resurrected body is imperishable, glorious, powerful and animated by the spirit (1 Cor. 15.42–44). Even if we conclude that these attributes are derived from Paul's experience of the risen Jesus, they were not based on observation because they are not perceptible and ponderable by human senses. Paul contrasts each of these descriptions to the properties of ordinary human bodies, which are perishable, dishonourable, weak and animated by the soul. Likewise, though the evangelists stress the palpable, fleshly character of Jesus' resurrected body, they nonetheless claim that this body was able to appear or vanish unexpectedly and could pass through the closed doors (Lk. 24.31, 36; Jn 20.19, 26). None of these qualities has any analogy in our current experience. Although we have mental and linguistic abilities to envisage and describe these properties of the resurrected body, we have no means of demonstrating them empirically.

In her discussion of the possibilities of applying historical analogy to the resurrection of Jesus, Sarah Coakley differentiates the resurrection of Jesus from the unique events in the strongest sense (i.e. those events which are completely incomprehensible so that they could not even be described) and the events which do not have parallels in our current experience but which could be reconstructed with the help of historical imagination. While Jesus' resurrected body that may be touched yet passes through solid objects can be conjured with the help of one's imagination, it is unique in the sense that 'it involves the violation of presently accepted scientific laws (which are assumed, until shown otherwise, to represent regularities of nature itself)'.[11]

There are attempts in modern discussions to reduce the weight of this objection through the concept of an open universe as an alternative to a closed system ruled by immutable laws. Ted Peters, for example, claims that 'if the God of Israel described by the Bible exists, then the laws of nature as we have come to know them are not the final word. They are not ultimate. The laws of nature belong to the creation, placed here by the Creator. In the event that the divine creator decides to change them, we can expect surprises.'[12] The concept of an open universe, however, does not alleviate the problem posed by the distinctiveness of Jesus' resurrection that has no analogy in ordinary human experience. Although, given the incompleteness of our knowledge of natural laws, the resurrection cannot be legitimately ruled out *a priori*, we are not able to demonstrate, for example, that Jesus' resurrected body was imperishable. No matter how many authentic reports about Jesus' appearances we have and no matter how early they are, the fact remains that they describe an eschatological reality that transcends life as we know it.

The principle of interconnectedness of all historical phenomena is also controversial because its application requires a historian's preference of natural over miraculous explanations of the phenomena. The apologists of the resurrection frequently take this principle as a prime example of why a theistic explanation of the resurrection is ruled out from the outset. Wolfhart Pannenberg, for example, claims that 'the negative judgement on the bodily resurrection of Jesus as having occurred in historical fact is not a result of the historical critical examination of the Biblical Easter tradition, but a postulate that precedes any such examination'.[13] However, if historical endeavour is influenced by someone's beliefs about God and the world, the criteria for evaluation of the evidence become highly subjective. This is what Troeltsch tried to avoid: 'When dogmatic apologetics stresses the "historical" character of Christianity in order to appeal to the secular appreciation of historical and social forces ... this is pure obscurantism ... Today all kinds of things are labeled as "historical" and as "facts" which are nothing of the kind, and which ought not to be so labeled, since they are miraculous in nature and can only be apprehended by faith.'[14] Even if faith convictions of a Christian historian impact her evaluation of historical evidence, these preconceived notions should not replace sound historical judgements that can be shared by all practitioners of the discipline, regardless of their worldviews and faith commitments. This means, in practical terms, that a belief in God's ability to suspend the known laws of nature and create a body that is completely different from an ordinary human body cannot be a factor in the evaluation of the available evidence because it is neither shared by everybody nor demonstrable by normal human senses. Historians can neither prove nor disprove God's involvement in historical events. Trying to do so would be a category mistake.[15] The following discussion is informed by this understanding of historical endeavour. We will start with the arguments for and against the historicity of the empty tomb.

2. Historicity of the Empty Tomb

The standard arguments for the historicity of the empty tomb can be summed up into the following six theses: (1) the sequence death–burial–resurrection in 1 Corinthians 15.3–4 implies the knowledge of the empty tomb; (2) Mark's account of the discovery of the empty tomb is unembellished and free of scriptural quotations, which demonstrates its primitive character; (3) women's testimony had little legal weight in Judaism, which suggests that the stories are authentic and not invented; (4) it would have been impossible to proclaim the resurrection of Jesus in Jerusalem had the tomb not been empty; (5) the earliest Jewish polemic recorded in Matthew 28.12–15 does not dispute that the tomb was empty, but only offers an alternative interpretation of it; and (6) the absence of a veneration of Jesus' site of burial supports the supposition that the tomb was empty.[16] The standard arguments against the historicity of the empty tomb include two major contentions: (1) Mark's report is a late creation that purports to explain the lack of knowledge of the empty tomb in the early church; and (2) Jesus' tomb was unknown given the widespread Roman practice to leave the victims of crucifixion either unburied or dumped into a common grave.[17] In the remainder of this section we will evaluate the strengths and weaknesses of each of these arguments.[18]

2.1. Paul's Presumed Knowledge of the Empty Tomb

While acknowledging that the pre-Pauline formula in 1 Corinthians 15.3–4 does not explicitly mention the empty tomb, some interpreters nevertheless insist that the reference to the resurrection after the reference to Jesus' burial implies the knowledge of the empty tomb. They also maintain that Paul, a former Pharisee, could not have proclaimed that Jesus was raised from the dead without also believing that the tomb was empty.

This argument cannot carry much weight because it is inconclusive. It is, indeed, reasonable to presume that Paul, and those who articulated this formula before Paul, believed that the tomb was empty, but it is impossible to demonstrate that they actually knew, or even heard, that it was empty. It is also difficult to ascertain whether the absence of any reference to women, who were, according to the gospel narratives, the primary agents in the discovery of the empty tomb, should be ascribed to patriarchal prejudice or to ignorance of such accounts. Since much of what Paul says in 1 Corinthians 15 is derived from his beliefs about the general resurrection of the dead, his assumption that the tomb was empty could likewise stem from the same beliefs. His silence on the subject of the empty tomb forces us to admit that we simply do not know whether he had any knowledge of its discovery.

2.2. The Unembellished Character of the Empty Tomb Narratives

Some scholars interpret the simplicity of the earliest account of the discovery of the empty tomb in Mark 16.1–8 as evidence of its primitive character. The absence of any legendary embellishments, scriptural allusions or references to eschatological hope is taken as a further proof of the matter-of-factness of the Markan tradition of the empty tomb discovery that supports its early date and bolsters its historical reliability.

This characterization of Mark 16.1–8 is certainly accurate. This account is strikingly simple and it is indeed devoid of apologetic interests, which are detectable in the later gospels. This simplicity, however, should not be exaggerated. Mark's narrative includes an angelophany, which could be the result of a later embellishment, or, as suggested in the previous chapter, of a transformation of an original Christophany to angelophany. Likewise, the absence of scriptural allusions cannot be taken as an indication of the account's historical reliability because, on this reading, the presence of such allusions would entail diminished historical reliability, which would be an unwarranted conclusion about Mark's passion narrative, for example. Moreover, the traditional material in 1 Corinthians 15.3–4 indicates that from the very beginning Jesus' resurrection was related to scripture. Another pre-Pauline formula in Romans 1.3–4 reveals that understanding Jesus' resurrection as a beginning of the general resurrection represents one of the earliest interpretations of this event. The absence of these features in Mark 16.1–8 does not therefore substantiate the assumption about its old age and traditional character.

2.3. The Discovery of the Empty Tomb by Women

The women's discovery of the empty tomb is probably the best-known argument for its historicity. Had the early Christians invented the story of the empty tomb, so the argument goes, they would not have portrayed women as discoverers of the missing body because female testimony had little weight in the first-century Jewish world. Since all four gospels consistently affirm that the tomb was found empty by a group of women, this report must be authentic. The potential embarrassment that this story could have caused bolsters its claim to historicity. A clear confirmation that such a story could have been embarrassing comes from the third-century writing *Contra Celsum* by Origen, in which the pagan Celsus ridicules his Christian opponents for relying on the testimony of 'a half-frantic woman' (Origen, *Cels.* 2.59).

This argument is quite persuasive. It is corroborated by Josephus' claim, 'From women let no evidence be accepted, because of the levity and temerity of their sex' (*Ant.* 4.219), as well as Luke's description of the male reactions to the women's report: 'But these words seemed to them an idle tale, and they did not believe them' (Lk. 24.11). The stories of the male verification of the women's testimony narrated in Luke 24.12 and John 20.3–10 represent later developments, which reveal discomfort that was felt by the account of the women's discovery of the missing body. It is certainly ironic that ancient prejudice against women provides the most convincing validation of the historical reliability of the accounts of the discovery of the empty tomb.

2.4. The Empty Tomb and the Proclamation of the Resurrection in Jerusalem

It is often argued that the proclamation of Jesus' resurrection in Jerusalem would have been virtually impossible had the tomb of Jesus not been empty. According to this reconstruction of the emergence of Christianity, had the body of Jesus still been in the grave, Jewish authorities could have easily produced it and discredited Christian preaching. Wolfhart Pannenberg, who has consistently laid great emphasis on this argument, asks: 'How could Jesus' disciples in Jerusalem proclaim his resurrection if they could be constantly refuted merely by viewing the grave in which the body was interred?'[19] The absence of the evidence that any such invalidation of Christian preaching was attempted is regarded as a decisive proof that the body disappeared, just as Jesus' followers said.

This argument presumes the historical reliability of the reports of Jesus' burial by Joseph of Arimathea and common knowledge of the location of the tomb in which Jesus was buried. It is sometimes objected that, even if the site of the burial had been generally known, by the time of Pentecost, when Jesus' followers began the public proclamation of Jesus' resurrection, empirical verification of the identity of the corpse could no longer have been made. This objection, though, appears unsubstantiated in light of the Mishnah's provisions for a secondary burial that was granted even to the executed criminals buried in a common grave: 'They used not to bury him in the burying-place of his fathers, but two burying-places were kept in readiness by the court, one for them that were beheaded or strangled, and one for them that were stoned or burnt. When the flesh had wasted away they gathered together the bones and buried them in their own place' (*m. Sanh.* 6.5-6). This regulation presumes that the family could identify the bones of their executed relative even after the flesh had decomposed.

The possibility of identifying Jesus' body or its remains, however, does not mean that Jewish authorities ever engaged in such an endeavour. In the absence of any evidence to the contrary, the scenario envisioned by modern scholars in which the opponents of the nascent Christian movement run to the tomb to produce the body in order to discredit the Christian preaching remains a fantasy. Had Jewish leaders ever gone to the tomb and found it empty, such a spectacular demonstration of the truthfulness of the Christian claim would not have remained unnoticed in the Christian literature. In this case the silence of the sources probably indicates that there was nothing to report. Jewish leaders either did not care or the empty tomb did not play any significant role in the Christian preaching. The fact that the empty tomb is neither mentioned in the pre-Pauline formula in 1 Corinthians 15.3–4 nor in the resurrection speeches in Acts 2.22–36 and 13.32–41 suggests that, for whatever reasons, this issue was not contentious.

2.5. Concurrence of Jewish Authorities that the Tomb Was Empty

A short report in Matthew 28.12–15 (along with its prequel in Mt. 27.62–66) is frequently regarded as a piece of early Jewish polemic. Jewish authorities described in this text do not dispute the report of the guard that the body disappeared from the tomb; rather, they bribe the soldiers to spread a lie that Jesus' disciples had stolen his body. The interpreters who ascribe an early date to this account conclude from this that the Jewish opponents of the early Christians did not contest the report of the empty tomb but only tried to explain it away.

The most problematic aspect of this argument is the assumption that Matthew's account describes the events that transpired in Jerusalem shortly after Jesus' crucifixion. This scenario is not very likely in light of several details that challenge the authenticity of this story. A Roman guard at the tomb of a crucified criminal is neither conceivable nor mentioned in any other gospel. It is difficult to imagine that the opponents of Jesus could have known his predictions of rising in three days, which Matthew, like other synoptic gospels, describes as being conveyed to the disciples in private. It is even more improbable that the Jews anticipated the proclamation of Jesus' resurrection. Finally, no other New Testament document mentions any Jewish accusation that the disciples of Jesus stole his body. The fact that only Matthew mentions it speaks strongly in favour of the assumption that this was a late rumour with limited impact, which arose in response to the Christian proclamation of Jesus' resurrection.

2.6. The Absence of the Veneration of Jesus' Tomb

The fact that no Christian source mentions any veneration of Jesus' burial place is sometimes interpreted as supporting evidence for the tomb's emptiness. Had Jesus' body remained in the tomb, his followers would have regarded it as a holy place – a shrine – worthy of adoration. Since they knew that his body was not there, they did not ascribe any religious value to it.

This is an argument from silence, which is inconclusive. While it is certainly true that there is no evidence that the followers of Jesus venerated Jesus' burial place, there is also no evidence that they did not. The belief that the Church of the Holy Sepulchre is built at the site of Jesus' crucifixion and burial presumes not only a viable tradition about the location of Jesus' grave but also a living memory of the place's religious significance. Moreover, the assumption that early Christians did not venerate the site of Jesus' burial could be used to support the opposite conclusion – that Jesus' burial place was unknown.[20] Either way, not much can be concluded from the silence of the source regarding religious services at the place of Jesus' burial.

2.7. Legendary Character of Mark's Account of the Discovery of the Empty Tomb

Some scholars contend that Mark 16.1–8 is a Christian invention devised to substantiate the proclamation of Jesus' bodily resurrection. On this reading, Mark's note about the women's silence serves as a literary device that explains the recent origin of the story: people did not hear of it before because the women said nothing to anyone.

In light of numerous legendary stories about disappearing bodies in antiquity, such as the ascensions of Enoch (Gen. 5.24; Heb. 11.5; *1 En.* 70.1–3; *3 En.* 6.1; 7.1) and Elijah (2 Kgs 2.11–12, 15–18; Josephus, *Ant.* 9.28), the disappearance of Moses (Josephus, *Ant.* 4.323–326), the unsuccessful search for the bodies of Job's children (*T. Job* 39.8–40.4), the assumptions of Ezra (*4 Ezra* 14.9, 48 Syr) and Baruch (*2 Bar.* 76.1–5), and the disappearances of Romulus (Ovid, *Metam.* 14.805–851; Plutarch, *Rom.* 27.7–28.3), Aristeas of Proconnesus (Plutarch, *Rom.* 28.4; Herodotus, *Hist.* 4.14–15), and Cleomedes of Astypaleia (Plutarch, *Rom.* 28.4–5; Pausanias, *Descr.* 6.9.6–9), the possibility that Mark's account could be a Christian legend cannot be easily dismissed. While many of these stories concern persons from the distant past or legendary figures, the *Dialogues* of Gregory the Great (540–640) contain an account about Gregory's contemporary, a Roman craftsman, who died and was buried in the Church of St Januarius the Martyr. Gregory reports that on the first night after the burial the sacristan heard loud shouting from the burial place. When the dead men's friends opened the grave, they found his clothes untouched but his body disappeared (*Dial.* 4.56). Pope Gregory assumes the accuracy of this story and even adds that anyone interested to check its veracity could do so, either by speaking with the witnesses or by examining the site of the burial. This is not just a medieval tale that could be simply brushed away. Matthew's accounts of the resurrected saints who exited their graves and appeared in Jerusalem after Jesus' resurrection (Mt. 27.52–53) or the guard at Jesus' tomb (Mt. 27.62–66; 28.4, 11–15) show that early Christians were capable of inventing stories for theological and apologetic purposes.

To be able to do something, however, does not also mean that something has been done. Many scholars, for example, find the suggestion that Mark invented the story of the discovery of the empty tomb unpersuasive. Jn 20.1–13 is not directly dependent on Mark, which raises the probability that it represents an independent tradition of the empty tomb's discovery. Several *hapax legomena* (Greek words that appear only once in the New Testament) in Mark 16.1–8, such as 'spices' (v. 1), 'roll away/back' (vv. 3–4) and 'terror' (v. 8), strengthen the hypothesis of the non-Markan origin of this account. To this list of reasons for the traditional character of Mark's account we can add Dale Allison's perceptive observation that 'no other logion or story in the canonical Jesus tradition justifies its recent appearance by pretending that people kept quiet about it'.[21] In light of these objections, the conjecture that Mark 16.1–8 represents a Christian invention *ex nihilo* fails to convince.

2.8. The Unknowability of Jesus' Burial Place

The supposition that Jesus' body was either left on the cross unburied or thrown into a mass grave reserved for executed criminals is based on the standard Roman practice of leaving the victims of crucifixion hanging on the cross, to be devoured by birds and animals (Suetonius, *Aug.* 13.2; Horace, *Ep.* 1.16.48; Josephus, *J.W.* 4.330–333; 4.360; 4.383; 5.518; 5.531). John Dominic Crossan applies the Roman practice of denying burial to crucified rebels to Jesus by investigating the trajectory of the burial tradition. The earliest layer of the tradition is, according to Crossan, preserved in *Gos. Pet.* 21 (which he ascribes to a hypothetical 'Cross Gospel'). This tradition presumes that Jesus' corpse was buried by the enemies (see also Acts 13.29). The next layer, preserved in Mark 15.42–47, transforms the burial by the enemies into a burial by a respected member of the Sanhedrin. The subsequent layer, preserved in Matthew 27.57–71, portrays Joseph of Arimathea as a rich man who was actually a disciple of Jesus. Finally, John 19.38–42 asserts that the tomb into which Jesus' body was laid was in a garden. The burial tradition thus developed 'from burial by enemies to burial by friends, from inadequate and hurried burial to full, complete, and even regal embalming'.[22] Crossan sees here an apologetic tendency that tried to hide the ugly truth: 'By Easter Sunday morning, those who cared did not know where it was, and those who knew did not care.'[23]

It is questionable, however, whether the Roman practice of denying burial to executed political enemies really applies to Jesus' case. At the time of Jesus' crucifixion Judea was not in an open rebellion against Rome. Deuteronomy 21.22–23 discloses a strong Jewish concern for the proper burial of the dead, both righteous and unrighteous, and a desire to avoid defilement of the land. Second Temple literature (11Q19 64.10–13; Philo, *Spec.* 3.151–152) confirms that Deuteronomy 21.22–23 was the law of the land. Josephus and Philo show that burial of the victims was frequently permitted, especially at festivals (*J.W.* 4.317; Philo,

Flacc. 83–85). The discovery of skeletal remains of a crucified man in a family tomb at Giv'at ha-Mivtar offers additional support to the supposition that burial could be granted to the victims of crucifixion. Even though Jesus was crucified as an insurrectionist, he did not lead an armed rebellion against Rome. All first-century sources are unanimous that Jesus was properly, even if hurriedly, buried. *Gospel of Peter* 21 ('Then they pulled the nails from the Lord's hands and placed him on the ground'), contrary to Crossan's assertion, says nothing about Jesus' burial. The burial of Jesus' body by Joseph of Arimathea, a pious member of the Sanhedrin, is thus not only plausible but also very likely.[24]

What, then, can we conclude about the historicity of the empty tomb? One obvious conclusion is that no argument is completely convincing. In each case, we are dealing with various degrees of probabilities. On the whole, however, the arguments for the historicity of the discovery of the empty tomb by a group of women appear more persuasive. This assessment of the evidence, if accepted, does not mean that we can also demonstrate that the reason for the disappearance of Jesus' body was its transformation into a new, resurrected body. This is just one among several possible interpretations of the tomb's emptiness. The body could have been relocated to another tomb, it could have been stolen, the women could have gone to a wrong tomb, etc. Some of these options have even been considered in our sources, despite their preference for the miraculous explanation. This is why the discovery of the empty tomb remains an ambiguous experience. To what extent this experience was formative for the emergence of the resurrection belief is at this point difficult to say. We will return to this question after we review the arguments for and against the objectivity of Jesus' post-resurrection appearances.

3. Objectivity of Jesus' Appearances

The disciples' radical transformation from despair to triumph, from fearfulness to courage – including the willingness to die for their beliefs – shows that something extraordinary must have happened to them that should be accounted for. Early Christian documents claim that this radical change was caused by the encounters with the risen Jesus who appeared to his followers on various occasions. The interpreters who assume historical reliability of the reports of Jesus' appearances argue that they were objective visions (i.e. sensory perceptions that have been caused by an external stimulus) and not subjective hallucinations or apparitions (i.e. sensory perceptions that have not been caused by an external stimulus). Some scholars even claim that these visions could have been recorded on a video camera.[25] This view is typically buttressed by the following arguments. The early date of the pre-Pauline tradition in 1 Corinthians 15.3–7 speaks against the legendary character of Jesus' post-mortem appearances. The fact that some of the witnesses mentioned in the traditional formula were still alive at the time of Paul's writing indicates that they could have been interrogated. Given that the traditional formula mentions Jesus' appearances to large groups, such as the twelve and five hundred, the visions of the risen Jesus could not have been hallucinations, because hallucinations are individual, not collective, perceptions of something that is not objectively present. Michael Licona succinctly articulates this oft-repeated argument: 'Since hallucinations are mental events with no external referent, one cannot share in the hallucination of another.'[26] The eyewitness testimony of the apostle Paul in conjunction with his discussion of the spiritual body (1 Cor. 15.35–57) is taken to mean that he had seen the risen Jesus in bodily form. Christian apologists are usually unwilling to recognize any significant differences between Paul's concept of the spiritual body and the evangelists' emphasis on Jesus' physicality. They also affirm the general reliability of the gospel narratives and, as a rule, do not question the accuracy of individual appearance accounts.[27]

On the other side of the spectrum are scholars who regard the appearances as subjective visions caused by a mixture of grief and guilt of Jesus' followers after his death and fuelled by the expectations of his vindication by God. Typically, these subjective visions are interpreted as individual or mass psychological delusions or hallucinations. Gerd Lüdemann, for example, argues that after Jesus' unexpected death Peter was so overwhelmed by grief and guilt that his subconscious generated an apparition of Jesus, who forgave him his sins.[28] Michael Goulder similarly alleges that both Peter and Paul experienced hallucinations produced by their guilt and self-doubt, which led them to change their life orientation. Peter transformed from a boastful denier of Jesus to a courageous champion of faith, while Paul converted from a persecutor of Christians, who had already developed a growing distaste for Judaism, to a fervent missionary to the Gentiles. Goulder regards these conversion visions as primary, in contrast to Jesus' appearance to his apostles or to five hundred brethren, which he regards as a secondary development that is comparable to the modern sightings of Mary, Bigfoot, UFOs and other collective delusions.[29] These explanations are examples of the so-called 'cognitive dissonance' theory derived from social psychology, which postulates a discrepancy between someone's inner fantasy world and reality.

Is there a way to find out whether the appearances of Jesus were objective visions or merely projections of the recipients' minds? The usual route taken by scholars is to compare the accounts of Jesus' post-resurrection appearances to similar phenomena in our contemporary experience because the latter have been studied by scientists and other modern researchers. Another route is to compare the New Testament accounts to similar stories from ancient literature. These analogies, even if only partially relevant, could nevertheless help us describe the disciples' experiences, regardless of our ability to explain them.

3.1. Contemporary Cross-Cultural Analogies

The most common analogies in cross-cultural studies are the apparitions of the recently deceased spouses that have been experienced by their bereaved widows. The first substantial study of this phenomenon was conducted by William Dewi Rees, who published his findings in 1971 in the *British Medical Journal*.[30] According to Rees's report, 47 per cent of a total of 293 interviewed widows reported apparitions of their dead husbands. Subsequent studies, which included both genders, confirmed Rees's findings: up to 50 per cent of the interviewed mourners have seen, heard or felt the presence of their dead spouses.[31] Some of the studies have shown that apparitions of the dead were not constricted to the grieving spouses but included different groups and ages of general population. The interviewees reported seeing, hearing, touching or even smelling the visions of the deceased. In some cases, more than one person experienced an apparition simultaneously.[32]

On the basis of various reports about post-mortem apparitions, published in both scientific and popular literature, Dale Allison compiled a list of parallels between the New Testament traditions about Jesus' appearances and cross-cultural apparitions of the departed: (1) both can be seen and heard; (2) both can be seen by one person and later by another; (3) both can be seen simultaneously by several percipients; (4) both are sometimes seen by only some persons in a larger group; (5) both appear to individuals who did not know them in life; (6) both create doubt in some percipients; (7) both offer reassurance and give comfort; (8) both give guidance and make requests; (9) both can be overwhelmingly real and indeed seemingly solid; (9) both appear and disappear in unusual and abrupt ways; (10) both could cause changes in belief; and (11) the frequency of both diminishes with the passage of time following the death of the person.[33]

While these parallels clearly show that, contrary to the assertions of some biblical scholars, Jesus' appearances are not without analogies, their relevance for understanding the New Testament resurrection stories is limited. We have no way of knowing whether any of the explanations of post-mortem apparitions and other similar phenomena, such as Christic visionary experiences[34] and apparitions of the Virgin Mary at Lourdes, Fatima and Medjugorje,[35] are applicable to the first-century Christian descriptions of the visions of the risen Jesus. Modern explanations of apparitions include Jungian archetype theory (psychic content from the unconscious that escapes control of our consciousness), psychoanalytic explanations (the Freudian view that a hallucination stems from a desire to gratify an unconscious wish), cognitive dissonance theory (discrepancy between fantasy and reality) and various neurophysiological explanations, such as hallucinations (defined in the Oxford English Dictionary as 'the apparent perception [usually by sight or by hearing] of an external object when no such object is actually present'). The last explanation – hallucination – frequently carries negative connotations because it is usually associated with mental disorders. Hallucinations are typically associated with delirium tremens (an acute episode of delirium), drug use, sensory deprivation, sleep deprivation, hypnosis, neurological disorders and schizophrenia.[36]

Various attempts to apply some of these theories to the early Christians have, in most cases, failed to convince the wider academic community. For example, many scholars rightly emphasize that the resurrection took Jesus' disciples by surprise. This turn of events was not what they were expecting or hoping for. Pious Jews expected the resurrection of the righteous at the end of the times, not a resurrection of a single individual in the midst of history. It is therefore difficult to explain Jesus' appearances as projections of the disciples' wishes and desires. Likewise, any attempt to reconstruct the disciples' state of mind is doomed to fail because our evidence is meagre and fragmentary. They may have felt disappointed, but they, or some of them, may have felt angry. It is also imaginable that some of them may have been much more concerned for their safety after the execution of their leader than coming to grips with their shattered religious beliefs. Each of these options remains a conjecture that is conceivable but not provable.

While these objections strengthen the apologists' case against naturalistic explanations of Jesus' appearances, they do not necessarily strengthen the case for the objectivity of these appearances. For example, it is not sufficient to point to the visual and palpable aspects of these experiences, because both sensations have been frequently reported by those who experienced post-mortem apparitions. The list of the earliest witnesses of Jesus' appearances in 1 Corinthians 15.5–7 is frustratingly terse; we only hear that Jesus appeared to certain individuals and groups. Equally terse is Paul's description of his own experience. He merely says that Jesus appeared to him (1 Cor. 15.8), that he has seen Jesus (1 Cor. 9.1) or that he was commissioned to proclaim the Son of God to the Gentiles (Gal. 1.16). In both cases, he appeals only to his visual and possibly auditory faculties. His description of the spiritual body does not clarify what specifically Paul has seen and on the basis of which distinguishing features he was able to identify Jesus, given the fact that he never met him before. Luke's accounts of Paul's experience (Acts 9.1–9; 22.6–11; 26.12–19) are also not of much help, because Luke portrays this event as a visionary experience that was only partially accessible to the bystanders and not as an appearance of the risen Jesus. Even if the gospel accounts preserve some early memories of the witnesses' experiences of the palpability of Jesus' body, they also repeatedly emphasize that Jesus could not be easily recognized. In light of this deconstructive aspect of the gospel narratives, which is especially evident in Luke and John, it is not surprising that both evangelists take great pains to demonstrate Jesus' identity. They accomplish this task, however, not by describing the physical appearance of Jesus' resurrected body, but by pointing to a familiar act (Lk. 24.30–31), a familiar word (Jn 20.16) or the marks of the crucifixion (Jn 20.20, 27 and possibly Lk. 24.39–40). The only unique aspect of the gospel narratives, when compared with the reports of contemporary apparitions, is Jesus' ability to eat, but this characteristic is only mentioned in Luke 24.41–43 (see Acts 10.40–41) and possibly John 21.12–13. In each case the late date and anti-docetic tendencies of the evangelists undermine the assumption that this is a genuine feature of the earliest experiences of Jesus' appearances.

The strongest support for the objectivity of Jesus' appearances is, according to Christian apologists, provided by the New Testament reports about collective visions of the risen Jesus (1 Cor. 15.5–6). Since hallucinations are private, individual events, collective hallucinations are quite rare, if not impossible. Even if the participants of such collective hallucinations claim to have had the same vision, such as the recipients of the Marian apparitions, this does not mean that each person had exactly the same hallucination. It is more likely that they had individual hallucinations that have been precipitated by similar expectations and emotional excitement. Since none of this applies to Jesus' collective appearances, they could not have been hallucinations but experiences of a reality independent of them.[37]

This argument is only partially convincing. Jesus' appearance to the eleven is indeed one of the best attested and most consistent appearances. The appearance to five hundred individuals, on the other hand, is not mentioned anywhere else except in 1 Corinthians 15.6, hence its reliability depends solely on the early age of the pre-Pauline formula and Paul's remark that many of the recipients of this collective Christophany were still living when he was writing 1 Corinthians, implying that they could have been interrogated. The main weakness of the above reasoning, however, is the unproven assumption that all recipients of collective Christophanies had exactly the same experience. We, however, have no way of knowing whether individual disciples or individuals who constituted the group of five hundred, if interrogated separately, would have said the same thing. Though it is true that Paul believed that his experience was of the same kind as the previous appearances, we know, for example, that Luke did not share this view. Moreover, Paul's portrayal of the spiritual body differs from the evangelists' emphasis on Jesus' fleshliness. While these disparities among different authors do not demonstrate the existence of disparities among the recipients of the collective Christophanies, they nonetheless indicate that this could have been a real possibility.

Another weakness of the apologetic argument is the insistence that collective visions of the risen Jesus could not have been triggered by any expectation or emotional excitement because Jesus' disciples were in a state of shock after Jesus' death. This description of the disciples' emotional state, however, is applicable only to the time before Jesus' first appearance. It is conceivable that Mary's or Peter's report about Jesus' initial appearance generated the disciples' expectation of the future appearances. The effect of their anticipation and excitement on their collective experiences of the risen Jesus could therefore not be excluded.

It appears, then, that the arguments for both objectivity and subjectivity of Jesus' appearances lack plausibility. Contemporary cross-cultural analogies cannot help us determine, much less prove, the character of Jesus' appearances. One reason for this setback is, once again, the fragmentary character of the sources. Another reason is that the recipients' perceptions of visions and apparitions depend, for the most part, on their understanding of reality as well as on the cultural assumptions that determine the content of a vision. It is therefore much more instructive to use emic criteria (i.e. criteria supplied by ancient authors) than etic criteria (i.e. criteria developed through cross-cultural studies) to assess early Christian reports about Jesus' appearances.

3.2. Ancient Analogies

Jewish literature, which provides the most relevant religious and social framework for the New Testament claims about Jesus' resurrection, contains two pertinent stories about post-mortem appearances. The account in 1 Samuel 28.4–19 describes Saul's invocation of the spirit of dead Samuel through a necromancer in order to get divine reassurance on the eve of his battle with the Philistines. Samuel indeed appears, but instead of offering reassurance he reprimands Saul for not obeying God's voice and predicts that the Philistines will defeat Saul's army and that he and his sons will die. The whole episode is presented as an illicit act, because the woman who serves as a medium initially objects: 'Surely you know what Saul has done, how he has cut off the mediums and the wizards from the land. Why then are you laying a snare for my life to bring about my death?' (1 Sam. 28.9; see 1 Sam. 28.3). This objection reflects the deuteronomic prohibition of necromancy as idolatrous: 'No one shall be found among you ... who consults ghosts or spirits. For whoever does these things is abhorrent to the LORD; it is because of such abhorrent practices that the LORD your God is driving them out before you' (Deut. 18.10–12). This prohibition, which functioned as the law of the land in ancient Israel, bans all appeals to the spirits of the departed along with other forms of compulsive manipulations of spiritual forces.

Another story of dead persons appearing after death is found in 2 Maccabees 15.12–16. In this account, Judas Maccabeus describes the appearances of the high priest Onias and the prophet Jeremiah, who give him the encouraging message of impending victory over his adversaries. The author of 2 Maccabees, however, emphasizes that Judas was 'relating a dream, a sort of vision, which was worthy of belief' (2 Macc. 15.11). This remark indicates that this story belongs to the genre of dream visions in which a holy man delivers a message that is pertinent to the actual situation of the person who has the vision.

It is, however, questionable whether these accounts of post-mortem apparitions provide appropriate analogies for the New Testament descriptions of Jesus' appearances. 1 Samuel 28.4–19 describes a forbidden practice, which requires a medium to contact the spirits of the dead. Moreover, the spirit of dead Samuel lacks any of the corporal features that characterize early Christian reports of Jesus' appearances. On the other hand, 2 Maccabees 15.12–16 classifies the appearances of Onias and Jeremiah into the category of dreams and visions, which are abundant in Jewish and Greco-Roman literature. Jesus' appearances are never presented as dreams and visions. The only exception is Luke's portrayal of Paul's experience on the Damascus road in Acts 9.1–9; 22.6–11; 26.12–19, which betrays Luke's desire to limit the appearances to the time period of forty days after the resurrection.

The closest parallels to Jesus' appearances are found in the Jewish texts that employ the verb 'appear to'. In the Septuagint, this verb is typically used in descriptions of the appearances of God or his messengers (Gen. 12.7; 17.1; 18.1; 26.2; Exod. 3.2; Judg. 6.12; 1 Kgs 3.5; 9.2; 2 Chron. 3.1). Of particular interest are stories of angels that appear in human form. In the narrative about the destruction of Sodom and Gomorrah, Abraham sees three men without recognizing that they are angels (Gen. 18.1–2). According to the Genesis account, these angels display normal human qualities: they have their feet washed and they eat (Gen. 18.3–15). Likewise, when two angels arrive at Sodom, Lot treats them as ordinary human beings. They again have their feet washed, they eat, and they drag Lot into the house when his life is endangered by the mob (Gen. 19.1–11). While Genesis 18 consistently uses the term 'men' for disguised angels (18.2, 16, 22), Genesis 19 employs the terms 'angels' (19.1, 15) and 'men' (19.5, 8, 10, 12, 16) interchangeably. A similar story is found in Judges 6.11–24, which describes the appearance of the angel of the Lord to Gideon. Gideon, who does not recognize the angel's true identity, treats him as an ordinary human being, repeatedly addressing him as 'sir' (vv. 13, 15). He perceives the truth only at the very end, when the angel vanishes from his sight. These motifs – human appearance and human attributes displayed by an angel and the failure of the protagonist to recognize the angel's identity – also appear in other Jewish texts, such as Judg. 13.16; Tob. 5.4–5; *T. Ab.* 2.2 (rec. A); Philo, *Abr.* 107–110, 113; and Josephus, *Ant.* 1.196–198. Especially prominent is the motif of eating/drinking (Gen. 18.8; 19.3; Philo, *Abr.* 110), although Second Temple and rabbinic writings regularly point out that angels only appear to devour food without really doing so (Tob. 12.19; *T. Ab.* 4.9–10 [rec. A]; Philo, *Abr.* 117–118; *QG* 4.9; Josephus, *Ant.* 1.197; *Tg. Neof. 1* and *Tg. Ps.-J.* on Gen. 18.8; *Gen. Rab.* 48.14).

The New Testament accounts about Jesus' appearances share several striking similarities with the stories about the appearance of angels in human form: (1) they appear to the recipients as ordinary human beings, as if having solid bodies and as if being able to consume food; (2) they could vanish unexpectedly; and (3) the recipients regularly fail to recognize/identify them. The fact that neither Paul nor the evangelists try to distinguish Jesus' appearances from the appearances of angels may suggest that earliest perceptions of the risen Jesus were akin to angelomorphism. This should not be surprising in light of various Jewish texts that envision the resurrected righteous like the angels and the stars (Dan. 12.3; *1 En.* 104.4; *1 En.* 39.3–5; *2 Bar.* 49.1–51.10). That early Christian interpreters were familiar with such traditions can be clearly seen in the story about Jesus' dialogue with the Sadducees about the resurrection, which is found in all three synoptic gospels (Mk 12.18–27; Mt. 22.23–33; Lk. 20.27–39). When Jesus was asked whose wife a woman married to seven brothers will be in the resurrection, he replied: 'For when they rise from the dead, they neither marry nor are given in marriage, but are like angels in heaven' (Mk 12.25; see Mt. 22.30; Lk. 20.34–36). It is therefore not too far-fetched to imagine that Christian interpreters could have used the standard motifs from the traditions about angels appearing in human form to describe the visions of the risen Jesus. While this suggestion does not resolve the question of whether Jesus' appearances were subjective or objective, it nonetheless moves the debate to the first-century world that shaped the earliest perceptions of Jesus' resurrected body and supplied the imageries to express it in linguistic terms.

4. Emergence of the Resurrection Belief

The central question that still remains to be answered is: why did Jesus' followers proclaim, from the very beginning, that Jesus had been raised from the dead? N. T. Wright eloquently articulates the traditional view on this subject:

> Neither the empty tomb by itself ... nor the appearances by themselves, could have generated the early Christian belief. The empty tomb alone would be a puzzle and a tragedy. Sightings of an apparently alive Jesus, by themselves, would have been classified as visions or hallucinations, which were well enough known in the ancient world. However, an empty tomb and appearances of a living Jesus, taken together, would have presented a powerful reason for the emergence of the belief.[38]

Wright further explains that both the empty tomb and the appearances provide the necessary conditions for the emergence of the resurrection belief, although by themselves they would have been insufficient to generate this belief. 'Bring them together, however, and they form, in combination, a sufficient condition.'[39]

Wright's claim that the discovery of the empty tomb would have been insufficient to generate the resurrection belief is certainly plausible. We have seen that a missing body could have been interpreted in many different ways. The empty tomb narratives also consistently show that this discovery regularly generated confusion, never faith. The only exception is the belief of the beloved disciple (Jn 20.8), but the next verse – 'for as yet they did not understand the scripture', 20.9 – clarifies that even this faith did not entail much comprehension. Wright's claim about the possible impact of Jesus' appearances, however, is less convincing. He does not distinguish between contemporary and ancient interpretations of such experiences. We have seen above, for example, that 2 Maccabees 15.12–16 categorizes the post-mortem appearances of Onias and Jeremiah as a dream–vision, which suggests a distinction between what is real and what is not (see Acts 12.9). To claim, however, that people in antiquity would regard experiences that have no basis in reality as 'hallucinations' imposes a modern category on the ancient texts. There is also no evidence in Jewish literature that 'such encounters were reasonably well known'.[40] Though visionary experiences were common, visions of the dead were quite rare. Wright's only example is Acts 12.15, but the disciples' supposition that Peter's angel was standing at the door does not mean that they thought that Peter had died but rather that they had been visited by his guardian angel.

The most significant aspect of Wright's argument, however, is his contention that both the empty tomb and the appearances were necessary for the emergence of the Christian resurrection belief. Scholars who share this view usually assume that without the empty tomb Christian proclamation would have been formulated as Jesus' vindication or the exaltation of his spirit to heaven and not as his resurrection. James D. G. Dunn, for example, entertains the following two alternatives: translation/rapture and vindication/exaltation.[41] He rejects the first option because Jewish texts that describe such individuals (Gen. 5.24; 2 Kgs 2.11–12; Josephus, *Ant.* 4.323–326; *4 Ezra* 14.9, 48 Syr; *2 Bar.* 76.1–5) exclude death, which would make them inapplicable to Jesus. The second alternative, however, seems to have been a real possibility. The classic version of a Hellenized Jewish concept of afterlife is found in Wisdom 3.1–9 and 5.1–5. These passages describe the destiny of the righteous, whose souls are in the hand of God. *Testament of Abraham* 20.10–11 describes the death of Abraham as a separation of his soul from his body: 'And immediately Michael the archangel stood beside him with multitudes of angels, and they bore his precious soul in their hands in divinely woven linen. And they tended the body of the righteous Abraham with divine ointments and perfumes until the third day after his death.' Similarly, the *Testament of Job* claims that when Job died, his soul was immediately taken to heaven, 'but his body, prepared for burial, was borne to the tomb' (*T. Job* 52.10–11).

If this was a real option, why did Jesus' followers claim that he was raised from the dead? The most intuitive answer seems to be: because they knew that the tomb was empty. Unfortunately, this conclusion frequently leads to an unwarranted emphasis on the empty tomb. Wright, for example, regards Jesus' appearances as 'a kind of necessary supplement to the discovery of the empty tomb'.[42] The New Testament documents, however, consistently downplay the significance of the empty tomb. The pre-Pauline formula in 1 Corinthians 15.3–7 does not even mention it. Although the emptiness of the tomb may be suggested by the sequence, 'he was buried, and ... he was raised on the third day in accordance with the scripture' (v. 4), we cannot ascertain whether the formula reflects the early Christian belief about the nature of the resurrection or the knowledge that the tomb was actually empty. If the latter is the case, as the apologists persistently claim, then the discovery of the empty tomb was either ignored (perhaps because of the unreliability of female testimony) or was considered inconsequential (perhaps because of the ambiguity of the empty tomb experience). Be that as it may, the formative influence of the empty tomb on the earliest stages of the proclamation of Jesus' resurrection cannot be established.

There is, in fact, no evidence in any of the sources before Mark that the empty tomb was common knowledge. To conclude from this, however, that the entire episode is a later invention is neither compelling nor warranted by the sources. Yet, the fact that the pre-Pauline formula in 1 Corinthians 15.3–7 enumerates the appearances without mentioning the empty tomb, while the earliest account of the discovery of the empty tomb in Mark 16.1–8 is transmitted without the reports of Jesus' appearance(s), suggests that these two traditions developed independently of each other. Their explicit fusion did not occur before the writing of the gospels of Matthew, Luke and John. This does not mean that these two traditions did not inform or support each other at a much earlier date, but such a conclusion is based on the overall assessment of the development of the early Christian movement rather than on the actual evidence provided by the sources.

Even the evangelists, who seek to establish the continuity between Jesus' missing body and his resurrected body by placing the discovery of the empty tomb before Jesus' appearances, or by narrating how Jesus' resurrected body appeared just outside the tomb from which his body disappeared, do not use the empty tomb as an explicit validation of Jesus' identity. When the characters are confounded or ask for a proof that the person they see is really their Lord who had been crucified a few days ago, the risen Jesus verifies his identity by showing them his hands, feet and side (Lk. 24.37–39; Jn 20.20), by inviting them to touch the marks of his crucifixion (Jn 20.24–29), or by consuming food in their presence (Lk. 24.41–43; Jn 21.12–13). In none of the accounts is a doubt concerning Jesus' identity alleviated by encouraging the witnesses to visit the empty tomb. Both Luke and John, who include the disciples' verification of the women's report about the missing body, place it before, not after, Jesus' appearances (Lk. 24.12; Jn 20.3–10). There is rather a sense that the mere experience of seeing Jesus alive, which is frequently characterized by a movement from disbelief to faith, was sufficient for the formation of the conviction that Jesus had been raised from the dead.

It seems, then, that Jesus' post-resurrection appearances were fundamental for the emergence of the resurrection belief. The discovery that Jesus' body disappeared from the tomb into which it was laid has certainly provided corroborating evidence, but how early and how widespread this knowledge was is difficult to reconstruct, especially if we take seriously Mark's concluding statement that the women, at least initially, 'said nothing to anyone' (Mk 16.8). Wright's claim that Jesus' appearances alone could not have persuaded the disciples that Jesus has been raised from the dead does not find much support in the sources, which repeatedly show that only the encounters with the risen Jesus were able to generate faith. In order to understand how Jesus' followers (or at least some of them) could have come to such a conclusion without also knowing that the tomb was empty, we have to take into account the religious and social context in which the appearances were experienced. Their meaning was determined not only by what the recipients saw or touched but also by what they believed about God and the world. Their worldview included an intensified eschatological expectation generated through Jesus' proclamation of the impending Kingdom of God. It also included the expectation of the resurrection of the righteous at the end of times. While Jesus' passion and resurrection predictions are, in their current form, formulated as *ex eventu* prophecies (Mk 8.31; 9.31; 10.32–34; Mt. 16.21; 17.22–23; 20.17–19; Lk. 9.22; 44; 18.31–33), they probably embody a genuine memory of Jesus' expectation of his speedy vindication by God. All these hopes supplied imagery and vocabulary that enabled the witnesses of the appearances to conceptualize their experiences. When they concluded that Jesus had been raised from the dead, they did not convey only what they believed had happened to Jesus, but also what they believed had happened to the entire creation – the dawn of God's vindication of the righteous and the beginning of the general resurrection of the dead.

5. Historicity of Jesus' Resurrection

Can a historian do more than just reconstruct the events that led to the emergence of the belief in Jesus' resurrection? Christian apologists generally believe that this can and should be done. The most prominent voice in this group is undoubtedly that of N. T. Wright. He concludes his investigation of Easter and history with the following claims:

> The question which must be faced is whether the explanation of the data which the early Christians themselves gave, that Jesus really was risen from the dead, 'explains the aggregate' of the evidence better than these sophisticated scepticisms. My claim is that it does. The claim can be stated once more in terms of necessary and sufficient conditions. The actual bodily resurrection of Jesus (not a mere resuscitation, but a transforming revivification) clearly provides a sufficient condition of the tomb

being empty and the 'meetings' taking place. Nobody is likely to doubt that. Once grant that Jesus really was raised, and all the pieces of the historical jigsaw puzzle of early Christianity fall into place. My claim is stronger: that the bodily resurrection of Jesus provides a necessary condition for these things; in other words, that no other explanation could or would do. All the efforts to find alternative explanations fail, and they were bound to do so.[43]

Michael R. Licona, who has produced a massive monograph of over 600 pages devoted to the historicity of Jesus' resurrection, reaches a similar conclusion:

I am contending that Jesus' resurrection from the dead is the best historical explanation of the relevant historical bedrock. Since it fulfills all five criteria [i.e., explanatory scope, explanatory power, plausibility, less ad hoc and illumination] for the best explanation and outdistances competing hypotheses by a significant margin in their ability to fulfill the same criteria, the historian is warranted in regarding Jesus' resurrection as an event that occurred in the past.[44]

Is Jesus' bodily resurrection from the dead really the best historical explanation of the available evidence? Many in the academy are reluctant to make such a bold claim, not because they do not believe that God is capable of bringing a dead person back to life but because they do not think that the historian's religious convictions should affect the evaluation of the data. Saying that 'questions pertaining to the cause behind the event (i.e. who or what raised Jesus), the mechanism behind the event (i.e. how precisely it was accomplished) and the precise nature of Jesus' resurrected state are beyond the reach of historians'[45] is making false claims of objectivity. Admitting the impact of one's beliefs or alleging that all historical judgements are subjective, on the other hand, is counterproductive. Despite Wright's claim that 'there is enough evidence to lure sceptics forward',[46] every debate on this subject has only confirmed the opposite. What counts as plausible is determined to a large extent by one's worldview. Since the claim that Jesus has been raised from the dead presumes divine agency, even when this is not explicitly stated, those who do not share this belief are not likely to be persuaded. This is, however, not a question of who can persuade whom but a question of the integrity of historical enquiry. Since historical judgements are never absolute, declaring that Jesus' resurrection is a historical event means that the resurrection probably happened, not that it certainly happened. It is therefore best to conclude with Alan F. Segal that 'the resurrection is neither probable nor improbable; it is impossible to confirm historically'.[47]

6. Summary and Conclusions

This chapter addresses one of the most contentious questions in the study of Jesus' resurrection: to what extent is the claim that Jesus has been raised from the dead an object of historical enquiry? The answer to this question depends on someone's understanding of the nature of historical investigation. Those who concur with Troeltsch's explanation of the character of historical judgements generally agree that the object of historical investigation can only be the emergence of the belief in Jesus' resurrection, not the resurrection itself. Those who believe that God's ability to suspend the known laws of nature should not be excluded from the repertoire of possible causes of the events under investigation are more prone to subject Jesus' resurrection to historical scrutiny.

Most practitioners in the discipline agree that the reports of the discovery of the empty tomb and the descriptions of Jesus' post-resurrection appearances belong to legitimate historical enquiry. After reviewing the standard arguments for and against the historicity of the empty tomb, the former appear to be more persuasive. What our sources consistently show, however, is that the discovery of the missing body was an ambiguous experience. This ambiguity, aided by ancient patriarchal prejudice regarding the reliability of female testimony, may have been a reason why the empty tomb is not mentioned in the early Christian proclamation. Historical investigation of the descriptions of Jesus' appearances includes their comparison with contemporary cross-cultural analogies as well as ancient analogies. Among the former, the reports about the apparitions of the dead to their grieving spouses and other family members are especially interesting. Even though their applicability to the disciples' experiences is quite limited, they nevertheless show that post-mortem apparitions could appear overwhelmingly real and solid to the recipients. Among ancient analogies, the closest parallels are provided by the Jewish texts that describe the appearance of angels in human form. Similar to Jesus' appearances, angels appear to the recipients as ordinary human beings, they can vanish unexpectedly and they are frequently not recognized until the very end. In light of various Jewish texts that compare the resurrected righteous to the angels, portraying Jesus' resurrected body with the help of angelomorphic imagery could have been a way of conceptualizing the appearances in eschatological terms.

The claim that both the empty tomb and the appearances provide not only sufficient but also necessary conditions for the emergence of the Christian resurrection belief, though plausible, remains nonetheless speculative. Since the empty tomb does not belong to the earliest Christian proclamation, it is difficult to demonstrate its formative influence on the development of the resurrection tradition. Even the evangelists who provide the accounts of the discovery of the empty tomb and narratively link the missing body to the resurrected body repeatedly emphasize that the resurrection faith was born only in the encounters with the risen Jesus.

The question of whether Jesus' resurrection itself can be the object of historical enquiry is a central issue of contention between those who insist that God's ability to intervene into the created world should not be excluded from the historian's worldview and those who hold that an understanding of history that does not comply with the principles of analogy and causality is not what the discipline is all about. This methodological disagreement hinders any constructive discussion between both groups. This is regrettable, because lay readers and audiences may get the erroneous impression that this is a contention between those who really believe in God and those who do not. But this is not a dispute about God's ability to suspend the natural laws; this is a dispute about the concept of historical enquiry and the boundaries of the discipline. Those who say that Jesus' resurrection is not accessible to historical investigation are in conformity not only with the modern understanding of the nature of historical enquiry but also with the New Testament documents themselves, which are unanimous that Jesus' resurrection was not an observable event but a divine act that can only be expressed through the confession that God raised Jesus from the dead.

Notes

1 The YouTube database includes the debates between Gary Habermas and Antony Flew (https://www.youtube.com/watch?v=BVb3Xvny8-k), William Lane Craig and John Shelby Spong (https://www.youtube.com/watch?v=zsXzu4tcOTI), William Lane Craig and Bart Ehrman (https://www.youtube.com/watch?v=vRTUrvTTRAQ), and John Dominic Crossan and Marcus Borg vs. James White and Jim Renihan (https://www.youtube.com/watch?v=waiM136MeuU).

2 Gary R. Habermas and Antony G. N. Flew, *Did Jesus Rise from the Dead?: The Resurrection Debate* (ed. Terry L. Miethe; San Francisco: Harper & Row, 1987); William Lane Craig, John Dominic Crossan and William F. Buckely, Jr, *Will the Real Jesus Please Stand Up?: A Debate between William Lane Craig and John Dominic Crossan* (ed. Paul Copan; Grand Rapids, MI: Baker, 1998); William Lane Craig and Gerd Lüdemann, *Jesus' Resurrection: Fact or Figment? A Debate Between William Lane Craig and Gerd Lüdemann* (eds Paul Copan and Ronald K. Tacelli; Downers Grove, IL: InterVarsity Press, 2000); John Dominic Crossan and N. T. Wright, *The Resurrection of Jesus: John Dominic Crossan and N. T. Wright in Dialogue* (ed. Robert B. Stewart; Minneapolis: Fortress, 2006). See also volume 3.2 (2005) of the *Journal for the Study of the Historical Jesus*, which is devoted to the discussion of Wright, *The Resurrection of the Son of God*, and volume 10.2 (2008) of *Philosophia Christi*, which is devoted to the discussion of Allison, *Resurrecting Jesus*.

3 William Lane Craig, *Assessing the New Testament Evidence for the Historicity of the Resurrection of Jesus* (SBEC 16; Lewiston, NY: Edwin Mellen, 1989); idem, *The Historical Argument for the Resurrection of Jesus* (TSR 23; Lewiston: Edwin Mellen, 1985).

4 John Dominic Crossan, *The Historical Jesus: The Life of a Mediterranean Jewish Peasant* (San Francisco: HarperSanFrancisco, 1991); idem, *The Birth of Christianity: Discovering What Happened in the Years Immediately after the Execution of Jesus* (San Francisco: HarperSanFrancisco, 1998).

5 Gerd Lüdemann, *The Resurrection of Jesus: History, Experience, Theology* (trans. John Bowden; London: SCM Press, 1994); idem, *The Resurrection of Christ: A Historical Inquiry* (Amherst, NY: Prometheus, 2004).

6 Wright, *The Resurrection of the Son of God*.

7 Allison, *Resurrecting Jesus*.

8 Michael R. Licona, *The Resurrection of Jesus: A New Historiographical Approach* (Downers Grove, IL: IVP Academic, 2010).

9 Ernst Troeltsch, 'Historical and Dogmatic Method in Theology', in *Religion in History* (trans. James Luther Adams and Walter F. Bense; Minneapolis: Fortress, 1991), 11–32.

10 Allison, *Resurrecting Jesus*, 338. It is therefore utterly baffling to see the confidence that is sometimes displayed by the scholars who seek to demonstrate the historicity of Jesus' resurrection. One recent example is the following assertion by N. T. Wright: 'We are left with the secure historical conclusion: the tomb was empty, and various "meetings" took place not only between Jesus and his followers (including at least one initial sceptic) but also, in at least one case (that of Paul; possibly, too, that of James), between Jesus and people who had not been among his followers. I regard this conclusion as coming in the same sort of category, of historical probability so high as to be virtually certain, as the death of Augustus in AD 14 or the fall of Jerusalem in AD 70' (*The Resurrection of the Son of God*, 710).

11 Sarah Coakley, 'Is the Resurrection a "Historical" Event? Some Muddles and Mysteries', in *The Resurrection of Jesus Christ* (ed. Paul Avis; London: Darton, Longman & Todd, 1993), 90.

12 Ted Peters, 'The Future of the Resurrection', in *The Resurrection of Jesus: John Dominic Crossan and N. T. Wright in Dialogue* (ed. Robert B. Stewart; Minneapolis: Fortress, 2006), 166.

13 Wolfhart Pannenberg, 'History and the Reality of the Resurrection', in *Resurrection Reconsidered* (ed. Gavin D'Costa; Oxford: Oneworld, 1996), 64 (emphasis removed).

14 Troeltsch, 'Historical and Dogmatic Method in Theology', 21.

15 See Alan F. Segal, 'The Resurrection: Faith or History?', in *The Resurrection of Jesus: John Dominic Crossan and N. T. Wright in Dialogue* (ed. Robert B. Stewart; Minneapolis: Fortress, 2006), 135–8.

16 Wolfhart Pannenberg, *Jesus – God and Man* (trans. Lewis L. Wilkins and Duane A. Priebe; Philadelphia: Westminster Press, 1968), 88–106; William Lane Craig, 'Did Jesus Rise from the Dead?', in *Jesus under Fire: Modern Scholarship Reinvents the Historical Jesus* (eds Michael J. Wilkins and J. P. Moreland; Grand Rapids, MI: Zondervan, 1995), 146–52; Wright, *The Resurrection of the Son of God*, 599–608.

17 There are other proposals that try to explain away the discovery of the empty tomb, such as the suggestion that Joseph of Arimathea removed

the body from the tomb into which he initially laid it and properly buried it in a shallow grave, or that the women went to a wrong tomb. While such alternative explanations of the emptiness of the tomb visited by the women are not impossible, they require a complete disregard of the New Testament evidence. For the arguments against the historicity of the empty tomb, see Jeffery J. Lowder, 'Historical Evidence and the Empty Tomb Story: A Reply to William Lane Craig', in *The Empty Tomb: Jesus Beyond the Grave* (eds. Robert M. Price and Jeffery J. Lowder; Amherst, NY: Prometheus, 2005), 261–306; John Shelby Spong, *Resurrection: Myth or Reality? A Bishop's Search for the Origins of Christianity* (San Francisco: HarperSanFrancisco, 1994), 225; Crossan, *The Historical Jesus*, 391–4; Adela Yarbro Collins, 'The Empty Tomb in the Gospel According to Mark', in *Hermes and Athena: Biblical Exegesis and Philosophical Theology* (eds. E. Stump and T. P. Flint; UNDSPR 7; Notre Dame, IN: University of Notre Dame Press, 1993), 107–37; Goulder, 'The Baseless Fabric of a Vision', 56; Kirsopp Lake, *The Historical Evidence for the Resurrection of Jesus Christ* (London: Williams & Norgate, 1907), 241–52.

18 For a comprehensive evaluation of these arguments, see Allison, *Resurrecting Jesus*, 311–31.

19 Pannenberg, *Jesus – God and Man*, 100.

20 See Lüdemann, *The Resurrection of Jesus*, 45.

21 Allison, *Resurrecting Jesus*, 304.

22 Crossan, *Historical Jesus*, 393.

23 Ibid., 394.

24 Craig A. Evans, 'Jewish Burial Traditions and the Resurrection of Jesus', *JSHJ* 3.2 (2005): 233–48; Allison, *Resurrecting Jesus*, 352–63; Jodi Magness, 'Ossuaries and the Burials of Jesus and James', *JBL* 124 (2005): 121–54.

25 N. T. Wright, 'The Transforming Reality of the Bodily Resurrection', in *The Meaning of Jesus: Two Visions* (eds Marcus Borg and N. T. Wright; New York: HarperCollins, 1999), 125.

26 Licona, *The Resurrection of Jesus*, 484.

27 Gary R. Habermas, *The Risen Jesus and Future Hope* (Lanham: Rowman & Littlefield, 2003), 10–11; Craig, 'Did Jesus Rise from the Dead?', 153–8.

28 Lüdemann, *The Resurrection of Jesus*, 49–84, 97–100.

29 Goulder, 'The Baseless Fabric of a Vision', 48–55.

30 William Dewi Rees, 'The Hallucinations of Widowhood', *British Medical Journal* 4 (1971): 37–41.

31 See, for example, Julian Burton, 'Contact with the Dead: A Common Experience?', *Fate* 35.4 (1982): 65–73; Richard Olson et al. 'Hallucinations of Widowhood', *Journal of the American Geriatric Society* 33 (1985): 543–7; Agneta Grimby, 'Hallucinations Following the Loss of a Spouse: Common and Normal Events Among the Elderly', *Journal of Clinical Geropsychology* 4 (1998): 65–74; Gillian Bennett and Kate Mary Bennett, 'The Presence of the Dead: An Empirical Study', *Mortality* (2000): 139–57; M. M. Ohayon, 'Prevalence of Hallucinations and Their Pathological Associations in the General Populations', *Psychiatry Research* 97 (2000): 153–64.

32 Richard A. Kalish and David K. Reynolds, 'Phenomenological Reality and Post-Death Contact', *Journal for the Scientific Study of Religion* 12 (1973): 209–21.

33 Allison, *Resurrecting Jesus,* 278–83. For each of these parallels, Allison offers lengthy footnotes that list relevant publications in books, scholarly journals and popular literature.

34 Phillip H. Wiebe, *Visions of Jesus: Direct Encounters from the New Testament to Today* (Oxford: Oxford University Press, 1997).

35 Michael P. Carroll, *The Cult of the Virgin Mary: Psychological Origins* (Princeton, NJ: Princeton University Press, 1986); Sandra Zimdars-Swartz, *Encountering Mary: From La Salette to Medjugorje* (Princeton, NJ: Princeton University Press, 1991).

36 Wiebe, *Visions of Jesus*, 172–211.

37 Gary R. Habermas, 'Explaining Away Jesus' Resurrection: The Recent Revival of Hallucination Theories', *Christian Research Journal* 23.4 (2001): 26–31, 47–9. This article is also available on Habermas' website: http://www.garyhabermas.com/articles/crj_explainingaway/crj_explainingaway.htm

38 Wright, *The Resurrection of the Son of God*, 686.

39 Ibid., 692.

40 Ibid., 690.

41 Dunn, *Jesus Remembered*, 866–8.

42 Wright, *The Resurrection of the Son of God*, 695 (original emphasis removed).

43 Ibid., 717 (original emphasis removed).

44 Licona, *The Resurrection of Jesus*, 610.

45 Ibid.

46 Wright, *The Resurrection of the Son of God*, 715.

47 Segal, 'The Resurrection: Faith or History?', 135.

6

Jesus' Resurrection and Theology

Because the claim that God raised Jesus from the dead lies at the heart of the Christian faith, the meaning of this event is of utmost importance for Christian identity. For many Christians today, Jesus' resurrection validates their belief in life after death. Yet, more often than not, this life after death is conceived not as bodily resurrection but as the soul going to heaven after death. While the doctrinal statements of most denominations include the expectation of bodily resurrection at the end of the age, a closer scrutiny shows that contemporary believers usually think that the term 'resurrection of the body' really means 'immortality of the soul'.

It may come as a surprise to some readers, but the belief in the immortal soul that goes to heaven after death is not derived from the New Testament but developed in the early church under the influence of Platonism. It is therefore imperative that we examine the meaning of Jesus' resurrection in its first-century context before we ask about its significance for us today. For the early Christians, Jesus' resurrection signalled the beginning of the general resurrection of the dead. Yet the general resurrection of the believers neither followed the resurrection of Jesus, as the first Christian generation quickly realized, nor has happened yet. What are the implications of this delayed completion of the resurrection for Christian hope? Moreover, if the early Christians believed that what happened to Jesus would also happen to them, why did they claim that Jesus was declared to be Son of God by the resurrection from the dead (Rom. 1.3–4), or that by raising Jesus God made him both Lord and Messiah (Acts 2.36)? In what way is Jesus' resurrection different from the expected resurrection of his followers? Related to this is the question of God's identity. If Jesus' resurrection was an act of God, how does this event shape our understanding of who God is? Why is God in the New Testament frequently identified as the one who raised Jesus from the dead (Rom. 4.24; 8.11; 2 Cor. 4.14; Gal. 1.1; Col. 2.12; 1 Pet. 1.21)? Finally, what is the relevance of the resurrection for Christian living? What does Paul mean when he says that 'just as Christ was raised from the dead by the glory of the Father, so we too might walk in newness of life' (Rom. 6.4)?

These questions can be classified into four distinct groups: (1) questions related to Jesus' resurrection as a guarantor of the resurrection of the believers (eschatology); (2) questions pertaining to Jesus' resurrection and his messianic identity (Christology); (3) questions about the significance to Jesus' resurrection for our understanding of God (theology); and (4) questions about the relevance of Jesus' resurrection to Christian living (ethics).

1. Jesus' Resurrection and Christian Hope

From the very start, Jesus' resurrection was understood as an event that marked the beginning of the general resurrection of the dead. This interpretation of the resurrection can be found in all layers of the New Testament. Paul describes the risen Jesus as 'the first fruits of those who have fallen asleep' (1 Cor. 15.20), a human being through whom the resurrection of the dead has come (1 Cor. 15.21), or 'the firstborn within a large family' (Rom. 8.29). By the same token, Jesus is portrayed as 'the firstborn from the dead' (Col. 1.18), 'the first to rise from the dead' (Acts 26.23), or 'the firstborn of the dead' (Rev. 1.5). Matthew conveys the same idea through a tale of the resurrection of the saints who, subsequent to Jesus' resurrection, came out of their tombs and appeared to the citizens of Jerusalem (Mt. 27.52–53).

At the same time, however, early Christian interpreters betray awareness that the general resurrection had not yet taken place, awareness that only grew in significance with the passage of time.

The author who directly and most profoundly addresses this problem is Paul. He uses the Adam–Christ analogy to develop a two-stage resurrection blueprint that begins with 'Christ the first fruits' and ends with the resurrection of believers (1 Cor. 15.20–23). As a result, the resurrection of the righteous, which is in Jewish literature understood as a single eschatological event, has been divided into two occurrences: first the resurrection of Jesus, then the resurrection of those who belong to him. Paul alleges that the completion of this process will take place when all enemies of Christ, who currently rules in heaven, are put under his feet. The final victory over the forces that oppose his reign will be achieved with the destruction of the last enemy – death, which in the context of Paul's argument most likely refers to the resurrection of believers (1 Cor. 15.24–28).

> But in fact Christ has been raised from the dead, the first fruits of those who have died. For since death came through a human being, the resurrection of the dead has also come through a human being; for as all die in Adam, so all will be made alive in Christ. But each in his own order: Christ the first fruits, then at his coming those who belong to Christ. Then comes the end, when he hands over the kingdom to God the Father, after he has destroyed every ruler and every authority and power. For he must reign until he has put all his enemies under his feet. The last enemy to be destroyed is death. For 'God has put all things in subjection under his feet.' But when it says, 'All things are put in subjection,' it is plain that this does not include the one who put all things in subjection under him. When all things are subjected to him, then the Son himself will also be subjected to the one who put all things in subjection under him, so that God may be all in all. (1 Cor. 15.20–28)

This passage explains the sequence of eschatological events that have been put in motion with Jesus' resurrection, but it does not fully explain the correlation between the resurrection of Jesus and the resurrection of those who belong to him. Paul addresses this question in the passage that precedes the one quoted above. In 1 Corinthians 15.12–19, Paul seeks to show that one cannot affirm Jesus' resurrection without also affirming the general resurrection of the dead because the former represents the first occurrence of the latter. This part of the argument, though somewhat circular, is relatively clear. The most ingenious aspect of Paul's argument, however, is his explanation of the link between the resurrection of Jesus and the resurrection of believers. When he eventually introduces Christian hope of the resurrection into the discussion, he does not simply say, 'For if the dead are not raised, your faith is futile and ... those who have died in Christ have perished', but he comes to this conclusion through the resurrection of Jesus as a mediating component (marked here in italics): 'For if the dead are not raised, *then Christ has not been raised. If Christ has not been raised,* your faith is futile and ... those who have died in Christ have perished" (vv. 16–18). Paul's explanation shows that Christian resurrection hope is not directly derived from eschatological expectation of the general resurrection of the dead but from a particular manifestation of this expectation in human history – the resurrection of Jesus.

We can thus conclude that bodily resurrection is the only form of belief in life after death that stands in continuity with the New Testament. This form of eschatological destiny of humanity affirms the goodness of the creation, the incarnation and Jesus' resurrection as a victory over the power of sin and death. When Paul declares that 'this perishable body must put on imperishability, and this mortal body must put on immortality' (1 Cor. 15.53), he describes the future destiny of the bodies of those who belong to Christ, not the future destiny of their souls. Only under this assumption does Paul's triumphant exclamation make sense: 'Death has been swallowed up in victory' (1 Cor. 15.54). Belief in the immortality of the soul marginalizes belief in resurrection by prioritizing the question of the soul's intermediate state after death and by turning the resurrection of the body into a secondary affair in the eschatological drama.

If belief in bodily resurrection represents the primary form of Christian hope, how can this hope be conceptualized in the modern world? We have seen that the emphasis on the corporeal character, even fleshliness, of Jesus' resurrected body that characterizes the gospel resurrection narratives differs from Paul's concept of the body animated by the spirit. These variances have a considerable bearing on the character of the eschatological destiny of humanity. The main difference between Jesus' resurrection and our resurrection is that Jesus' body was brought back to life after three days while our dead bodies will eventually decompose. Though the speed of corpse decay depends on various factors, every tissue of the human body will eventually disappear. When this aspect of the general resurrection is considered, the idea of the empty tomb, which plays such an important role in contemporary discussions about the historicity of Jesus' resurrection, becomes almost irrelevant. Much more pertinent is Paul's comparison of the earthly body to a bare seed that does not epitomize 'the body that is to be' (1 Cor. 15.37), as well as his claim that 'God gives it a body as he has chosen' (1 Cor. 15.38). Paul's contentions, however, merely provide a helpful start in modern discussions about the future resurrection of the dead. One of the central questions in these conversations is the nature of personal identity. If human self is an embodied self, what/who safeguards the continuity between our earthly lives and our resurrected lives? Some physical residuum of our earthly bodies? Our consciousness? Our moral character? God's memory of who we are? Are the new bodies going to be mere replicas of our old bodies or will God create enhanced bodies? How will the resurrection affect people with disabilities? Will their disabilities be eliminated or retained?[1] None of these questions can be addressed here, but they effectively illustrate the complexity of an ongoing dialogue between biblical interpreters, theologians, and scientists about the nature of the eschatological resurrection of the dead.[2]

2. Jesus' Resurrection and His Messianic Identity

Although the early Christians interpreted Jesus' resurrection as the beginning of the general resurrection of the dead, they also regarded it as a distinctive event that uniquely disclosed his messianic identity. As an occurrence that is both categorically and chronologically distinguished from the resurrection of believers, Jesus' resurrection is an exclusive event that carries Christological significance. The tradition that Paul received included the confession that Christ (the Greek term for the Messiah) was raised on the third day in accordance with the scriptures (1 Cor. 15.3–4). In Luke 24.46, the risen Jesus explains to his disciples that 'it is written, that the Messiah is to suffer and to rise from the dead on the third day'. In Acts 17.3, Paul claims 'that it was necessary for the Messiah to suffer and to rise from the dead'. These claims are astounding, because there is no evidence before the rise of Christianity that anybody expected the resurrection of the Messiah. While both the expectation of the Messiah and the hope for the resurrection of the dead at the end of time are well attested in Jewish literature, these two expectations are nowhere linked together except in some texts that claim that the resurrection of the righteous will take place during or at the conclusion of the messianic age (4Q521 frg. 2 2.12; *4 Ezra* 7.26–32). Why then did the early Christians claim that Jesus' resurrection confirmed his messianic identity?

The answer to that question depends, to a large extent, on one's reconstruction of Jesus' earthly ministry. In view of the variety of Jewish messianic hopes, it is not surprising that Jesus' preaching and activity aroused all kinds of messianic expectations. The main disagreement among the scholars concerns the question of how Jesus responded to these expectations. While some interpreters insist that a messianic self-claim was not part of Jesus' message, others allege that, despite the lack of overt messianic declarations, Jesus nevertheless acted and spoke as Israel's Messiah.[3] Regardless of whether we think that Jesus regarded himself as the Messiah or not, however, all four gospels are unanimous that he was executed as a messianic pretender. The inscription of the charge against him was 'The King of the Jews' (Mk 15.26; Mt. 27.37; Lk. 23.38; Jn 19.19). In light of this well-attested charge, it is very likely that Jesus' followers understood his resurrection as a divine vindication of his ministry and a divine affirmation of the cause for which he was crucified – his messiahship. Consequently, they attributed to him a new messianic dignity that he received through his resurrection.

While this historical reconstruction remains tentative, there are three New Testament passages that provide explicit arguments for Jesus' messiahship on the basis of his resurrection from the dead. One is found in the letters of Paul (Rom. 1.3–4) and two in the speeches in Acts (2.29–36; 13.30–37).[4] Though the belief in Jesus' messiahship functions as a preconceived notion that makes these arguments intelligible, they give us a glimpse into the rationale of the conflation between the confession of Jesus' messianic identity and the claim that he was raised from the dead.

2.1. Romans 1.3–4

Paul's self-presentation in the opening lines of his letter to the Romans includes an early Christian confession that juxtaposes Jesus' Davidic origin with his status as the Son of God with power by virtue of his resurrection from the dead (written in italics):

> Paul, a servant of Christ Jesus, called to be an apostle, set apart for the gospel of God, which he promised beforehand through his prophets in the holy scriptures concerning his Son, *who was born of the seed of David according to the flesh, and who was declared to be Son of God in power according to the spirit of holiness since the resurrection of the dead*, Jesus Christ our Lord ... (Rom. 1.1–4)[5]

The pre-Pauline material, which may not have included the phrase 'in power' as a qualifier of the title 'Son of God', consists of two parallel statements: (1) Jesus was born of the seed of David according to the flesh, and (2) Jesus was declared to be Son of God according to the spirit of holiness since the resurrection of the dead.[6] The first statement is usually understood as a description of Jesus' earthly career as a Davidic Messiah and the second statement as a description of his heavenly reign as Son of God. This type of Christology is called a two-stage Christology because it presumes that Jesus' existence consists of two consecutive stages: his earthly life of humiliation and his resurrected state of exaltation. Jesus' resurrection functions as a temporal demarcation between these two stages. It should be noted that this is the only New Testament passage in which the designation for the general resurrection ('the resurrection of the dead') stands for Jesus' resurrection. The use of this formulation, which was later replaced by a clearer expression, 'the resurrection from the dead' (1 Pet. 1.3), indicates that for the early Christians, Jesus' resurrection marked the beginning of the general resurrection. This was not an isolated event, but the first instalment of the eschatological resurrection of the dead.

Scholars who read Romans 1.3–4 as an expression of a two-stage Christology typically attribute the declaration 'born of the seed of David' to Jewish–Christian communities who regarded Jesus as the Davidic Messiah who fulfilled Jewish nationalistic hopes.[7] They also allege that the emphasis in the formula falls on the second stage, i.e. on Jesus' exalted status as the Son of God. Eduard Schweizer, for example, claims that 'the earthly existence of the Son of David has clearly been regarded as the lowly first stage which was fulfilled only by exaltation to the Sonship of God'.[8] On this reading, when Jesus was raised from the dead, he was not just declared to be the Son of God but he was actually appointed to be the Son of God. At his resurrection, Jesus acquired a status that he did not have before. If the original formula did not include the phrase 'in power', it declared that Jesus' divine sonship originated from his resurrection. If the original formula included the phrase 'in power', it declared that Jesus' divine sonship in power originated from his resurrection. Either way, 'the resurrection of Jesus was regarded as of central significance in determining his divine sonship, either as his installation to a status and prerogatives not enjoyed before, or as a major enhancement of a sonship already enjoyed'.[9]

It is, however, questionable whether only the first part of the traditional formula refers to the Davidic Messiah. The expression 'the seed of David' is not a synonym for the messianic title 'Son of David' but a genealogical marker that stipulates the condition that any claimant to the Davidic throne must fulfil. A Davidide becomes a king not by virtue of his birth but by virtue of his enthronement as the rightful Davidic heir. Moreover, Psalm 2.7 indicates that in ancient Israel the enthronement ceremony was viewed as a divine adoption of a newly installed king. In this text, God recognizes the new status of the monarch by declaring 'You are my son; today I have begotten you.' The similarity between the divine adoption of a royal figure (who is called God's 'anointed' in Ps. 2.2) at his enthronement and the installation of Jesus to a position of divine sonship at his resurrection is conspicuous. If, however, the second part of the formula in Romans 1.3–4 alludes to Psalm 2.7, as many scholars recognize, then the designation 'Son of God' functions as a messianic title.

Although there is not much evidence in pre-Christian Jewish sources for a messianic interpretation of Psalm 2.7, early Christian interpreters consistently read this verse as a messianic text (Acts 13.33; Heb. 1.5; 5.5). This understanding is consistent with God's promise to David in 2 Samuel 7.12–16 that God will raise up David's seed after him and that his seed will be a son of God. The first element of the promise – Davidic descent – became a major component in expectations of the Davidic Messiah. The second element – the father–son relationship between the Davidic king and God – though mentioned less frequently than the Davidic descent, was also important for the development of Davidic messianism. In 4Q174 1.10–11, for example, the author combines the quotations of 2 Samuel 7.12 (which mentions David's offspring), 2 Samuel 7.13b (which refers to the endless duration of the Davidic throne) and 2 Samuel 7.14 (which expresses God's promise to adopt David's descendant) to clarify the identity of the Davidic Messiah, who is here called 'the Shoot of David'. When the Davidic origin and a divine adoption are juxtaposed, Davidic ancestry merely establishes one's messianic credentials; in and of itself it does not authenticate one's messianic claim. For this reason, it is the second, not the first, part of Romans 1.3–4 that establishes Jesus' messianic identity. Jesus' Davidic descent is affirmed through a non-titular acknowledgement of his origin: he 'was born of the seed of David according to the flesh'. Jesus' resurrection, however, is here presented as the moment at which he was installed to the position of the Son of God and thereby became the Messiah. The phrase 'according to the spirit of holiness' functions either as a reference to the activity of the Spirit through which Jesus' enthronement took place or as an indicator of the eschatological character of his messianic reign.

In light of these considerations, it is certainly appropriate to speak about the two 'stages' of Jesus' life – one that started with his birth and one that began with his resurrection. In Romans 1.3–4, however, these two stages are not conceived of as two independent phases in Jesus' career, one as a Jewish Messiah and one as the Son of God, but as two closely related facets of his messianic identity. More specifically, it is the second stage – Jesus' enthronement and the divine adoption at the resurrection – that ascertains his messianic status.

2.2. Acts 2.29–36

Although Luke ascribes the speeches in Acts to various individuals who were active in the first few decades of the early Christian movement, they betray many theological concerns that emerged by the end of the first century. It is thus not surprising that most scholars regard the speeches in Acts as Luke's own compositions. In each case, however, Luke sought to construct a 'speech in character', i.e. a speech that was appropriate to the character of the speaker and the occasion at which the oration was delivered.

Peter delivers the first major speech in Acts on the occasion of the coming of the Holy Spirit at Pentecost (Acts 2.14–36). It consists of two subunits, the so-called 'Pentecost speech' (vv. 14–21) and the 'resurrection speech' (vv. 22–36). The 'resurrection speech' begins with a short synopsis of Jesus' life ('Jesus of Nazareth, a man attested to you by God with deeds of power, wonders, and signs that God did through him among you' – v. 22), death ('this man, handed over to you according to the definite plan and foreknowledge of God, you crucified and killed by the hands of those outside the law' – v. 23) and resurrection ('but God raised him up, having freed him from death, because it was impossible for him to be held in its power' – v. 24). The rest of the speech, however, does not tackle the first two topics but focuses exclusively on Jesus' resurrection. Peter's entire argument consists of various biblical quotations that he invokes to prove that the resurrection is foretold in Israel's Scripture. Peter first quotes the Greek translation of Psalm 16.8–11, in which David expresses confidence that God will not abandon his soul to Hades or let his Holy One experience corruption (vv. 25–28). The Hebrew text of this psalm envisions God's saving intervention in life-threatening circumstances experienced in the present. The psalmist does not describe life after death but expects God's healing and avoidance of death. The Greek translation of this psalm, however, uses several expressions, such as 'my flesh will live in hope' (Ps. 15.9b LXX) or 'you have made known to me the ways of life' (Ps. 15.11a LXX), which could be interpreted as references to resurrection, regardless of whether they were intended as such by the translators. This is, in fact, how Peter interprets the text. He does not understand this psalm as David's prayer for his own healing but as David's prophecy of the resurrection of the Messiah.

> Fellow Israelites, I may say to you confidently of our ancestor David that he both died and was buried, and his tomb is with us to this day. Since he was a prophet, he knew that God had sworn with an oath to him that he would put one of his

descendants on his throne. Foreseeing this, David spoke of the resurrection of the Messiah, saying,

'He was not abandoned to Hades, nor did his flesh experience corruption.' This Jesus God raised up, and of that all of us are witnesses. Being therefore exalted at the right hand of God, and having received from the Father the promise of the Holy Spirit, he has poured out this that you both see and hear. For David did not ascend into the heavens, but he himself says, 'The Lord said to my Lord, "Sit at my right hand, until I make your enemies your footstool."' Therefore let the entire house of Israel know with certainty that God has made him both Lord and Messiah, this Jesus whom you crucified. (Acts 2.29–36)

Peter supports the claim that David spoke not of himself but of the Messiah by creating a paraphrase of Psalm 15.9–10 LXX in which the term 'flesh' is no longer linked to the idea of living in hope, as was the case in the original quotation of Psalm 15.9 LXX ('moreover my flesh will live in hope' – Acts 2.26b), but to the term 'corruption' ('nor did his flesh experience corruption' – Acts 2.31). Since the image of flesh experiencing corruption is highly suggestive of death, the opposite image – flesh not experiencing corruption – is suggestive of resurrection. But this is only the first step in Peter's argument. In order to demonstrate that David did not foresee his own resurrection but the resurrection of the Messiah, Peter reminds the audience that David died and was buried. The public knowledge of David's tomb here serves as proof that he cannot be God's 'Holy One' who will not experience corruption (Acts 2.27). Peter then declares that the person about whom David spoke is one of his descendants whom God promised to put on his throne (see Ps. 132.11 [131.11 LXX]), which allows him to conclude that this individual must be no one else but the Messiah.

Peter's argument for the resurrection of the Messiah is not only innovative but also ingenious. By paraphrasing the original quotation of Psalm 15.9–10 LXX and by claiming that David's prediction is not applicable to him personally but to the promised Davidic offspring that will sit on his throne, Peter arrives at the conclusion that is not documented in any extant Jewish writing – that scripture envisions the resurrection of the Messiah. This reasoning is most likely the rationale behind the claim of the risen Jesus in Luke's Gospel that 'it is written, that the Messiah is to suffer and to rise from the dead on the third day' (Lk. 24.46).

Only after Peter has established that David prophesied about the resurrection of the Messiah does he mention Jesus to demonstrate that he must be the Messiah because his resurrection literally fulfils the words of the psalm. He accomplishes this by simply declaring 'This Jesus God raised up, and of that all of us are witnesses' (Acts 2.32). Peter's argument presumes that Jesus' body did not remain in the grave long enough to decompose because only so can the words of the psalm, 'nor did his flesh experience corruption' (v. 31), be literally fulfilled. This aspect of the resurrection is unique to Jesus because the resurrection of believers at the end of time clearly presumes decomposition of their corpses. Peter's argument, in fact, neither presupposes nor depends on the understanding of the resurrection of Jesus as the beginning of the general resurrection. His argument, however, depends on the idea of the resurrection of the flesh. Since these two features – dissociation of Jesus' resurrection from the resurrection of believers and the concept of the resurrection of the flesh – do not characterize the early Christian proclamation of Jesus' resurrection, they betray a later development that is consistent with the resurrection narratives in the gospels of Luke and John.

Had Peter's goal been merely to prove Jesus' messiahship on the basis of his resurrection from the dead, he could have ended his speech in v. 32. At this point he has effectively demonstrated that since Jesus has been raised in the manner described in Psalm 16.8-11 (15.8-11 LXX), which has just been shown to speak of the resurrection of the Messiah, Jesus must be the Messiah. Peter indeed makes this conclusion, but not immediately after v. 32 where it logically belongs, but at the end of his speech, when he declares that 'God has made him ... Messiah, this Jesus whom you crucified' (v. 36). Between these two points – the final piece of evidence in the argument for Jesus' messiahship and the logical conclusion of that argument – Peter inserts another scriptural argument based on Psalm 110.1, which allows him to add the title 'Lord' to his closing statement about the identity of the crucified and risen Jesus.

The argument for Jesus' lordship begins with Peter's assertion 'Being therefore exalted at the right hand of God, and having received from the Father the promise of the Holy Spirit, he has poured out this that you both see and hear' (v. 33). It is not entirely clear whether Jesus' resurrection and exaltation are here presented as two simultaneous or successive events. The first option is plausible under the assumption that Luke incorporates traditional material, which regularly equates Jesus' resurrection and exaltation (Phil. 2.9; Heb. 1.3–13; 8.1). The second option, however, is more plausible within the literary and theological framework of Luke–Acts, which differentiates between Jesus' resurrection and Jesus' ascension. This interpretation is also supported by the reference to the fulfilment of the promise of the Holy Spirit in the second half of v. 33. On this reading, vv. 32–33 describe three separate events: Jesus' resurrection, Jesus' exaltation (equated here with his ascension) and the outpouring of the Holy Spirit at Pentecost. Peter supports his claim about Jesus' exaltation at the right hand of God with the quotation of Psalm 110.1, in which the Lord (God) invites someone, who is also called 'Lord', to sit at his right hand. Peter alleges that the second Lord is Jesus because, unlike David, who did not ascend into heaven, Jesus has been exalted to God's presence upon his resurrection.[10] This interpretation allows him to conclude that 'God has made him both Lord and Messiah, this Jesus whom you crucified' (v. 36).

Peter's 'resurrection speech' thus makes two distinct though related claims. Jesus' resurrection demonstrates, on the one hand, that he is the Messiah and, on the other hand, that he is Lord. Both claims are intelligible only in the light of scripture. Psalm 16.8–11 (15.8–11 LXX) provides the scriptural support for the declaration that Jesus is the Messiah, while Ps. 110.1 provides the scriptural support for the claim that he is Lord.

2.3. Acts 13.30–37

Paul's speech in the synagogue of Pisidian Antioch (Acts 13.16–41) begins with a survey of major events from Israel's history (prosperity in Egypt – exodus – wandering in the wilderness – possession of Canaan – judges – King Saul – King David [vv. 17–22]), followed by a synopsis of Jesus' life, death and resurrection, whose purpose is to show that by raising Jesus from the dead God finally and conclusively fulfilled his promise to David (vv. 23–37). The content of this promise is not explicated, but the formulation 'from the seed of this man [David]'[11] (v. 23) clearly alludes to Nathan's oracle in 2 Sam. 7.12–16. Similar to Peter's 'resurrection speech' in Acts 2, Paul employs the Greek translation of Psalm 16, but he quotes only one verse from this text. His scriptural proof also includes the quotations of Psalm 2.7 and Isaiah 55.3, which are not used in Acts 2. The primary purpose of these citations is not to demonstrate that Jesus is the Messiah but that 'what God promised to our ancestors he has fulfilled for us, their children, by raising Jesus' (vv. 32b–33a). These differences between Acts 13 and Acts 2 indicate that Paul's speech is not a mere repetition of Peter's. The Lukan Paul presumes the audience's familiarity with the argument for Jesus' messiahship, which allows him to shift the focus from Jesus' identity to the fulfilment of the Davidic promises.

> But God raised him from the dead; and for many days he appeared to those who came up with him from Galilee to Jerusalem, and they are now his witnesses to the people. And we bring you the good news that what God promised to our ancestors he has fulfilled for us, their children, by raising Jesus; as also it is written in the second psalm, 'You are my Son; today I have begotten you.' As to his raising him from the dead, no more to return to corruption, he has spoken in this way, 'I will give you the holy promises made to David.' Therefore he has also said in another psalm, 'You will not let your Holy One experience corruption.' For David, after he had served the purpose of God in his own generation, died, was laid beside his ancestors, and experienced corruption; but he whom God raised up experienced no corruption. (Acts 13.30–37)

Paul's claim that God raised Jesus from the dead echoes the primitive Christian proclamation of Jesus' resurrection. God is the active subject and Jesus is the recipient of God's intervention on his behalf. This declaration is supported only by a reference to Jesus' appearances to his followers and their role as witnesses to the people. Paul is not focused on proving that Jesus has been raised from the dead but on clarifying the meaning of this event. His explanation involves three scriptural quotations: Psalm 2.7, Isaiah 55.3 and Psalm 16.10 (15.10 LXX) (vv. 33b–35). The presumed context of Psalm 2.7 is a royal enthronement ceremony at which God adopts a newly installed king as his son. In Paul's speech, the adverb 'today' that appears in the quotation of this psalm ('You are my Son; today I have begotten you' – Acts 13.33b) most likely refers to Jesus' resurrection. The pre-Pauline confession in Romans 1.3–4 indicates that a link between Jesus' resurrection as his messianic enthronement was established very early, but only in Acts 13.33b is the resurrection portrayed as divine begetting. By quoting Psalm 2.7 in support of his contention that by raising Jesus God fulfilled his promise to the forefathers, Paul interprets Jesus' resurrection as a royal enthronement that completes God's promise to adopt David's offspring (2 Sam. 7.14). This argument is very similar to Romans 1.3–4, but it is much more developed. Rather than merely alluding to Psalm 2.7, the Lukan Paul not only supplies the full quotation of this psalm but also introduces it with a statement that explains its hermeneutical function.

The other two biblical quotations – Isaiah 55.3 and Psalm 15.10 LXX – are introduced with a declaration that the risen Jesus will no more return to corruption (v. 34). The notion of not returning to corruption seems to be particularly significant in Paul' argument because he repeats it in his comments after these two scriptural citations, not just once but twice: first in reference to David (he saw corruption – v. 36) and then in reference to the risen Jesus (he did not see corruption – v. 37). The purpose of this increased emphasis on seeing/not seeing corruption cannot be merely to show that by declaring 'You will not let your Holy One experience corruption' (v. 35) David did not speak of himself but of someone else, as was the case in Peter's sermon in Acts 2. The main objective of Paul's synagogue homily is to demonstrate that Jesus' resurrection fulfils the prophecy from Isaiah 55.3 ('I will give you the holy promises made to David'), which is quoted before Ps. 15.10 LXX. The Isaiah quotation functions here as a recognizable reference – almost like a shortcut – to God's everlasting covenant with David (2 Samuel 7.12–16). This abridged reference to Nathan's oracle emphasizes the everlasting character and irrevocable nature of God's promise to David, which plays a prominent role not only in 2 Sam. 7.12–16 but also in other scriptural references to the Davidic covenant (2 Sam. 23.1–5; 2 Chron. 13.5; 21.7; Ps. 89.4–5, 27–30; 132.11; and Amos 9.11–12). Paul claims that by raising Jesus, who will no more return to corruption, God finally fulfilled the promise to David of an everlasting kingdom.[12]

In comparison with Romans 1.3–4 and Acts 2.29–36, which also present Jesus' resurrection as a fulfilment of God's promise to David, Paul's Pisidian Antioch sermon offers not only the most sophisticated but also the most complete argument for this function of the resurrection. Unlike Romans 1.3–4 and Acts 2.29–36, which focus only on Jesus' Davidic descent and his status as the Son of God attained at his resurrection, the Lukan Paul demonstrates that Jesus fulfils all three components of Nathan's oracle in 2 Samuel 7.12–16. He is David's offspring (Acts 13.23), he has been enthroned and declared God's son by virtue of his resurrection from the dead (Acts 13.32–33) and his dominion is everlasting because he will no more return to corruption (Acts 13.34–37). Within the narrative framework of Luke–Acts, Paul's sermon provides a direct response to the angelic announcement in Luke 1.32–33: 'He will be great, and will be called the Son of the Most High, and the Lord God will give to him the throne of his ancestor David. He will reign over the house of Jacob forever, and of his kingdom there will be no end.'

3. Jesus' Resurrection and the Character of God

Karl Barth claims that 'in the resurrection of Jesus Christ we have to do with a movement and action which took place not merely in human history but first and foremost in God Himself'.[13] Thorwald Lorenzen sums up the ideas of Eberhard Jüngel, Jürgen Moltmann and Robert Jenson when he says that by raising the crucified Jesus 'God exposed his very being to the estranging power of death, yet without ceasing to be God'.[14] The assumption that the resurrection of Jesus discloses the character of God is corroborated by several confessional statements in which the claim that God raised Jesus from the dead functions as a divine predicate: 'It will be reckoned to us who believe in him who raised Jesus our Lord from the dead' (Rom. 4.24); 'If the Spirit of him who raised Jesus from the dead dwells in you, he who raised Christ from the dead will give life to your mortal bodies also through his Spirit that dwells in you' (Rom. 8.11); 'we know that the one who raised the Lord Jesus will raise us also with Jesus' (2 Cor. 4.14); 'through Jesus Christ and God the Father, who raised him from the dead' (Gal. 1.1); 'through faith in the power of God, who raised him from the dead' (Col.

2.12); 'Through him you have come to trust in God, who raised him from the dead' (1 Pet. 1.21). In each of these statements, God is either described or identified through his act of raising Jesus from the dead.

In Romans 4.13–25, Paul compares the experience of Abraham to the experience of believers in order to demonstrate that not only Jews but also Gentiles have access to justification through faith. The former are described as 'the adherents of the law' and the latter as 'those who share the faith of Abraham' (v. 16). Corresponding analogies include the act of believing, the character of God, and the consequences of believing. The first analogy – the act of believing – provides the foundation of Paul's argument. Abraham believed God's promise that he would become the father of many nations despite two insurmountable obstacles: his own body 'was already as good as dead' because he was almost 100 years old and his wife Sarah was barren (v. 19). Unlike Paul's elaborate explication of Abraham's faith, which is at one point described as 'hoping against hope' (v. 18), the faith of Christian believers – both Jewish and Gentile – is merely asserted. After Paul declares that Abraham's faith was reckoned to him as righteousness, he alleges that it will be also 'reckoned to us who believe' (v. 24).

The second analogy – the character of God – is of primary importance here. The God in whom Abraham believed is portrayed as 'the God ... who gives life to the dead and calls into existence the things that do not exist' (v. 17). The God in whom Christians believe is identified as the one 'who raised Jesus our Lord from the dead' (v. 24). These descriptions of God's character are directly relevant to the third analogy – the consequence of believing. God revitalized Abraham's body and opened Sarah's womb to conceive a child, whose birth demonstrated that God acted in accordance with his character. God who gives life to the dead and calls into existence things that do not exist gave reproductive ability to Abraham's body that was already as good as dead and to Sarah's barren womb to create a new life – Isaac.

The link between God's character and the consequence of believers' faith, however, is less transparent. Paul does not say that because we believe in him who raised Jesus from the dead we will also be raised from the dead, though this conclusion is certainly implied, but that Jesus' resurrection enables our justification (v. 25).[15] The concept of justification has a strong correspondence to the recurring motif of Romans 4 that Abraham's faith was reckoned to him as righteousness (vv. 3, 9, 10, 11, 22, 23, 24). Paul's identification of God as the one who raised Jesus from the dead enables him to relate the faiths of Abraham and Christian believers in order to show that believing in the same God as Abraham – the God who has confirmed his trustworthiness by raising Jesus from the dead – leads to justification. By demonstrating that the one who raised Jesus from the dead (the object of faith for both Jewish and Gentile believers) is the same God who gives life to the dead (the object of faith of Abraham), Paul validates his claims in Romans 3.28–30 that the God of Jews is also the God of Gentiles and that this God will justify both the circumcised and the uncircumcised 'by faith apart from the works prescribed by the law' (v. 28). These considerations shed light on the nature of the analogy between the birth of Isaac and believers' justification: both outcomes lead to the creation of Abraham's progeny, i.e. the people of God.[16]

The correlation between God's character that has been revealed through raising Jesus from the dead and the soteriological implications of Jesus' resurrection is much clearer in Romans 8.11: 'If the Spirit of him who raised Jesus from the dead dwells in you, he who raised Christ from the dead will give life to your mortal bodies also through his Spirit that dwells in you.' The most remarkable aspect of this statement is that it does not mention the word 'God'. Rather, God is identified through the act of raising Jesus, both in the protasis (condition) and the apodosis (consequence) of this conditional sentence. Paul replaces the word 'God' with a descriptive characterization of God because he wants to show that by raising Jesus from the dead God is true to his character as a life-giver, so that believers can be reassured through God's Spirit that what happened to Jesus will also happen to them.

Paul's assertion in 2 Corinthians 4.14 serves the same purpose. He claims that 'we know that the one who raised the Lord Jesus will raise us also with Jesus, and will bring us with you into his presence'. Like in Romans 4.24 and 8.11, the term 'God' is here replaced by a substantive clause, 'the one who raised the Lord Jesus'. God's act of raising Jesus from the dead not only expresses the character of God but also identifies God. In this way, God's very being guarantees the correspondence between the resurrection of Jesus, as a past event, and the resurrection of believers, as a future event.

In Galatians 1.1, Paul introduces himself to his readers as 'an apostle – sent neither by human commission nor from human authorities, but through Jesus Christ and God the Father, who raised him from the dead'. In this formulation, God is not only characterized through his act of raising Jesus from the dead but also identified as the Father. The latter is most likely a term that explains the relationship between Jesus Christ and God. Since the text does not mention the redemptive benefits of Jesus' resurrection, the emphasis falls solely on God's fatherhood of Jesus that is displayed through his act of raising Jesus from the dead.[17]

Unlike the previous references, the characterization of God through his act of raising Jesus from the dead in Colossians 2.12 appears in a statement that portrays Christian baptism as a metaphorical burial and resurrection with Christ. The author of this letter, whether Paul or a close associate of Paul, tells his readers: 'when you were buried with him in baptism, you were also raised with him through faith in the power of God, who raised him from the dead'. God's ability to re-enact the resurrection of believers is plainly presumed, but the emphasis falls not on the future resurrection of believers but on their present experience of new life in Christ.

Finally, in 1 Peter 1.21 the author reminds the audience that through Jesus Christ they 'have come to trust in God, who raised him from the dead and gave him glory, so that your faith and hope are set on God'. God's character that has been revealed through the resurrection of Jesus is here presented as the foundation of Christian faith and hope. Although the text does not explicate the content of this faith and hope, an earlier reference in the letter, which mentions 'a salvation ready to be revealed in the last time' (1 Pet. 1.5), seems to suggest that the eschatological resurrection of believers is in view.

In each of these declarations, God is either identified or described through the act of raising Jesus from the dead. This way of speaking about God is derived from the principle *esse est operari*, or being-in-act. God's divine being is disclosed through God's acts, and God's acts enable humans to perceive God's character. Speaking about God in functional rather than ontological terms is not unique to Christianity. 'I am the LORD your God, who brought you out of the land of Egypt' is a standard self-presentation of God in the Jewish Scriptures (Exod. 20.2; 29.46; Lev. 11.45; 19.36; 25.38;

26.13; Num. 15.41; Deut. 5.6; Ps. 81.10). In other instances, God is identified though the acts of creation (2 Chron. 2.12; Pss 115.15; 121.2; 124.8; 146.5–6; Isa. 44.24; 45.18; Josephus, *Ag. Ap.* 2.121; *Jos. Asen.* 12.1–2). Of these two types of divine predication, the identification of God as the one who brought the Israelites out of Egypt provides a closer analogy to the Christian identification of God as the one who raised Jesus from the dead because their theological purposes are similar. In Christian literature, the resurrection of Jesus is portrayed as the essential aspect of God's being because it is constitutive for the emergence of the Christian community, similar to the way in which God's bringing the Hebrew slaves out of Egypt was constitutive for the emergence of Israel. Likewise, in each case God's redemptive activity in the past provides the basis for the expectation of redemptive acts on behalf of God's people in the present and the future. This aspect of the characterization of God is especially prominent in the New Testament, because the statements that use the resurrection of Jesus as the unique identifier of God regularly present it as the sole basis for Christian hope. The portrayal of God as the one who raised Jesus from the dead thus defines God's being in relation to those who have been redeemed through Jesus Christ. By raising Jesus, God's being has been revealed as God's being for us.[18]

4. Jesus' Resurrection and Christian Living

One of the most remarkable aspects of the early Christian interpretation of the resurrection is that it is presented not only as a past event that happened to Jesus or a future event that will happen to believers but also as an event that characterizes Christian living between these two poles, i.e. in the eschatological tension between the 'already' and the 'not yet'. Paul describes a life transformed by the resurrection as walking in the newness of life.

> Do you not know that all of us who have been baptized into Christ Jesus were baptized into his death? Therefore we have been buried with him by baptism into death, so that, just as Christ was raised from the dead by the glory of the Father, so

we too might walk in newness of life. For if we have been united with him in a death like his, we will certainly be united with him in a resurrection like his. We know that our old self was crucified with him so that the body of sin might be destroyed, and we might no longer be enslaved to sin. For whoever has died is freed from sin. But if we have died with Christ, we believe that we will also live with him. We know that Christ, being raised from the dead, will never die again; death no longer has dominion over him. The death he died, he died to sin, once for all; but the life he lives, he lives to God. So you also must consider yourselves dead to sin and alive to God in Christ Jesus. (Rom. 6.3–11)

In this passage, Paul describes Christian baptism as a symbolic dying and rising with Christ. Immersion into water (downward movement) symbolizes the believer's participation in Christ's death, while rising out of water (upward movement) symbolizes the believer's participation in Christ's resurrection. It is clear that both analogies – death and resurrection of Jesus – here function as metaphors. The first analogy – dying with Christ – describes the destruction of the old self, which Paul calls 'the body of sin', which brings freedom from sin (v. 6). The second analogy – rising with Christ – explains what this freedom from sin means. Since Christ, over whom death no longer has dominion, lives to God, those who have undergone baptism should also consider themselves dead to sin and alive to God (vv. 9–11). What Paul describes here is a radically transformed life that is lived for the glory of God. Speaking about the new life of the baptized believer as a metaphorical resurrection does not mean that bodily resurrection has been replaced by spiritualized resurrection or that eschatology has been dissolved into ethics. Along with his depiction of the resurrection as a metaphor for the newness of life (v. 4), Paul continues to speak about the resurrection with Christ that will be experienced in the future (v. 5). 'For Paul', clarifies Leander E. Keck, 'baptism does not end mortality; it begins a new morality, one that must be actualized.'[19]

What are the characteristics of the life that has been transformed by the resurrection of Jesus? Paul summons his readers to live 'as those who have been brought from death to life' by engaging in a struggle against all life-denying forces dominated by sin (Rom.

6.12–13). The author of 1 Peter speaks about 'a new birth into a living hope through the resurrection of Jesus Christ from the dead' (1 Pet. 1.3). This new life, which is traditionally described as spiritual rebirth through the Spirit, is a life that participates in the transformation of the creation that has been set in motion with Jesus' resurrection. Thorwald Lorenzen aptly articulates multiple dimensions of Christian praxis that affirm Christ's victory over the destructive forces of sin and death.

> If we 'are raised with Christ' then this resurrection reality takes shape in our relationship with God, with each other, with nature, and with history. Christian praxis must reflect these relationships. The praxis of faith, therefore, includes an existential involvement with God (conversion, worship, prayer), an intentional commitment to the neighbor (mission, evangelism, justice, liberation), a concern for nature (ecological lifestyle), and responsibility for the future (politics, economic justice).[20]

Affirming the resurrection of Jesus cannot therefore be reduced to a mere intellectual or confessional assent to its past reality. Neither can it be reduced to a hope of bodily resurrection on the last day. Affirming the resurrection also means affirming its transformative power in the present through an intentional living that upholds its promise. When we feed the hungry, love the unlovable and work for justice, we acknowledge that human bodies matter and that they will be restored by God's power to raise the dead. Through such acts we proclaim the triumph of God's justice over the systems and ideologies that promote death in all its forms. This process will be completed with God's final victory over death that will be won, in Paul's words, 'when this perishable body puts on imperishability, and this mortal body puts on immortality' (1 Cor. 15.54).

5. Summary and Conclusions

The early Christian interpreters are unanimous that the resurrection of Jesus was an act of God. By raising Jesus from the dead God has, on the one hand, pronounced judgement on Jesus' adversaries and, on the other hand, vindicated Jesus' claims and the cause for which he was crucified. This turn of events took everyone by surprise. Though many Jews believed in resurrection, nobody expected that a single individual, however extraordinary, would be raised from the dead to a new eschatological life in the midst of history. The confession that God raised Jesus from the dead can therefore be regarded as a religio-historical *novum*.[21] Yet the meaning of this new and unexpected act of God could only be conveyed through the linguistic and conceptual categories that were derived from the existing religious worldview of Jesus' followers.

The earliest formulas and confessions indicate that the early church regarded Jesus' resurrection as the beginning of the general resurrection of the dead. This is especially visible in the statements that emphasize Jesus' 'firstness', such as 'the first fruits of those who have fallen asleep' (1 Cor. 15.20) or 'the firstborn from the dead' (Col. 1.18). Within this conceptual framework, the *novum* of Jesus' resurrection consists in its timing. Jesus was raised first and those who belong to him will be raised in much the same way at the end of time. On further reflection, however, there is one significant difference between Jesus' resurrection and our resurrection. While his dead body did not undergo decay, our bodies will most certainly decompose. This difference is pertinent to our understanding of the empty tomb. While the empty tomb plays a significant role in the gospel narratives, it is questionable whether it has any relevance for the eschatological resurrection of the dead. Another issue that has emerged in modern discussions of the Christian resurrection hope is the nature of personal identity with respect to the embodied self. This question is especially germane in the conversations about the resurrection of people with disabilities, but it also has a wider significance for the understanding of the continuity between our earthly and resurrected bodies.

The *novum* of Jesus' resurrection is particularly evident in the early Christian interpretations of Jesus' messianic identity. In this regard, the resurrection of Jesus was understood as an exclusive event that uniquely determined his messiahship. It seems that the early Christians reached this conclusion on the basis of their understanding of the resurrection as God's vindication of the charge – the King of the Jews – for which Jesus was crucified, which they further elaborated through their interpretation of Israel's Scripture. Most instrumental in this process were the texts that are derived from God's promise to David in 2 Samuel 7.12–16, which includes David's offspring (i.e. David's 'seed'), divine adoption and an everlasting kingdom. We have seen that Romans 1.3–4, which gives us a glimpse into the earliest Christian exegesis, presents Jesus' resurrection as a fulfilment of the first two elements of this promise. God's act of raising Jesus from the dead is here portrayed as Jesus' royal enthronization at which he was declared to be the Son of God, similar to the divine adoption of a newly inaugurated king described in Psalm 2.7. Later texts, such as the speeches in Acts (2.29–36 and 13.30–37), further elaborate this idea with the help of Psalm 16.8–11, Psalm 110.1 and Isaiah 55.3. Peter's speech in Acts 2.29–36 portrays Jesus' resurrection as his exaltation to the right hand of God. Paul's speech in Acts 13.30–37 augments the idea of Jesus' messianic identity with the concept of an everlasting kingdom. The scriptural argument in this passage shows that by raising Jesus, God has fulfilled – wholly and conclusively – his promise to David that one of his descendants will reign over his kingdom forever.

The New Testament authors also portray Jesus' resurrection as an event that disclosed the character of God. The *novum* of various declarations that either describe or identify God as the one who raised Jesus from the dead consists in their exclusive focus on this particular act of divine self-revelation. God is portrayed not only as the one 'who gives life to the dead and calls into existence the things that do not exist' (Rom. 4.17) in general but the one 'who raised Jesus our Lord from the dead' (Rom. 4.24) in particular. The passages that portray God with reference to Jesus' resurrection regularly emphasize the redemptive purpose of this act of divine self-disclosure. By raising Jesus from the dead God has given us an assurance that this will happen to us too. This idea is most clearly expressed in 2 Corinthians 4.14, where Paul asserts that 'we know that the one who raised the Lord Jesus will raise us also with Jesus, and will bring us with you into his presence'. In theological terms, by raising Jesus from the dead God has revealed Godself not only as the Creator but also as the Redeemer.

Finally, in some passages, such as Romans 6.3–11 and 1 Peter 1.3, Jesus' resurrection functions as a metaphor for the newness of life. By raising Jesus from the dead God has started the new creation, in which we are called to participate. This participation includes the acts of worship and service within the community of believers as well as a struggle against all structures that promote death, be it though violence, political oppression, social injustice or other forms of dehumanization of life. While some Jewish texts, such as Ezekiel 37.1–14 and Hosea 6.1–3, use the resurrection of the dead as a metaphor for the restoration of Israel, the *novum* of the Christian metaphorical understanding of the resurrection consists in its applicability to Christian life as a participation in God's transformation of the creation.

Affirming Jesus' resurrection therefore means believing that God has decisively acted by raising one particular individual – Jesus of Nazareth – from the dead to a new eschatological life, hoping that we too will be raised from the dead like Jesus, acknowledging Jesus' messiahship stemming from his resurrection, trusting God's faithfulness to act on our behalf as he once acted on behalf of Jesus, and living as resurrection people who affirm the fullness of life and struggle against all forms of death.

Notes

1 See Amos Yong, *Theology and Down Syndrome: Reimagining Disability in Late Modernity* (Waco, TX: Baylor University Press, 2007), 259–92. Yong claims that '[t]o say that people with disabilities ... will no longer be disabled in heaven threatens the continuity between their present identities and that of their resurrected bodies' (ibid., 269).

2 See the collection of essays edited by Ted Peters, Robert John Russell and Michael Welker, *Resurrection: Theological and Scientific Assessments* (Grand Rapids, MI: Eerdmans, 2002).

3 See, for example, the exchange on this subject between Marcus J. Borg and N. T. Wright in *The Meaning of Jesus: Two Visions*, 31–76.

4 For a comprehensive analysis of scriptural arguments in these passages, see Lidija Novakovic, *Raised from the Dead According to Scripture: The Role of Israel's Scripture in the Early Christian Interpretations of Jesus' Resurrection* (JCT 12; London: Bloomsbury T&T Clark, 2012), 133–46, 198–213.

5 My translation.

6 The structure of Rom. 1.3–4 is similar to the structure of 1 Tim. 3.16 ('He was revealed in flesh, vindicated in spirit') and 1 Pet. 3.18 ('He was put to death in the flesh, but made alive in the spirit').

7 Robert Jewett, 'The Redaction and Use of an Early Christian Confession in Romans 1:3–4', in *The Living Text: Essays in Honor of Ernest W. Saunders* (eds. Dennis E. Groh and Robert Jewett; Lanham, MD: University Press of America, 1985), 104; Georg Strecker, *Theology of the New Testament* (ed. Friedrich Wilhelm Horn; trans. M. Eugene Boring; Louisville: Westminster John Knox, 2000), 69.

8 Eduard Schweizer, *Lordship and Discipleship* (SBT 28; London: SCM, 1960), 59.

9 James D. G. Dunn, *Christology in the Making: A New Testament Inquiry into the Origins of the Doctrine of Incarnation* (2nd edn; London: SCM, 1989), 35 (emphasis removed).

10 The idea that Jesus is seated at the right hand of God is found in numerous New Testament passages that either quote (Mk 12.36; Mt. 22.44; Lk. 20.32–43; Acts 2.34–35; Heb. 1.13) or allude to Ps. 110.1 (Mt. 26.64; Mk 14.62; Lk. 22.69; Acts 2.33; 5.31; 7.55–56; Rom. 8.34; Eph. 1.20; Col. 3.1; Heb. 1.3; 8.1; 10.12–13; 12.2; 1 Pet. 3.22; Rev. 3.21). In all these texts, the imagery of Christ seated at God's right hand conveys the idea of his messianic enthronization.

11 My translation.

12 For a thorough interpretation of the role of the quotation of Isa. 55.3 in Paul's synagogue homily, see Evald Lövestam, *Son and Saviour: A Study of Acts 13,32–37* (trans. Michael J. Petry; ConBNT 18; Lund: Gleerup, 1961), 48–81.

13 Karl Barth, *Church Dogmatics* IV/1 (trans. Geoffrey W. Bromiley; Edinburgh: T&T Clark, 1956), 304.

14 Thorwald Lorenzen, *Resurrection and Discipleship: Interpretative Models, Biblical Reflections, Theological Consequences* (Maryknoll, NY: Orbis, 1995), 257.

15 Michael F. Bird, '"Raised for Our Justification": A Fresh Look at Romans 4:25', *Colloquium* 35 (2003): 31–46.

16 J. R. Daniel Kirk, *Unlocking Romans: Resurrection and the Justification of God* (Grand Rapids, MI: Eerdmans, 2008), 75.

17 Martinus C. de Boer, *Galatians: A Commentary* (NTL; Louisville, KY: Westminster John Knox, 2011), 24–5.

18 Eberhard Jüngel, *God's Being Is in Becoming: The Trinitarian Being of God in the Theology of Karl Barth* (trans. John Webster; Edinburgh: T&T Clark, 2001), 120.

19 Leander E. Keck, *Romans* (ANTC; Nashville: Abingdon Press, 2005), 161 (original emphasis removed).

20 Lorenzen, *Resurrection and Discipleship*, 229.
21 Jürgen Moltmann, *Theology of Hope: On the Ground and the Implications of a Christian Eschatology* (trans. James W. Leitch; London: SCM Press, 1967), 179; Lorenzen, *Resurrection and Discipleship*, 116–26.

BIBLIOGRAPHY

Allison, Dale C., Jr. *Resurrecting Jesus: The Earliest Christian Tradition and its Interpreters*. London: T&T Clark, 2005.
Asher, Jeffrey R. *Polarity and Change in 1 Corinthians 15: A Study of Metaphysics, Rhetoric, and Resurrection*. Hermeneutische Untersuchungen zur Theologie 42. Tübingen: Mohr Siebeck, 2000.
Avery-Peck, Alan J. and Jacob Neusner, eds. *Death, Life-After-Death, Resurrection and the World-to-Come in the Judaisms of Antiquity*. Part 4 of *Judaism in Late Antiquity*. Handbuch der Orientalistik I/49. Leiden: Brill, 2000.
Barth, Karl. *Church Dogmatics* IV/1. Translated by Geoffrey W. Bromiley. Edinburgh: T&T Clark, 1956.
Bennett, Gillian and Kate Mary Bennett. 'The Presence of the Dead: An Empirical Study'. *Mortality* (2000): 139–57.
Bird, Michael F. '"Raised for Our Justification": A Fresh Look at Romans 4:25'. *Colloquium* 35 (2003): 31–46.
Bode, Edward Lynn. *The First Easter Morning: The Gospel Accounts of the Women's Visit to the Tomb of Jesus*. Analecta Biblica 45. Rome: Biblical Institute Press, 1970.
Boer, Martinus C. de. *Galatians: A Commentary*. The New Testament Library. Louisville, KY.: Westminster John Knox, 2011.
Brock, Ann Graham. *Mary Magdalene, the First Apostle: The Struggle for Authority*. Harvard Theological Studies 51. Cambridge, MA: Harvard University Press, 2003.
Brown, Raymond E. *The Gospel according to John (xiii–xxi)*. The Anchor Bible 29A. Garden City, NY: Doubleday, 1970.
Bultmann, Rudolf. *The History of the Synoptic Tradition*. Translated by John Marsh. New York: Harper & Row, 1963.
Bultmann, Rudolf. *The Gospel of John: A Commentary*. Translated by G. R. Beasley-Murray et al. Philadelphia: Westminster Press, 1971.
Burton, Julian. 'Contact with the Dead: A Common Experience?' *Fate* 35.4 (1982): 65–73.
Carroll, Michael P. *The Cult of the Virgin Mary: Psychological Origins*. Princeton, NJ: Princeton University Press, 1986.

Cavallin, Hans C. C. *Life After Death: Paul's Argument for the Resurrection of the Dead in 1 Cor 15, Part I: An Enquiry into the Jewish Background*. Coniectanea Biblica: New Testament Series 7. Lund: Gleerup, 1974.
Charlesworth, James H., ed. *The Old Testament Pseudepigrapha*. 2 vols. New York: Doubleday, 1983–85.
Charlesworth, James H. et al. *Resurrection: The Origin and Future of a Biblical Doctrine*. Faith and Scholarship Colloquies. London: T&T Clark, 2006.
Coakley, Sarah. 'Is the Resurrection a "Historical" Event? Some Muddles and Mysteries' in *The Resurrection of Jesus Christ*. Edited by Paul Avis. London: Darton, Longman & Todd, 1993, 85–11.
Collins, Adela Yarbro. 'The Empty Tomb in the Gospel according to Mark' in *Hermes and Athena: Biblical Exegesis and Philosophical Theology*. Edited by E. Stump and T. P. Flint. University of Notre Dame Studies in the Philosophy of Religion 7. Notre Dame: University of Notre Dame Press, 1993, 107–37.
Collins, Adela Yarbro. 'Apotheosis and Resurrection' in *The New Testament and Hellenistic Judaism*. Edited by Peder Borgen and Søren Giversen. Peabody, Mass.: Hendrickson, 1995, 88–100.
Collins, Adela Yarbro. *Mark: A Commentary*. Hermeneia. Minneapolis: Fortress, 2007.
Collins, John J. *Daniel: A Commentary on the Book of Daniel*. Hermeneia. Minneapolis: Fortress, 1993.
Craig, William Lane. *The Historical Argument for the Resurrection of Jesus*. Texts and Studies in Religion 23. Lewiston, NY: Edwin Mellen, 1985.
Craig, William Lane. *Assessing the New Testament Evidence for the Historicity of the Resurrection of Jesus*. Studies in Bible and Early Christianity 16. Lewiston, NY: Edwin Mellen, 1989.
Craig, William Lane. 'Did Jesus Rise from the Dead?' in *Jesus under Fire: Modern Scholarship Reinvents the Historical Jesus*. Edited by Michael J. Wilkins and J. P. Moreland. Grand Rapids, MI: Zondervan, 1995, 141–76.
Craig, William Lane and Gerd Lüdemann. *Jesus' Resurrection: Fact or Figment? A Debate between William Lane Craig & Gerd Lüdemann*. Edited by Paul Copan and Ronald K. Tacelli. Downers Grove, IL: InterVarsity Press, 2000.
Craig, William Lane, John Dominic Crossan and William F. Buckely, Jr. *Will the Real Jesus Please Stand Up? A Debate between William Lane Craig and John Dominic Crossan*. Edited by Paul Copan. Grand Rapids, MI: Baker, 1998.

Crossan, John Dominic. 'Empty Tomb and Absent Lord' in *The Passion in Mark: Studies on Mark 14–16*. Edited by Werner H. Kelber. Philadelphia: Fortress, 1976, 134–52.
Crossan, John Dominic. *The Historical Jesus: The Life of a Mediterranean Jewish Peasant*. San Francisco: HarperSanFrancisco, 1991.
Crossan, John Dominic. *The Birth of Christianity: Discovering What Happened in the Years Immediately after the Execution of Jesus*. San Francisco: HarperSanFrancisco, 1998.
Crossan, John Dominic and N. T. Wright. *The Resurrection of Jesus: John Dominic Crossan and N. T. Wright in Dialogue*. Edited by Robert B. Stewart. Minneapolis: Fortress, 2006.
Dalferth, Ingolf U. 'The Resurrection: The Grammar of "Raised"' in *Biblical Concepts and Our World*. Edited by D. Z. Phillips and Mario von der Ruhr. Claremont Studies in the Philosophy of Religion. New York: Palgrave Macmillan, 2004, 190–212.
Davies, W. D. and Dale C. Allison Jr. *A Critical and Exegetical Commentary on the Gospel According to Saint Matthew*. International Critical Commentary. 3 vols. Edinburgh: T&T Clark, 1988–7.
Delobel, Joël. 'The Corinthians' (Un)Belief in the Resurrection' in *Resurrection in the New Testament*. Edited by Reimund Bieringer, Veronica Koperski and Bianca Lataire. Bibliotheca Ephemeridum Theologicarum Lovaniensium 165. Leuven: Peeters, 2002, 343–55.
Dunn, James D. G. *Christology in the Making: A New Testament Inquiry into the Origins of the Doctrine of Incarnation*. 2nd edn. London: SCM, 1989.
Dunn, James D. G. *Jesus Remembered*. Vol. 1 of *Christianity in the Making*. Grand Rapids: Eerdmans, 2003.
Ehrman, Bart D. and Zlatko Pleše, trans. *The Apocryphal Gospels: Texts and Translations*. Oxford: Oxford University Press, 2011.
Endsjø, Dag Øistein. 'Immortal Bodies before Christ: Bodily Continuity in Ancient Greece and 1 Corinthians'. *Journal for the Study of the New Testament* 30 (2008): 417–36.
Enslin, Morton Scott. *Christian Beginnings*. New York: Harper & Brothers, 1938.
Evans, Craig A. 'Jewish Burial Traditions and the Resurrection of Jesus'. *Journal for the Study of the Historical Jesus* 3.2 (2005): 233–48.
García Martínez, Florentino and Eibert J. C. Tigchelaar. *The Dead Sea Scrolls: Study Edition*. 2 vols. Leiden: Brill, 1997–8.
Ginsberg, Harold L. 'The Oldest Interpretation of the Suffering Servant'. *Vetus Testamentum* 3 (1953): 400–4.
Goulder, Michael. 'The Baseless Fabric of a Vision' in *Resurrection Reconsidered*. Edited by Gavin D'Costa. Oxford: Oneworld, 1996, 48–61.

Grimby, Agneta. 'Hallucinations Following the Loss of a Spouse: Common and Normal Events among the Elderly'. *Journal of Clinical Geropsychology* 4 (1998): 65–74.

Gundry, Robert H. 'Trimming the Debate' in *Jesus' Resurrection: Fact or Figment*. Edited by Paul Copan and Ronald K. Tacelli. Downers Grove, IL: InterVarsity Press, 2000, 104–23.

Habermas, Gary R. 'Explaining Away Jesus' Resurrection: The Recent Revival of Hallucination Theories'. *Christian Research Journal* 23.4 (2001): 26–31, 47–9.

Habermas, Gary R. *The Risen Jesus and Future Hope*. Lanham, MD: Rowman & Littlefield, 2003.

Habermas, Gary R. and Antony G. N. Flew, *Did Jesus Rise from the Dead? The Resurrection Debate*. Edited by Terry L. Miethe. San Francisco: Harper & Row, 1987.

Harrington, Daniel J. 'Afterlife Expectations in Pseudo-Philo, 4 Ezra, and 2 Baruch, and their Implications for the New Testament' in *Resurrection in the New Testament*. Edited by Reimund Bieringer, Veronica Koperski, and Bianca Lataire. Bibliotheca Ephemeridum Theologicarum Lovaniensium 165. Leuven: Peeters, 2002, 21–34.

Hays, Richard B. *First Corinthians*. Interpretation. Louisville: John Knox Press, 1997.

Holmes, Michael W., trans. *The Apostolic Fathers: Greek Text and English Translations*. 3rd edn. Grand Rapids, MI: Baker Academic, 2007.

Jewett, Robert. 'The Redaction and Use of an Early Christian Confession in Romans 1:3–4' in *The Living Text: Essays in Honor of Ernest W. Saunders*. Edited by Dennis E. Groh and Robert Jewett. Lanham, MD: University Press of America, 1985, 99–122.

Jüngel, Eberhard. *God's Being Is in Becoming: The Trinitarian Being of God in the Theology of Karl Barth*. Translated by John Webster. Edinburgh: T&T Clark, 2001.

Kalish, Richard A. and David K. Reynolds, 'Phenomenological Reality and Post-Death Contact'. *Journal for the Scientific Study of Religion* 12 (1973): 209–21.

Keck, Leander E. *Romans*. Abingdon New Testament Commentaries. Nashville: Abingdon Press, 2005.

Keener, Craig S. *The Gospel of John: A Commentary*. 2 vols. Peabody, MA: Hendrickson, 2003.

Kirk, J. R. Daniel. *Unlocking Romans: Resurrection and the Justification of God*. Grand Rapids, MI: Eerdmans, 2008.

Koester, Craig R. 'Jesus' Resurrection, the Signs, and the Dynamics of Faith in the Gospel of John' in *The Resurrection of Jesus in the Gospel of John*. Edited by Craig R. Koester and Reimund Bieringer.

Wissenschaftliche Untersuchungen zum Neuen Testament 222; Tübingen: Mohr Siebeck, 2008, 47–74.

Koester, Helmut. *Ancient Christian Gospels: Their History and Development*. London/ Philadelphia: SCM/Trinity Press International, 1990.

Lake, Kirsopp. *The Historical Evidence for the Resurrection of Jesus Christ*. London: Williams & Norgate, 1907.

Lehmann, Karl. *Auferweckt am dritten Tag nach der Schrift: Früheste Christologie, Bekenntnisbildung und Schriftauslegung im Lichte von 1 Kor. 15,3–5*. Quaestiones disputatae 38. Freiburg: Herder, 1968.

Licona, Michael R. *The Resurrection of Jesus: A New Historiographical Approach*. Downers Grove, IL: IVP Academic, 2010.

Lindars, Barnabas. *The Gospel of John*. New Century Bible. London: Oliphants, 1972.

Lorenzen, Thorwald, *Resurrection and Discipleship: Interpretative Models, Biblical Reflections, Theological Consequences*. Maryknoll, NY: Orbis, 1995.

Lövestam, Evald. *Son and Saviour: A Study of Acts 13.32–37*. Translated by Michael J. Petry. Coniectanea Neotestamentica 18. Lund: Gleerup, 1961.

Lowder, Jeffery J. 'Historical Evidence and the Empty Tomb Story: A Reply to William Lane Craig' in *The Empty Tomb: Jesus Beyond the Grave*. Edited by Robert M. Price and Jeffery J. Lowder. Amherst, NY: Prometheus, 2005, 261–306.

Lüdemann, Gerd. *The Resurrection of Jesus: History, Experience, Theology*. Translated by John Bowden; London: SCM Press, 1994.

Lüdemann, Gerd. *The Resurrection of Christ: A Historical Inquiry*. Amherst, NY: Prometheus, 2004.

Magness, Jodi. 'Ossuaries and the Burials of Jesus and James'. *Journal of Biblical Literature* 124 (2005): 121–54.

Martin, Dale B. *The Corinthian Body*. New Haven, CT: Yale University Press, 1995.

Metzger, Bruce M. *A Textual Commentary on the Greek New Testament*. 2nd edn. Stuttgart: Deutsche Bibelgesellschaft/United Bible Societies, 1994.

Moltmann, Jürgen. *Theology of Hope: On the Ground and the Implications of a Christian Eschatology*. Translated by James W. Leitch; London: SCM Press, 1967.

Nickelsburg, George W. E. 'Judgment, Life-After-Death, and Resurrection in the Apocrypha and the Non-Apocalyptic Pseudepigrapha' in *Death, Life-After-Death, Resurrection and the World-to-Come in the Judaisms of Antiquity* (part 4 of *Judaism in Late Antiquity*. Edited by Alan J. Avery-Peck and Jacob Neusner. Handbuch der Orientalistik I/49. Leiden: Brill, 2000, 141–62.

Nickelsburg, George W. E. *1 Enoch 1: A Commentary on the Book of 1 Enoch, Chapters 1–36; 81–108.* Hermeneia. Minneapolis: Fortress, 2001.

Nickelsburg, George W. E. *Resurrection, Immortality, and Eternal Life in Intertestamental Judaism and Early Christianity.* Expanded edition. Harvard Theological Studies 56. Cambridge, MA: Harvard University Press, 2006.

Nickelsburg, George W. E. and James C. VanderKam. *1 Enoch: A New Translation.* Minneapolis: Fortress, 2004.

Novakovic, Lidija. *Raised from the Dead According to Scripture: The Role of Israel's Scripture in the Early Christian Interpretations of Jesus' Resurrection.* Jewish and Christian Texts in Contexts and Related Studies Series 12; London: Bloomsbury T&T Clark, 2012.

Ohayon, M. M. 'Prevalence of Hallucinations and their Pathological Associations in the General Populations'. *Psychiatry Research* 97 (2000): 153–64.

Olson, Richard et al. 'Hallucinations of Widowhood'. *Journal of the American Geriatric Society* 33 (1985): 543–7.

Pannenberg, Wolfhart. *Jesus – God and Man.* Translated by Lewis L. Wilkins and Duane A. Priebe. Philadelphia: Westminster Press, 1968.

Pannenberg, Wolfhart. 'History and the Reality of the Resurrection' in *Resurrection Reconsidered.* Edited by Gavin D'Costa. Oxford: Oneworld, 1996, 62–72.

Peters, Ted. 'The Future of the Resurrection' in *The Resurrection of Jesus: John Dominic Crossan and N. T. Wright in Dialogue.* Edited by Robert B. Stewart. Minneapolis: Fortress, 2006, 149–69.

Peters, Ted, Robert John Russell and Michael Welker, eds. *Resurrection: Theological and Scientific Assessments.* Grand Rapids, MI: Eerdmans, 2002.

Plank, Karl A. 'Resurrection Theology: The Corinthian Controversy Reexamined'. *Perspectives in Religious Studies* 8 (1981): 41–54.

Puech, Émile. *La croyance des Esséniens en la vie future: Immortalité, résurrection, vie éternelle? Histoire d'une croyance dans le Judaïsme ancient.* Études Bibliques 21–22. 2 vols. Paris: Gabalda, 1993.

Rees, William Dewi. 'The Hallucinations of Widowhood'. *British Medical Journal* 4 (1971): 37–41.

Reid, Barbara E. *Choosing the Better Part? Women in the Gospel of Luke.* Collegeville, MI: Liturgical Press, 1996.

Schenkel, Daniel. *A Sketch of the Character of Jesus: A Biblical Essay.* London: Longmans, Green, 1869.

Schweizer, Eduard. *Lordship and Discipleship.* Studies in Biblical Theology 28. London: SCM, 1960.

Segal, Alan F. *Life after Death: A History of the Afterlife in the Religions*

of the West. The Anchor Bible Reference Library. New York: Doubleday, 2004.
Segal, Alan F. 'The Resurrection: Faith or History?' in *The Resurrection of Jesus: John Dominic Crossan and N. T. Wright in Dialogue*. Edited by Robert B. Stewart. Minneapolis: Fortress, 2006, 149–69.
Sellin, Gerhard. *Der Streit um die Auferstehung der Toten*. Forschungen zur Religion und Literatur des Alten und Neuen Testaments 138. Göttingen: Vandenhoeck & Ruprecht, 1986.
Smith, Daniel A. *Revisiting the Empty Tomb: The Early History of Easter*. Minneapolis: Fortress, 2010.
Smith, D. Moody. *John*. Abingdon New Testament Commentaries. Nashville: Abingdon, 1999.
Spong, John Shelby. *Resurrection: Myth or Reality? A Bishop's Search for the Origins of Christianity*. San Francisco: HarperSanFrancisco, 1994.
Strecker, Georg. *Theology of the New Testament*. Edited by Friedrich Wilhelm Horn. Translated by M. Eugene Boring. Louisville: Westminster John Knox, 2000.
Talbert, Charles H. *Luke and the Gnostics: An Examination of Lucan Purpose*. Nashville: Abingdon, 1966.
Troeltsch, Ernst. 'Historical and Dogmatic Method in Theology' in *Religion in History*. Translated by James Luther Adams and Walter F. Bense. Minneapolis: Fortress, 1991, 11–32.
Tuckett, Christopher M. 'The Corinthians Who Say "There Is No Resurrection of the Dead" (1 Cor 15,12)' in *The Corinthian Correspondence*. Edited by R. Bieringer. Bibliotheca Ephemeridum Theologicarum Lovaniensium 125. Leuven: Peeters, 1996, 247–75.
Wedderburn, A. J. M. 'The Problem of the Denial of the Resurrection in 1 Corinthians XV'. *Novum Testamentum* 23 (1981): 229–41.
Westcott, Brooke F. and Fenton J. A. Hort. *The New Testament in the Original Greek*. 2 vols. Cambridge: Macmillan, 1881.
Wiebe, Phillip H. *Visions of Jesus: Direct Encounters from the New Testament to Today*. Oxford: Oxford University Press, 1997.
Wright, N. T. 'The Transforming Reality of the Bodily Resurrection' in *The Meaning of Jesus: Two Visions*. Edited by Marcus Borg and N. T. Wright. New York: HarperCollins, 1999, 111–27.
Wright, N. T. *The Resurrection of the Son of God*. Vol. 3 of *Christian Origins and the Question of God*. Minneapolis: Fortress, 2003.
Yong, Amos. *Theology and Down Syndrome: Reimagining Disability in Late Modernity*. Waco, TX: Baylor University Press, 2007.
Zimdars-Swartz, Sandra. *Encountering Mary: From La Salette to Medjugorje*. Princeton, NJ: Princeton University Press, 1991.

INDEX

Jewish Scriptures/Old Testament

Genesis
1–2	71
1.13	55
2.7	70, 71
5.24	138, 150
12.7	62, 148
17.1	62, 148
18	148
18.1–2	148
18.1	62, 148
18.2	148
18.3–15	148
18.8	148
18.16	148
18.22	148
19	148
19.1–11	148
19.1	148
19.3	148
19.5	148
19.8	148
19.10	148
19.12	148
19.15	148
19.16	148
22.4	55
26.2	62, 148
31.22	55
34.25	55
40.20	55
42.18	55

Exodus
3.2	62, 148
19.11	55
19.15	55
19.16	55
20.2	179
29.46	179

Leviticus
7.17	55
7.18	55
11.45	179
19.6	55
19.7	55
19.36	180
25.38	180
26.13	180

Numbers
7.24	55
15.41	180
19.12	55
19.19	55
29.20	55

Deuteronomy
5.6	180
18.10–12	147
21.22–23	139
26.14	7

Joshua
3.2	55
9.17	55

INDEX

Judges
5.20	14
6.11–24	148
6.12	62, 148
6.13	148
6.15	148
13.16	148
20.30	55

1 Samuel
20.12	55
30.1	55
28.3	147
28.4–19	146, 147
28.9	147

2 Samuel
1.2	55
7.12–16	168, 174, 175, 176, 184
7.12	169
7.13	169
7.14	169, 175
23.1–5	175

1 Kings
3.5	62, 148
3.18	55
9.2	62, 148
12.12	55

2 Kings
2.11–12	138, 150
2.15–18	138
20.5	55
20.8	55

2 Chronicles
2.12	180
3.1	62, 148
10.12	55
13.5	175
21.7	175

Ezra
6.15	55

Esther
5.1	55

Job
14.12–14	8
17.16	14
26.5–6	7
38.7	14

Psalms (Hebrew Bible)
2.2	168
2.7	168, 174, 175, 184
16	174
16.8–11	170, 172, 173, 184
16.9–10	8
16.10	8, 174
73.23–26	8
81.10	180
88.11	7
89.4–5	175
89.27–30	175
106.28	7
110.1	172, 173, 184, 186 n.10
115.15	180
121.2	180
124.8	180
132.11	171, 175
146.5–6	180

Psalms (LXX)
15.8–11	172, 173
15.9–10	171
15.9	170, 171
15.10	8, 174, 175
15.11	170
131.11	171

Proverbs			12.2	13, 14, 43, 57
2.18	7		12.3	13, 14, 20, 40, 44, 45 n.5, 46 n.5, 149
9.18	7			
21.16	7			

Ecclesiastes
9.5–10   8

Hosea
6   11
6.1–3   8, 10, 185
6.2–3   56
6.2   10, 55, 56, 74

Isaiah
14.9   7
24–27   11
26.14   7, 11, 12
26.16–18   11
26.18   11
26.19   8, 11, 12, 57
26.21   11
44.24   180
45.18   180
52.13–53.12 46 n.5
53.11   45 n.5
55.3   174, 175, 184, 186 n.12

Amos
9.11–12   175

Jonah
2.1   55

Apocrypha/Deuterocanonical Books

Tobit
5.4–5   148
5.9   79
12.19   148

Wisdom of Solomon
3.1–9   151
5.1–5   151

Ezekiel
37   11, 124
37.1–14   8, 185
37.1–10   8–9, 11
37.5–14   71
37.5   71
37.6   71
37.8   71
37.9   71
37.10   71
37.11–14   9, 27
37.12   57

Sirach
17.28   8
41.4   8

2 Maccabees
3.26   79
3.33–34   79
6.18–31   22
6.26–28   22
7   22, 23, 44, 124
7.9   23
7.10–11   23
7.14   23
7.22–23   24, 71
7.28–29   24

Daniel
8.10   14
8.15–16   79
11.32–35   14
11.33   46 n.5
12.1–3   8, 12, 14, 15, 17, 35, 43

7.28	24	28.5–8	96
14.37–46	23	28.5	85
14.46	23, 71	28.6	85
15.11	147	28.7	52, 85
15.12–16	147, 150	28.8–10	122
		28.9–10	61, 96, 104

New Testament

		28.9	124
Matthew		28.11–15	80, 83, 138
4.8	105	28.12–15	132, 136
5.1	105	28.16–20	61, 85, 105, 118, 119, 121
8.1	105		
12.40	54, 75 n.2	28.16	105
14.23	105	28.17	106, 123
15.29	105		
16.13–19	75 n.5	*Mark*	
16.21	54, 83, 153	8.31	54, 153
17.1	105	9.31	54, 153
17.22–23	153	10.32–34	153
17.23	54, 83	10.34	54
20.17–19	153	12.18–27	149
20.19	54, 83	12.25	149
22.23–33	149	12.36	186 n.10
22.30	149	14.28	81
22.44	186 n.10	14.62	186 n.10
24.3	105	15.26	166
24.7	84	15.40	79
26.32	85	15.42–47	77, 139
26.64	186 n.10	15.47	79
27.37	166	16.1–8	79, 94, 95, 96, 97, 125, 133, 134, 137, 138, 139, 151
27.50–53	57		
27.51–53	84		
27.52–53	138, 162		
27.57–71	139	16.1	138
27.59–61	77	16.2	54
27.62–66	82, 136, 138	16.3–4	138
27.63–64	54	16.6	52, 87
27.64	84	16.7	78, 81, 118, 119
28.1–10	83, 85	16.8	78, 81, 96, 97, 101, 138, 152
28.1–8	94, 95		
28.1	54	16.9–19	78
28.2–3	96	16.12	123
28.2	96		
28.4	96, 138		

Luke

1.12–13	87
1.29–30	87
1.32–33	176
2.9–10	87
5	75 n.5
5.1–11	75 n.5, 121
8.1–3	87
9.16	109
9.22	54, 87, 153
9.44	87, 153
18.31–33	75 n.2, 87, 153
18.33	54
20.27–39	149
20.32–43	186 n.10
20.34–36	149
22.19	109
22.69	186 n.10
23.4	124
23.14–15	124
23.38	166
23.41	124
23.47	124
23.53	77
24.1–12	86, 94, 95
24.1	54
24.2	86
24.3	86
24.4–7	96
24.4	86
24.5	86, 87
24.6–7	54
24.6	88
24.9–11	96
24.11	98, 134
24.12	88, 91, 93, 98, 101, 135, 152
24.13–35	63, 107–8, 112, 122
24.13–15	108
24.13	54
24.16	123
24.21	55, 108, 123
24.22–23	87
24.24	88, 91, 93, 101, 109
24.25–27	92, 110
24.25–26	123
24.27	108
24.30–31	145
24.30	108
24.31	108, 125, 130
24.33	110
24.34	60
24.35	106, 121
24.36–49	61, 63, 109–10, 118, 119, 121
24.36–43	122
24.36	110, 125, 130
24.37–39	152
24.39–40	145
24.39	110, 123, 124
24.41–43	106, 124, 145, 152
24.44–47	92, 110
24.44	111
24.45–46	49
24.45	123
24.46	54, 75 n.2, 165, 172
24.47	120
24.49	111
24.50–53	113

John

1.50	102 n.9
2.22	49, 52
4.48	102 n.9
4.53	102 n.9
5.21	71
5.44	102 n.9
6.1	117
6.36	102 n.9
6.47	102 n.9
6.64	102 n.9

9.38	102 n.9	20.25	102 n.9, 113, 114, 124
10.25	102 n.9		
10.26	102 n.9	20.26	55, 125, 130
11.15	102 n.9	20.27	124, 145
11.40	102 n.9	20.28	116
14.29	102 n.9	20.29	93, 102 n.9, 116
19.19	166	21	75 n.5, 116
19.31–37	114	21.1–19	75 n.5
19.35	102 n.9	21.1–14	116–7, 119, 121
19.38–42	78	21.1	119
20	116, 117	21.4	117, 123
20.1–13	89, 94, 95, 138	21.12–13	124, 145, 152
20.1–2	96	21.14	52, 117
20.1	54	21.15–19	121
20.2–10	90, 91		
20.2–3	98	*Acts*	
20.2	80	1.1–11	113
20.3–10	96, 135, 152	1.3–9	119
20.3	90, 101	1.3	103
20.8	92, 93, 150	1.6–11	63
20.9	92, 93, 150	1.8	120
20.11–18	61	2	174, 175
20.11–13	96	2.1–4	115
20.11	90	2.14–36	170
20.13	80, 101, 123	2.14–21	170
20.14–18	96, 111–2, 122	2.22–36	136, 170
20.14	125	2.22	170
20.15	80	2.23	170
20.16	145	2.24	51, 170
20.17	104, 112, 120, 124	2.25–28	170
		2.26	171
20.19–29	118, 119	2.27	171
20.19–23	61, 113–4, 118, 121	2.29–36	166, 169, 170–1, 175, 176, 184, 184
20.19	54–5, 120, 125, 130	2.31	8, 171, 172
20.20	114, 123, 124, 145, 152	2.32–33	173
		2.32	172
20.21	115	2.33	172, 173, 186 n.10
20.22	120		
20.24–29	61, 106, 115, 119, 123, 152	2.34–35	186 n.10
		2.36	162, 172, 173
20.24	114	2.42	109

2.46	109	*Romans*	
3.14–15	51	1.1–4	167
3.26	51	1.3–4	57, 134, 162, 166, 167, 168, 169, 175, 176, 184, 185 n.6
5.31	186 n.10		
7.55–56	186 n.10		
9	63		
9.1–9	63, 122, 129, 144, 147	3.28–30	178
		3.28	178
9.3	63	4	178
9.7	63	4.3	178
10.40–41	63, 110, 145	4.9	178
10.40	51, 54	4.10	178
10.41	124	4.11	178
12.9	150	4.13–25	177
12.15	150	4.16	177
13	174	4.17	71, 177, 184
13.16–41	173	4.18	177
13.17–22	173	4.19	177
13.23–37	173	4.22	178
13.23	173, 176	4.23	178
13.29	139	4.24	51, 162, 176, 177, 177, 178, 184
13.30–37	166, 173, 174, 184, 184		
		4.25	52, 177
13.32–41	136	6.3–11	180–1, 184
13.32–33	51, 174, 176	6.4	52, 162, 181
13.33–35	174	6.5	181
13.33	168, 175	6.6	181
13.34–37	176	6.9–11	181
13.34	175	6.12–13	181–2
13.35	175	7.4	53
13.36	175	8.11	51, 71, 162, 176, 178
13.37	175		
17.3	165	8.29	58, 162
20.7	109	8.34	53, 113, 186 n.10
22.6–11	63, 122, 144, 147	10.9	51
22.6	63		
22.9	63	*1 Corinthians*	
26.12–19	63, 122, 144, 147	6.14	51
26.13	63	9.1	62, 122, 144
26.19	63	15	57, 58, 59, 64, 74, 125, 133
26.23	58, 162		
		15.1–11	64
		15.2	65

15.3–8	59, 62, 125	15.40–41	68
15.3–7	59, 99, 141, 151	15.42–44	130
15.3–4	53, 97, 132, 133, 134, 136, 165	15.42	69
		15.44	69
15.4	11, 53, 55, 56, 151	15.45–49	69–70
		15.45	70, 71
15.5–8	119	15.47–49	71
15.5–7	54, 117, 118, 122, 144	15.49	72
		15.50	72, 73, 124
15.5–6	145	15.51–57	72–3
15.5	60, 119, 121	15.53	164
15.6	145	15.54	73, 164, 182
15.7	60, 61, 122		
15.8	62, 122, 144	2 Corinthians	
15.11	65	4.14	52, 162, 176, 178, 184
15.12–28	64		
15.12–19	58, 64, 65, 66, 163	Galatians	
15.13	66	1.1	51, 162, 176, 179
15.14	1, 49	1.15–16	62, 122
15.16–18	164	1.16	144
15.17–18	49		
15.20–28	66, 163	Ephesians	
15.20–23	163	1.20	52, 186 n.10
15.20	53, 58, 66, 162, 183	Philippians	
15.21–22	71	2.8–9	113
15.21	162	2.9	173
15.22	67	3.20–21	72
15.23–28	67		
15.23	64, 67	Colossians	
15.24–28	163	1.18	58, 162, 183
15.24	67	2.12	52, 162, 176–7, 179
15.26	67		
15.27	72	3.1	186 n.10
15.35–58	67		
15.35–57	141	1 Thessalonians	
15.35–49	72	1.10	52
15.36–38	68		
15.36	68	1 Timothy	
15.37	130, 165	3.16	185 n.6
15.38	165		
15.39	68, 69		

Hebrews

1.3–13	173
1.3	186 n.10
1.13	186 n.10
1.5	168
5.5	168
8.1	173, 186 n.10
10.12–13	186 n.10
11.5	138
12.2	186 n.10

1 Peter

1.3	167, 182, 184
1.5	179
1.21	52, 162, 177, 179
3.18	71, 185 n.6
3.21–22	113
3.22	186 n.10

Revelation

1.5	58, 162
3.21	186 n.10

Pseudepigrapha

1 Enoch

1–36	15
22	15
22.1–13	15–6, 17, 20
22.3	17
22.13	17
24.2–25.7	17
25.3–7	17–8
37–71	20
39.3–5	20, 149
51.1	20
51.5	20
58.3	21
62.15	21
70.1–3	138
85–90	18
90.21	14
90.33	18
90.37–38	18
91–105	19
102.4–5	19
103.2–4	19
103.3–4	22
104.2–6	14
104.2	19
104.4	19, 149

3 Enoch

6.1	138
7.1	138

Jubilees

23.16–31	21
23.30–31	21

Pseudo-Philo, *Liber Antiquitatum Biblicarum*

3.10	34–35
9.10	98
19.12–13	35
23.13	34
33.3	34
42.5	98
44.10	34

4 Ezra

4.36	36
7	41
7.26–44	36
7.26–32	166
7.32	37
7.37–38	37
7.37	37
7.78–80	36
7.91	36
7.101	36
8.51–54	37
14.9	138, 150
14.48 (Syr)	138, 150

2 Baruch

21.13–15	38

21.17	38
21.23	38
30.1–5	38
49.1–51.10	149
49.1–51.6	39–40, 114
51.9–10	40
51.10	44
76.1–5	138, 150

Testament of Simeon
6.7	27

Testament of Judah
25.1	27, 28
25.4	27

Testament of Zebulon
10.1–4	27–8
10.2	28

Testament of Benjamin
10.6–10	28
10.6–7	28
10.7	28
10.8	28

Testament of Job
39.8–40.4	138
52.10–11	151

Testament of Abraham
2.2 (rec. A)	148
4.9–10 (rec. A)	148
20.10–11	151

Psalms of Solomon
3.10–12	29

Sibylline Oracles
4.179–191	41

Pseudo–Phocylides
100–108	41–2
112–115	42

Joseph and Aseneth
12.1–2	180

Qumran Literature

1QS
4.7–8	25

1QH^a
14.34	25
19.12	25

4Q174
1.10–11	169

4Q385
frg. 2 lines 2–9	26

4Q386
frg. 1 1.1–10	46 n.14

4Q388
frg. 7 lines 2–7	46 n.14

4Q521
frg. 2 2.1	26
frg. 2 2.10–13	25
frg. 2 2.10	26
frg. 2 2.12	25, 166

11Q19
64.10–13	139

Philo

On the Special Laws
3.151–152	139

Against Flaccus
83–85	139–40

On the Life of Abraham
107–110	148
110	148
113	148
117–118	148

Questions and Answers of Genesis
4.9	148

Josephus

Against Apion
2.121	180
2.218	30, 31

Jewish War
2.152	33
2.153	33
2.154–155	32, 33
2.163	31
2.165	31
3.362	30
3.372	30
3.374–375	30
4.317	139
4.330–333	139
4.360	139
4.383	139
5.518	139
5.531	139

Jewish Antiquities
1.196–198	148
1.197	148
4.219	60, 98, 134
4.323–326	138, 150
5.277	79
5.279	79
9.28	138
18.14	31
18.16–17	31
18.18	33

Rabbinic Works

m. Sanhedrin
6.5–6	135

m. Šebuʻot
4.1	60

m. Roš Haššanah
1.8	60

y. Berakot
5.2	10, 56

y. Sanhedrin
11.6	10

b. Sanhedrin
97a	10

b. Roš Haššanah
31a	10

Pirqe Rabbi Eliezer
51 (73b–74a)	10, 56

Midrash Psalms
22.5	10, 56

Genesis Rabbah
14.5	9, 71
48.14	148
56.1	10, 56
91.7	10, 56

Leviticus Rabbah
14.9	9

Deuteronomy Rabbah
7.6	10

Esther Rabbah
9.2	10, 56

Targum Neofiti 1: Genesis
18.8   148

Targum Pseudo-Jonathan: Genesis
18.8   148

Targum to Hosea
6.2   10, 56

Targum to Ezekiel
37.1–14   9

Christian Works

Gospel of Peter
21   139, 140
34–49   50
59–60   118

Gospel of Thomas
114   61

Gospel of Mary
9.16–18   61
10.7–17.7   61
17.18–22   61

Pistis Sophia
1–3   61

Epistula Apostolorum
10   102 n.8

Ignatius, *Smyrnaeans*
2.1–3.3   124–5

Justin, *First Apology*
52   9

Irenaeus, *Against Heresies*
5.15.1   10

Tertullian, *The Resurrection of the Flesh*
29–30   10

Origen, *Contra Celsum*
2.59   134

Augustine, *Harmony of the Gospels*
3.24.69   92, 95–6

Gregory the Great, *Dialogues*
4.56   138

Greco-Roman Works

Aristophanes, *Pax*
832–834   14

Chariton, *Chaereas and Callirhoe*
3.3.3–5   80–1

Cicero, *De republica*
6.13–17   14

Herodotus, *Historiae*
4.14–15   138

Horace, *Epistulae*
1.16.48   139

Ovid, *Metamorphoses*
14.805–851   138

Pausanias, *Description of Greece*
6.9.6–9   138

Plutarch, *Romulus*
27.3–28.6   65
27.7–28.3   138
28.4–5   138
28.4   138
28.6–8   5–6
28.6   65
28.8   65

Suetonius, *Divus Augustus*
13.2   139